FRED T
JANE

AN ECCENTRIC VISIONARY

Fred T Jane

FRED T JANE

AN ECCENTRIC VISIONARY

BY RICHARD BROOKS

ISBN 0-1706-1751-8
"Jane's" is a registered trade mark

Typeset by
Jane's Information Group Ltd

Printed and bound in the UK by
Biddles Ltd, Guildford and King's Lynn

Credits
Dennis Bunn: inside back cover, p140 (grave), pp68, 86 (wargame). Dennis
Bunn also copied many of the illustrations reproduced from Jane's novels, all
of which are now out of copyright. Jane's Information Group appreciates the
help of Portsmouth City Library, The British Newspaper Library and The Royal
Naval Museum, Pastimes of Southsea, Portsmouth City Museums and Record
Service.

From his own collection, author Richard Brooks provided the illustrations
featured on pp. 26, 32, 68, 94, 115, 123, 130, 131, 158
Andrew Howard, p24
Peter Howard, pp8, 9, 70, 71, 197, 201
Anthony Tory, pp162, 163
Beaulieu Motor Museum, pp124, 136
Peter Rogers, p123
J A Hewes, p196

Copyright
Illustrated London News, pp28, 32, 167, 204
Jane's Information Group, pp8, 9, 24, 66, 70, 71, 82, 86, 87, 114, 140, 197,
201
Portsmouth City Libary, p33
Exeter School, p16
Royal Marines Museum, p12
E A Tory, pp162, 163
Daily Mirror, p142

Publisher's note: Every effort has been made to trace the owners of
Copyright of works used in this book. If there are any errors or omissions,
please inform Jane's Information Group, Sentinel House, 163 Brighton Road,
Coulsdon, Surrey CR5 2NH, UK.

CONTENTS

AUTHOR'S PREFACE AND ACKNOWLEDGEMENTS

I first came across Jane's *Fighting Ships* when I bought a battered reprint of the 1898 issue in a second hand book shop, more than twenty years ago. Little realising I was following in the footsteps of its editor, I used the book to design misshapen models of the curious warships that Jane had sketched, and fought naval wargames on the floor. On moving to Portsmouth my interest was rekindled on finding that many of the City Library's collection of early issues of *Fighting Ships* were originally collated in a house not far from my own.

The resulting book is something of a pioneering work being the first biography published of Fred T Jane. Known worldwide as founder of *Jane's Fighting Ships*, he turned out to be much more than just a naval expert. In an age that celebrated eccentricity he was notorious for his pungently expressed views, and his freakish sense of humour. Today people are often afraid of humour, lest it prevents them being taken seriously. Fred T Jane, however, had no time for such self-importance, and like his better known contemporary George Bernard Shaw often used humour to make his most telling points.

As there are no readily available personal sources, such as diaries or letters, I have used published works, newspaper reports and local historical sources to reconstruct Jane's life. This is a valid approach, for Jane put much of his own life and views into his writing, while his doings often featured in the local press. The main source used is the series of columns Jane contributed to the *Hampshire Telegraph* between 1907 and 1915. As will appear, these not only dealt with naval matters of the day, but with a wide variety of subjects ranging from Esperanto to Teetotalism.

Jane's approach to his work always remained that of the visual artist. It is especially pleasing to be able to present many of his drawings which have long been unavailable. These deserve to be republished as they demonstrate Jane's immense energy and powers of imagination better than any amount of words. The variety of his output also brings out the personal side of this very human naval expert.

Primary unpublished material used includes:
(1) Signed letters of Fred T Jane held by the Portsmouth Museum and Record Service, cited as PCRO 832A.
(2) Copies of documents held by Biscoe-Smith, Heather & Bellinger, cited as Biscoe-Smith.
(3) The Edmonds Papers held by Kings College London. References to these appear by permission of the Trustees of the Liddell Hart Centre for Military Archives, University of London, King's College.

Biographical sketches of Fred Jane were written by Francis E McMurtrie who eventually succeeded Fred as editor of *Fighting Ships*, and Lionel Cecil Jane, Fred's brother. These may be viewed as primary evidence, written as they were by men who had known their subject intimately.

I have used a large number of direct quotations not only to allow the reader to see Jane's character between the lines, but also to bring out the flavour of the period. The present author's interjections into quotations where needed for clarity are enclosed in square brackets. Footnotes are used almost exclusively for source notes.

Acknowledgements:
One of the most pleasant features of writing this book has been the encouragement and help I have received from all quarters. In particular, I would like to thank the following individuals and institutions for their assistance without which the book could not have been written:
Ed Bartholomew
William Henry Bartlett
Beaulieu Motor Museum
Brian C Bellinger
The Bodleian Library, Oxford

The British Newspaper Library, Colindale
The Rev J T Carre, Fred T Jane's nephew
Dave Carson
Bob Cordery - wargame developments
The Engineer
Bradley G Gardner
Hammersmith & Fulham Archive and Local History Centre
Illustrated London News
David C Isby
Jane's Information Group
    Dennis Bunn
    Dr Kathleen Bunten
    Diana Burns
    Penny Carrington
    Marc Firmager
    Peter Howard
    Rachael Hogg
    Jane Lawrence
    Jeff Pye
    David Ward
Kent County Council, Arts and Libraries Department
Kensington and Chelsea Library
King's College London
Alan King and the staff of Portsmouth City Library
Bill Leeson
John Jago (retired Headmaster of Exeter School)
Newcastle upon Tyne, Central Library
Steve Paine
John Pile
Sarah Quail and the staff of the Portsmouth Museum and Record Service
Scientific American
Peter Rogers
Geoff Salter
Andy Sawyer of the Science Fiction Foundation Collection University of Liverpool
Maureen Kincaid Speller of the British Science Fiction Association
Brian Stableford
Rev. John Stone
Edward Anthony Tory, son of Fred T Jane's widow Muriel

AUTHOR'S PREFACE AND ACKNOWLEDGEMENTS

Andrew Trotman
West Country Studies Library
Derek Williams (Bursar of Exeter School)
I must also thank my father Ken Brooks for his magisterial review of the draft, and my wife Eileen. Without her support I would never have started, let alone finished, my search for the man who once lived down the road, and was known for writing books about ships, although he did many other things besides.

Richard Brooks
Southsea
April, 1997

INTRODUCTION

In 1898 our founder, Frederick Thomas Jane, published the first edition of *Jane's Fighting Ships*. Now, Jane's Information Group is proud to publish Richard Brooks' biography of Fred T Jane.

The first edition of *Jane's Fighting Ships* took some 10 years to compile and covered 22 navies in 221 pages. The book contained no photographs, all of the ship illustrations being hand drawn by Jane. This edition was so successful that it was reprinted four times.

The company that Fred T Jane founded thrived over the next few years and the editorial lessons learned during that time still influence today's business practice. Accuracy, impartiality and authority are highly valued within the company, as is the timely flexibility so essential to our customers in today's fast changing environment.

Jane's produces in excess of 200 publications throughout the year, including: annual yearbooks, monthly and weekly magazines, newsletters, information updates, special reports, fortnightly reports and binder products. All of these are available in several formats including our "new generation" CD-ROM that has text, imagery and enlarging capabilities.

Technical innovations have significantly altered the presentation of our information. Delivery systems such as the Internet and On-line services have been used to reach a wider audience. The next 100 years will undoubtedly bring changes, some unimaginable, in delivery and also in collection, production and presentation.

INTRODUCTION

Our Web site already contains news, archive and video and before long we will have a 24-hour news and analysis service in a wide variety of media including virtual reality, satellite imagery and mapping animation.

The latest environment in which Jane's data can be seen is the Corporate Intranet. These are areas where ministries, corporations and military organisations are fed with data direct from Jane's and incorporated into their own operating systems. Based on the World-wide Web, Intranet technology includes searchable databases, updated daily from Jane's. These cross time zones and are available at the start of every working day anywhere in the world.

Such changes in world connectivity means the Company has also changed and developed its business practices. Jane's is already planning and developing its product line well into the 21st century in order that customer requirements are met instantly.

Fred T Jane would be justifiably proud of his legacy and that the Company he founded is at the leading edge of multimedia information for governments, the military and commerce. This biography is a fascinating insight into the way we were and the man who started "the closest thing to a commercial intelligence agency".

Alfred Rolington
Managing Director
Jane's Information Group

CHAPTER I

RED SKY IN THE MORNING

HE surname of Fred T Jane, the founding editor of *Fighting Ships*, must be known to millions of people around the world, but the man himself is practically unknown. This is more than a little paradoxical. Professionally, he set new standards for the clear and accurate presentation of information in *Fighting Ships* and *All the World's Aircraft*. Personally, he was a colourful character, with a reputation as the "biggest joker in Portsmouth", and the "only man in the country who uses a racing car as a runabout".[1] However, no biography appears under his name in the British Library's Biographical Bibliography, and the most surprising errors about his life persist: his date of birth is generally misrepresented; the German press referred to him as "the well known British naval officer Fred T Jane",[2] while a 1939 clipping from the *Portsmouth Evening News*, about half of which is true, bears the intriguing note: "The picture below is not much like Fred T Jane. I knew him. He lived first in Nightingale Road and later at 'Cat and Fiddle' House Bedhampton where he died. He worked for the Naval Intelligence Department and had agents all over the world".

Some of the errors must be laid at his own door. He was not averse to spreading misinformation, for example dropping numerous dark hints about his dubious experiences as a war correspondent in South America. At a dinner for former pupils of Exeter School he was admonished by the president for: "indulging

1

in amusing but in some cases apocryphal anecdotes of some present".[3] Consequently, would-be biographers may never be sure whether they are the victim of inadequate evidence or one of their subject's practical jokes.

Jane's contribution to naval technical literature was immense, not just in his own day, but as one of the first civilian defence analysts, he had a commitment to providing complete and accurate public information, regardless of political party or service interest.

Fighting Ships was the first book to successfully provide technical information about warships in a structured and integrated way giving its users a consistent and rational basis for comparison. Certainly it was not the first attempt to do this, and Jane owed much to *Brassey's Naval Annual* and Laird Clowes' *Naval Pocket Book*. However, *Fighting Ships* was the first to hold all the information about a particular ship once, and in the same place, with a variety of logical paths into the data, to suit the user's immediate need and level of knowledge. It was also the most complete work of its kind, painstakingly documenting the sort of obscure auxiliary and minor warship which is often neglected, particularly in peacetime. Jane insisted that *Fighting Ships* should include: "everything in naval service on the same principle that a dictionary includes words on account of the mere fact of their existence".[4]

Jane was a prolific author, producing at least 19 other titles on naval matters and nine novels in a publishing career spanning 26 years. He developed a naval wargame which was used officially by major navies around the world, and is still played by enthusiasts today. For almost a decade his weekly column in the *Hampshire Telegraph & Naval Chronicle* documented naval developments, not only tactical or material changes, but also the political and social reforms necessary for the Royal Navy to become a modern professional force. The same publication also recorded the role he played in local affairs in Southsea, as Parliamentary candidate, organiser of the new Boy Scout movement, spycatcher, and practical joker.

Jane does not appear to have been a typical Edwardian. He was much too direct to have any patience with the intellectual limitations imposed by an uncritical and deferential society. In *Heresies of Sea Power* he ruthlessly exposed the half-baked logic and careless use of evidence that lay behind the Blue Water school of naval strategy. He had little time for half-measures and compromise and hence for politicians, democracy or the niceties of international law. In 1914, he was one of the few to prophesy a long war, characterised, at sea, by an absence of major surface actions.[5] Less correctly, as it turned out, the lengthening casualty lists of 1915 would lead him to the logical conclusion that polygamy would become a feature of post-war Britain.[6] Although a self-confessed Tory (Conservative) prone to tirades against Radicals and Socialists alike, he had no respect for the class distinctions rife in society in general, and acutely so within the Royal Navy. This stood him in good stead when researching technical details of ships' actual performance as opposed to the trial speeds quoted in other reference works. His contacts among naval personnel included not just executive branch officers, but engineers, and representatives of the lower deck, especially among the long-serving warrant and petty officers. These contacts, and his intolerance of injustice, led him into campaigns against a variety of grievances over recruitment, pay and conditions of service within the navy, often to the annoyance of other more single minded reformers.

Sometimes Jane's forthrightness caused difficulties for him when, in the heat of the moment, he abandoned the careful circumlocutions of Edwardian debate. His eminently practical suggestions for retaliation against interference with British commerce received a hostile reception at the Royal United Services Institute, an institution he had already pained by his likening of the new King Edward VII class battleships to prize gooseberries: "all very well to make the neighbours stare, but of limited practical use".[7] This originality, however, provides the key to much of Jane's success, going further than just being a 'breezy style' or a penchant for forthright comments.

After his death a hostile newspaper commented unkindly on his love of paradoxes, but these were often illuminating for their waywardness: "the less the Navy appears to do, the more it is actually doing" provides an excellent characterisation of British naval supremacy in 1914. Applied to the problems of ship recognition his originality produced a revolutionary set of concepts to answer the needs of those who need to know quickly, not only what that ship is on the horizon, but what level of threat it might represent.

Jane worked immensely hard to bring his ideas to fruition,

sometimes as long as 18 hours a day. Even his success with *Fighting Ships* provided little respite as the prefaces record: every year a mass of updates and corrections poured in from an "unprecedented number of correspondents" requiring continual and extensive rework. Although he should have derived a measure of financial security from these efforts, he continued to work for a wide variety of newspapers and periodicals. After the outbreak of the First World War his exhausting round of propaganda work in the press and on tour contributed to the collapse of his health and early death.

As was only proper, Jane's obituaries dwelt upon his warmer qualities. His descriptions of life on board torpedo boats, or in the mean streets of Holborn in London, and his often satirical columns in the *Naval Chronicle*, also leave little doubt that he was an entertaining raconteur with a ready turn of wit. Perhaps most striking to the modern reader is the practical, not to say downright hazardous, nature of his humour: the wargames played with real guns and torpedoes, the abductions of Members of Parliament and alleged spies, and most inexplicable of all, the mousetrap set for a motor cycle club.

It is important to strike a balanced note when assessing the significance of a man like Jane. Perhaps the best way to see Jane is, in his own words, as a spectator able to see more of the game from the side lines. He was, after all, a journalist. He was not in a position of power and should not be held responsible for the decision making process.

Fred T Jane was a mirror of his times. His writings provide a more complex view of the period than do standard works dealing with a few key establishment figures, such as Winston Churchill, or Lord Fisher, First Sea Lord from 1904 to 1910. Jane shows that the variety of different views on the naval issues of the day were the product of a genuine debate within the Royal Navy. They cannot usefully be categorised as a simple clash between far-seeing reform and blind reaction. Jane's work also shows how the Edwardian period foreshadowed much of the subsequent history of the 20th Century. The type of analysis and technical information Jane provided is still needed today, not only for the naval 'man in a hurry', but also to inform the societies and leaders that send him out to do their work.

* * *

Fred T Jane was born into a world which in retrospect appears to have been a much safer place than that of the late 20th century. However, the mid-Victorians were subject to social and political strains every bit as acute as those of today. Their technology, quaint as it may now appear, was far more revolutionary in its effects than the technical progress of the last 50 years. Fred T Jane's generation had to face the problems of their 'modern' world, with an outlook rooted in the world of the sailing ship and well-bred horse.

Although the British Isles were still insulated from the power struggles in Europe, the 1860s saw the beginning of a process that, within Jane's own lifetime, would destroy British isolation (splendid or otherwise) for ever. Prussia had begun the process of German unification in a manner that showed the hollow nature of British pretensions to maintain the European balance of power, rebuffing British efforts to mediate in the Schleswig-Holstein War of 1864. More seriously for Europe as a whole, the successful use of force in the Seven Weeks War of 1866 and the Franco-Prussian War of 1870 brought about the collapse of the post-Napoleonic map of Europe, legitimising violence as a means of settling international disputes. The result converted Europe into an armed camp, about which Otto von Bismarck, the first Chancellor of the modern German Empire 1871–90, had to admit: "The great powers of our time are like travellers, unknown to one another, whom chance has brought together in a carriage. They watch each other, and when one of them puts his hand into his pocket, his neighbour gets ready his own revolver in order to be able to fire the first shot".[8]

Until the 1860s it had been possible to believe that economic progress and free trade would make wars increasingly irrelevant, at least in the 'civilised' world.[9] However, from 1870, diplomacy was no longer a means of avoiding war, but of ensuring its optimum timing, while arms races became a more or less permanent feature of European politics.[10]

These were not just the result of political tension. They were fuelled by forces of technological change that were apparently beyond anyone's control, bringing revolution in their wake. The railway reduced travelling times by an extent never subsequently rivalled. Richard Cobden, the Radical politician, found in 1862 that he could travel from London to Edinburgh in about 10 hours by rail, compared with the 48 hours required by stage coach: "Our successors can have no such gain on our present travelling even if they are shot like a cannon ball through a pneumatic tube".[11] By 1871 there were 48,860 miles of rail in the USA, 19,000 of these were west of the Mississippi.

It is no wonder that railway stations became the cathedrals of the age, or that a confirmed secularist like Fred T Jane, should later defend their claim to be: "visited every bit as much as St Paul's, the Abbey or the Tower . . . [being] as worthy a memento of this century, as those buildings are of the days that are gone".[12] At sea, steam power had similarly dramatic effects. In his idiosyncratic book *Heresies of Sea Power*, Jane studied the lessons of wars fought with galleys because, like steam ships, they had traded endurance for independence of the weather. Strategically naval operations were no longer intermittent, at the mercy of the wind, as in the days of Nelson, while tactically an enemy could approach from all 32 points of the compass.[13] The social consequences of steam at sea were no less radical. The pre-eminence of the seaman, inevitable in the days of sail, was threatened by new fighting specialists, and, even worse, by the greasy denizens of the engine room.

The increase in speed of communications via the telegraph, was even more remarkable: messages could now travel at near light speed, instead of the speed of a horse. Global shrinking began to produce a single world market for information. The first successful transatlantic cable was laid in 1866, the year after Jane's birth. In 1869, when Fred T Jane was four, the Press Association was formed to provide British provincial papers with the latest national and international news via the telegraph. London became the news centre of the British Empire, and in effect of the world.[14] In the long run, however, the new technology proved a mixed blessing for maritime powers, such as Great Britain, as it strengthened the position of continental powers, notably Germany, which could now move troops more quickly and cheaply by rail than by sea.

New types of warship were also developed. Jane documented the development of the battleship during the successive regimes of Sir Edward Reed, Sir Nathaniel Barnaby, and Sir William White, the Royal Navy's Chief Constructors between 1864 and the turn of the century.[15] A comparison of HMS *Bellerophon*, launched in the year of Jane's birth, with HMS *Revenge*, completed in the month of his death shows this evolutionary change:[16]

	Bellerophon	*Revenge*
Date completed	1866	1916
Displacement	7,550 tons	25,750 to 33,500 tons
Complement	730	908 to 998
Length	300 feet	624 feet
Beam	56 feet	88 feet
Mean draught	26.5 feet	27 feet
Horsepower	6,520	42,962
Belt armour	6 inches iron	13 inches steel
Speed	14.17 knots	21.9 knots
Fuel	650 tons (coal)	900 to 3,400 tons (oil)
Cost	£322,701	£2.5m
Wt of main guns	120 tons (10 x 9″ RML)	968 tons (8 x 15″ BL)

The adoption of steam by the French Navy had caused the first of many naval panics back in the 1840s. The changes of the next 50 years gave rise to a whole series of more or less serious war scares. Often these were based on ignorance, partly of 'enemy' intentions and partly of their capabilities. In 1888, the British Government was reduced to asking Prince Bismarck, of all people, whether the French really meant to attack the Royal Navy's Mediterranean Fleet.[17] There was at that time no means of comparing the real fighting value of potentially hostile fleets, containing as they did a hotchpotch of more or less obsolescent designs. Contemporary war stories exploited the confusion to maximise public paranoia, their hostile squadrons often including vessels later dismissed by *Fighting Ships* as of "limited fighting value".

Rapid change characterised not only the naval world. In a special edition marking Queen Victoria's Diamond Jubilee in 1897, the *Hampshire Telegraph* listed over 30 Victorian inventions which had shaped the world in which Fred T Jane grew up. These included sewing machines, tramways, Lucifer matches, chloroform, x-rays, Cook's Tours, free education, lady barbers, and motor cars.[18] Some of these affected Jane's life more directly than others. The 1870 Education Act, passed five years after his birth, was aimed at ensuring that the mass electorates created by the Reform Acts of 1867 and 1884 were able to exercise their new rights with some degree of understanding. In the USA, illiteracy rates fell from 20 per cent in 1870 to 13.3 in 1890 and 7.7 in 1910. The growth of literacy resulted by the 1890s in a massive increase in all types of publication. Writing in 1896, Jane commented on the "numerous coteries of papers that the last decade has produced".[19] Of direct relevance to himself, the years between 1888 and 1898 saw more books published on naval subjects than had appeared in the previous 30 years.[20] Unfortunately these works were all too often sensational scare stories, such as the 'Siege of Portsmouth' published in the *Southern Evening News* as part of the proprietor's election campaign of 1895.[21] Jane himself contributed to several examples of these *guerres imaginaires*.

War scares may have been partly caused by ignorance, but there was also a growing sense that the British position in the world was being eroded. German unification had created a new force in Europe, stretching from the Vosges to the Vistula, its 41 million population outnumbering every political entity in Europe except Russia. With its rapidly developing industry, German commercial rivalry was soon perceived as a significant threat to British trade. Demographic trends left Great Britain more vulnerable to external threats. The population left the countryside, geographically by moving into the cities, and gastronomically by eating food imported from Canada, New Zealand, Australia, and the USA. Specialising in manufacture and commerce at the

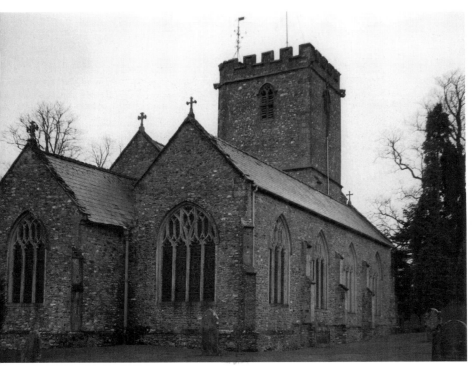

The parish church of St Mary the Virgin at Upottery in Devon

expense of agriculture, Great Britain lost her self-sufficiency in food. By 1914, some 60 per cent of British foodstuffs, by calorific value, were imported.[22]

Personally, Jane contributed to the process of social specialisation by leaving Devon's countryside for the city, and by following a career which met the needs of a more complex society. Technical naval problems were now so complex that they justified full time study. When Admiral Sir Edmund Fremantle protested in the *Times* against a civilian: "darkening counsel by expressing decided opinions on naval tactics", Jane defended himself on the grounds that he was: "professionally compelled to devote hours and days to the study of points which the average Naval Officer can only spend as many minutes on".[23] Such a confident assertion of civilian expertise would have been unimaginable in the pragmatic days of sail.

* * *

The old vicarage, Upottery

One of the most frequently repeated statements about Fred T Jane is that he was the son of the Vicar of Upottery, but this is misleading. Jane's father, John Jane, was a curate at St John's Church in Richmond, Surrey, near London, when his eldest son was born. This event did not occur in 1870, as often claimed, but on 6 August 1865. As was usual then, the baby was born at home, in Gothic House, facing the Green at Richmond. Although registered as John Frederick Thomas Jane, the child was always known simply as Fred. John Jane did not in fact become Vicar at Upottery until 4 January 1886, by which time Jane had taken the railway train to London. It is quite fair, however, to speak of his father as a West Country clergyman, as he held a variety of appointments in his native Cornwall, and subsequently in Devon.

The family name is Cornish, being listed as one of the "peculiar names mostly confined to this county".[24] It derives from the Middle English 'Jan', a form of John. Jane did not become a specifically feminine name until the 17th century.[25] At that time there had been a notable Liskeard family of the name who had acted as County Commissioners and Members of Parliament in the time of King Charles I and Cromwell.[26] Fred T Jane himself traced his ancestry back for 600 years, including the original Vicar of Bray a cleric said to have kept his living by changing allegiance as required.[27] Although Edwardian genealogy is often suspect, there was indeed a late 17th century divine, the Reverend Doctor William Jane who successfully advanced his career regardless of the period's changes of regime. Appointed Regius Professor of Divinity by the crypto-Catholic King Charles II, he managed to end his life as chaplain to the Calvinist William III, despite an intervening proscription by the fanatically Popish James II.[28] It is doubtful whether the wily Doctor's more outspoken descendant would have weathered the political storms of the Glorious Revolution so successfully.

Another possible ancestor, of more nautical significance, may have been the Iohn Iane (sic), merchant, who accompanied the Elizabethan explorer John Davies. In the 1580s, he made a series of voyages in search of the North West Passage, to the "Isles of the Moluccas and the Coast of China", which he documented in Hakluyt's '*Principall Navigations, Voiages and Discoveries of the English Nation*' (sic). Jane's successor as editor, Francis McMurtrie, referred in *Fighting Ships 1947–48* to an Admiral Sir Richard Hughes, who would certainly be an interesting family connection. Not only did he command the Leeward Islands station when a young Captain Nelson was there in the 1780s, but he poked out one eye, trying to kill a cockroach with a dinner fork.[29] Unfortunately, the current writer can find no evidence to verify the supposed kinship between the admiral and Fred T Jane's mother.[30]

There were Janes in the Royal Navy as early as a Henry Jane who was captain of HMS *Seahorse* in the war of 1739–48.[31] Another Henry Jane commanded HMS *Indian* in 1812, leaving a monument at Lanteglos, in Cornwall, not far from St Winnow, where Jane's father was born in November 1840. However, John Jane came in fact from yeoman stock. His father, Thomas Jane, was a farmer's steward at Lanhydrock, marrying a daughter of the innkeeper there. In 1873 two Thomas Janes were listed in the Return of Owners of Land at Lanhydrock, having 114 acres between them, worth £64 a year. This was rather less than the average landholding in Cornwall, although considerably more than the three acres owned at Lanhydrock by a John Jane who may have been Fred's father. The family can be traced back in Lanhydrock to the period of Queen Anne, at the start of the 18th century. Jane's great-great-uncle, a John Jane baptised in 1777, can be identified as a naval lieutenant of 1815. Jane's father, however, was called to the Church, studying at St Aidan's Theological College in Birkenhead, and being ordained priest in 1865, the year of his first son's birth. The previous year, he had married Caroline Sophia Todd, in Bristol. Together they had seven children, one of whom died in childhood. Caroline did have extensive naval connections, but her clerical relations were of more immediate significance in Jane's life. At the age of one, he was taken from Richmond to the sea air of St Austell, in Cornwall, where his father became curate in 1866. St Austell was a large parish of some 6000 souls: "situate on the southern slope of a hill, is of comparatively modern date, and owes its prosperous condition to the numerous tin and copper mines, and china clay works in the surrounding district . . . A great part of the labouring population of St Austell Parish, men, women and children, as young as ten years of age, are employed in manufacturing and saving clay".[32]

The vicar of St Austell was the Rev Fortescue Todd. Although there appears to be no direct tie between him and Caroline Jane's father, the Rev James Frederick Todd, it seems likely that family interest played some role in John Jane's appointment. Like Caroline's father, Fortescue Todd came from a Durham family recently moved south. James Frederick Todd had been Vicar of St Austell's neighbouring parish of Liskeard, where Caroline was born in 1842. He was suspended from his clerical duties in 1844 for missing out a crucial part of the burial service said over an erstwhile parishioner. Subsequently he devoted his time to writing numerous religious works,[33] dying rather suddenly at his home in Exeter in 1863.[34] The Rev James Frederick Todd set precedents for Fred T Jane both as an author and in his difficulties

Fred T's great-great uncle Major Andrew Kinsman, RM

with established authority. He also allowed Jane to claim Russian descent, as his own mother had been a native of Mitau in the Baltic province of Courland, now part of Latvia.[35] Jane's maternal grandmother, the Reverend James Todd's wife, had been born Caroline Warren Kinsman, providing links with an extensive naval family. Her father was Captain John Kinsman of Callington, one of three brothers who between them had served in the Navy, Marines and Excise. Commander John Knill Kinsman, as he appears in the Navy List, saw service in the Egyptian campaign of 1801, and was later mentioned for his part in an epic action almost straight from the pages of C S Forester's Hornblower series of novels. After a two day chase, HMS *Cleopatra*, a 32 gun frigate, caught up with the *Ville de Milan*, of 46 guns. The British ship had the better of the duel, until, during an attempt to rake the Frenchman's bow, an unlucky shot disabled her wheel. She was forced to strike her colours, in moments becoming: "a perfect wreck, not a spar standing but the mizen mast; and her commander fully expecting she would have foundered . . . The following morning the French ship had only her fore-mast and bowsprit standing; and was otherwise so much cut up as to be incapable of offering the slightest resistance when fallen in with by Captain Talbot of the *Leander* . . . which also recaptured the *Cleopatra*".[36]

John Kinsman's brother, Robert, also had his share of excitement while in command of the Revenue cutter *Active*. In 1809 he took a French privateer from St Malo, *Les Deux Freres*, of 29 crew and two carriage guns, recapturing several prizes the Frenchman had taken, before they could reach home.[37] A painting survives of the third brother, Major Andrew Kinsman RM, which reveals a striking facial resemblance to Jane himself. Caroline Todd may well have told her grandson of her uncles' exploits, as she lived on in Bristol until the 1880s, when Jane's father acted as her executor. Colonel William Kinsman RM, another relative, lived in Torquay, quite near to Teignmouth in Devon, where Jane moved at the age of six.[38]

In 1871 Teignmouth was a fashionable watering place, with its "fascinatingly ugly octagonal church of St James",[39] where John Jane was curate. *Kelly's Commercial Directory* described the town as irregularly built: "some of the streets are narrow and ill-paved, it contains some good shops, and a number of villas, several fine terraces, and other residences; it is lighted with gas and has a good water supply."

Shipbuilding had ceased there in 1852, after a three masted ship ran aground off the harbour. Although the traditional fishing boats still went out for whiting, herrings and mackerel, fishing was already giving way to tourism as the main source of revenue. Altogether, the town sounds like a more pleasant place for growing children than the white-capped spoil heaps of St Austell's clay pits. The Janes lived at number 8, Catherine Terrace, where Henry Edgar, the longest lived of the family, joined Jane, and his younger brother and sister, George Hugh and Helen Caroline, who had been born at St Austell.

When Jane was nine he began an association with the city of Exeter which would last until he left home. In 1874 John Jane was finally appointed to a parish of his own, Bedford Chapel in the centre of Exeter. Although the city had lost its importance as centre of the woollen industry during the Napoleonic Wars this was fortunate for the environment: "The entrances to the city are good from every point; the streets are particularly clean. The salubrity of the air and its proximity to many delightful watering places, tend greatly to enhance its eligibility as a place of residence for the invalid, as well as the nobility and gentry".[40]

It is indicative of the close-knit nature of English society at the time, if not necessarily of nepotism, that a second cousin of Jane's mother, Richard Byrn Kinsman, was a senior member of the cathedral close, the Bishop himself being patron of Bedford Chapel. A son of the commander of the Revenue cutter *Active*, he had followed Caroline's father at Trinity College, Cambridge, and become a prebendary at Exeter in 1870. Even if John Jane owed his position to family influence, there is no reason to doubt his ability. Appointed rector to the parish of St John with St George, also in central Exeter, he became Rural Dean in 1877, responsible for maintaining parochial standards throughout the diocese. On leaving the joint parish in 1878, he received an illuminated testimonial inscribed by 70 of his parishioners, and more usefully, a set of 12 solid silver fish knives and forks: "as a tribute of respect to their worthy rector . . . they were all sorry to lose Mr Jane, for it was no small blessing to have a good Protestant clergyman amongst them, and they all knew their rector had endeavoured to act, preach and teach the Protestant doctrines of the Church of England".

Fred T Jane and his father appear to have shared both their energy and an ability to relate to all classes of society. The Rev

Jane: "was known by his sympathy with all classes and the confidence with which the poor approached him as their guide and counsellor. There was nothing of the upstart priest about their faithful rector, and he touched the hearts of all by the true feeling he put into his work".[41] John Jane inspired affection throughout his career, the historian of his final parish at Upottery noted that he had been much beloved, a man "of notable presence and personality... Well equipped with natural genius". In 1997 Fred's father was remembered in Upottery as "a big, square set and kindly man". One particular talent he shared with his son, Fred T Jane, was being a fair hand with oils and water colours.

His latest move, to Upton Pyne on the north-west of Exeter, was distinctly upwards. The value of the benefice was set down in Crockford's Clerical Directory as £551 a year, compared with £175 a year for his old, inner-city parish. The 1881 census shows that three servants were kept at the Rectory; the establishment prescribed by Mrs Isabella Mary Beeton (1836–65), an authority on cooking and household management, for an income of £500 a year. There was a cook, house and parlour maid, and a nursemaid for Jane's youngest brother, Lionel Cecil, born the previous year.

Jane appeared in the census, as a scholar aged 15, for at this time he was still attending Exeter School which he entered on 12 September 1877, shortly after his 12th birthday. It is not clear how he had been educated until then, but the school required that on admission boys should be able to read fluently, write fairly, and work the first four rules of arithmetic. Fees were 8 guineas a year for general work; 2 guineas for drawing, and 5 shillings for the drill sergeant. In general, the school addressed the needs of the local middle classes. The parents of a sample of 20 day-scholars included: an ironfounder, post office surveyor, physician, clergyman, stockbroker, solicitor, and a captain in the army.[42] Jane's social background, therefore, was entirely typical of the intake. Although he was a day boy, he seems to have suffered none of the harassment suffered by the novelist Anthony Trollope, another day boy at Harrow School in the 1820s.[43]

When Jane first went there, Exeter school was still housed in the old 12th century Hospital of St John on the High Street just inside the East Gate: "a fine old Tudor [actually Gothic] style red sandstone building in High Street, where the Post Office now is. Inside it was rather like a medium sized church... with a transept partitioned off".[44] In the hall, over a great fire place, hung a

Famous Exonians: Fred T Jane kneeling bottom right

The new Exeter School built by William Butterfield

portrait of Hugh Crossing, founder of the school. Beneath this, offending boys were caned, a punishment only the headmaster could inflict. One day Fred T Jane, who suffered much in this respect, took his revenge by rearranging old Hugh's features with a piece of chalk. Inevitably he was detected: "The Head bit his lip (in anger as I then thought). My form master put his hand over his face (weeping for my crime I supposed) . . . 'Jane major' said the Head, 'we read in Scripture of certain unfortunate creatures called demoniacs. I am inclined to think that you are one. I shall not cane you, because it is customary to extend a certain leniency towards those who are not in full possession of their mental faculties. Stand there, and let your school fellows see what an idiot looks like'."[45]

The school had fallen on hard times and much of it was in a ruinous condition, theoretically out of bounds. However, for any right-minded boy this served only as a challenge: "Some of the staircases had tumbled away, but it was still possible to get to the top of the house. Here there was a room full of old school books and a great hole in the floor. The joke used to be to get up there, wait until some other explorer came along far below and then try to drop a book on his head! It was a fine game till one day someone dropped an extra big dictionary on the head of a fellow with an extra thin skull and knocked him senseless!".[46]

Jane himself fell into a trap dug in the headmaster's overgrown garden by some seniors, and "lay there expecting to die" until found by chance. He does seem to have been accident prone, as on another occasion he put a bottle of sulphuric acid upside down in his pocket, bearing the scars for the rest of his life. Perhaps the acid was intended for the manufacture of explosives, an activity which allegedly resulted in his exclusion from the chemistry laboratory.[47] He also showed a: "tendency to untidiness in dress which persisted as a characteristic in later life".[48]

Jane's school career was not a success in the academic sense: "at school I was an awful thickhead. I could never understand Euclid. I was whacked. I was called an idiot. I was punished in all kinds of ways, but it never got me any further".[49]

In later years he would recall having to learn and write out Bacon's 'Essay on Truth', "many times as a punishment for general inattention",[50] although he did remember the Greek history that 'Bulldog' Pearson his mathematics teacher pursued as a sideline.[51] Jane's talents lay in other directions. He produced a panorama: "of sufficient merit to induce his schoolfellows to pay for admission".[52]

He must also have shown a considerable degree of literary ability as in 1881 his school mates elected him editor of the new school magazine, *The Exonian*. This was scotched by the Headmaster who: "indicated horribly clearly that the editor must come out of the sixth and not from the bottom of Form IV A". In retaliation Jane started a rival paper called *Toby*, presumably named after Mr Punch's dog, as it was "illumined with jokes stolen out of back numbers of *Punch* [a satirical magazine, recently brought back to life after years of not being published] and from an antique work called The Penny Anecdotes". This undercut the *Exonian*, selling for twopence instead of threepence, gaining: "much success by reason both of its illustrations and its disregard of veracity and the law of libel in dealing with the school authorities".[53]

However, it paid its way: "And when C. Burch minor and T. Burch terts both came into the venture with a small printing press which lived in a summer house in their back garden-well Toby really hit the Exonian quite hard . . . C. Burch minor and I used to set up the type. Burch terts used to scrub the type after use, also being smaller, he was handy to whack when mistakes were made. We still 'graphed' the pictures, but everything else was printed...".[54] Here Jane learned the mysteries of typesetting, discovering that: "while it was quite a simple job to put straight something which ran: 'wE qrobuce this NumBer HobIng thAtour ReEdeRs' and so on . . . knocking out a single word in the middle of a paragraph meant a great deal more! Knowing that is worth far more to anyone who aspires to make a living by writing than any amount of command of the King's English".[55]

On the games field, however, Jane enjoyed a more conventional form of success playing rugby football. He was selected for the 'mauls', as a forward in the XVs of 1881 and 1882, and as a half-back in his last season, 1883. The *Exonian* of the day paid him this interesting tribute: "A plucky and straight running half-back, who always makes ground, but through over-eagerness is apt to get too near the scrimmage",[56] an observation that would be borne out on more than one occasion in his life.

An indication of organising talents that would be subsequently called into play was Jane's membership of the Games Committee and the Committee of the Debating Society. He was a frequent speaker at the latter, which was run on Parliamentary lines. Jane himself was the Honourable Member for Wick. Generally he proved out of tune with conventional wisdom, opposing the introduction of electric street lighting or tramlines along Exeter High Street. He gave early proof of his lifelong anti-radical sentiments by speaking out against the Liberal Government's 'Corrupt and Illegal Practices Prevention' Bill of 1883. This sought to prohibit the congenial electoral custom of 'treating', that is, rendering the voters insensible with drink. Jane's maiden speech had supported the anti-Darwinian notion, "that monkeys are degenerate men". Not surprisingly the Speaker of the House had some difficulty in preventing personal recriminations.

By this stage of Jane's school career there had been several changes of scene for his family. His father had relinquished the rectory at Upton Pyne in favour of a curacy at Alphington, on the southern edge of the city. It is not clear whether he had fallen out with his patron, Sir Stafford Northcote, a Conservative Lord Chancellor, or whether with several sons at school in Exeter it was more convenient to move closer to town. Their new address in Denmark Road was conveniently placed for the new site to which Exeter School had moved in 1880. The old Hospital was increasingly unsatisfactory, running: "parallel with and against the high street, the windows opening on that side, and owing to a cabstand immediately outside . . . liable to disagreeable and noisy interruption".[57]

Despite the efforts of several headmasters to update the curriculum with modern subjects, such as French, German, drawing and music, the numbers of boys had dwindled to a mere dozen at the beginning of 1877. Jane had joined the school as it was reorganised under a new headmaster, the Reverend Edward Harris. More importantly for the school's recovery, a new site of 20 acres had been purchased at Victoria Park for £7,600. Here fashionably High Victorian Gothic buildings, designed by William Butterfield the architect responsible for Keble College Oxford, were erected at the enormous cost of £16,750. One of Jane's contemporaries, whose first memory of going to school was the drip on the headmaster's nose, also recalled Jane inviting him to go pistol shooting in the garden at Denmark Road: "putting up bottles on the wall, we proceeded to practise, until an urgent message came from the Shrubbery to say that Mrs Pope and her daughter were in danger of their lives, the bullets having come across the Barnfield into their garden". In later life Jane went on to heavier stuff, amassing a fair collection of naval ammunition, ranging from a 1 lb to a 40 lb shell.[58]

With this interest in weaponry it is perhaps not surprising that Jane should reveal an early and all too practical interest in naval warfare. In 1904, he explained the genesis of his naval wargame in these terms: "When I was a small boy ... I had the boat sailing craze. A school fellow had a better boat than I; I mounted a gun in mine and committed an act of piracy on a duck pond. My chum was a sportsman, and after punching my head, proceeded to arm his ship also. We took to armour plates made from biscuit tins, and to squadrons instead of single ships. In the battle that ensued our fleets annihilated each other, and depleted finances forbade their renewal".[59]

In *The Port Guard Ship* Jane provided more precise details of the manufacture of shells and fuzes from simple household effects such as sugar, weedkiller, lead foil (for the shells) and wax matches (for the fuzes). A very similar game, played at a similar period using sailing ships and shotgun ammunition is also described in PC Wren's novel *Beau Geste*. However, in young Jane's case, invention born of economic necessity led him on to make-believe battles, and the evolution of an indoor naval wargame, rather than joining the Foreign Legion. He did however try to join the British Army, an earlier attempt to enter Britannia, the Royal Navy's cadet training ship, failing for unspecified health reasons. He failed the Sandhurst examinations, more predictably: "I played the ass in my salad days. Had I dug out when I was at the Army coach's, I should have been a Major today [written in 1909] with brevet Lieutenant Colonel not so very far off. Instead I painted things red, with the result that I have become an inkslinger, and have to convince other people beside the Income Tax Collector, that the 'Pen is mightier than the Sword'".[60]

Even though he had learned to handle the Rifle Volunteers' ancient Lancaster rifles, with their sword bayonets, and drilled in the dark grey uniform they shared with the School Cadet Corps, Jane's "neglected Maths and Piccadilly" failed him for Sandhurst. His father, with four other children, soon to be joined by another daughter, apparently suggested his idle son should join the 256,000 other Britons who emigrated each year during the 1880s.[61] Two of Jane's contemporaries, one of them the genius of the class, did go to the colonies: "earning a precarious livelihood . . . as a hotel porter, and subsequently . . . as an odd job man. In this latter capacity he was attended to professionally by a local magistrate who a dozen years or so before had been shipped out to the Colonies as worthless, and who incidentally had been the dunce and rotter of the same form of which the genius had been so distinguished an ornament".[62]

Jane did not go overseas, however. He left Devon for another destination, affording similar prospects of personal catastrophe or advancement: London.

CHAPTER II

MANOEUVRES IN THE DARK
THE MEMOIRS OF A TORPEDO MAN

RED T Jane left home in 1885, at the age of 20. At that time home was still in Exeter, in the Cathedral Close, where his sister Gwendoline was born that January. The Reverend Jane did not become vicar of Upottery until the following year. Despite its idyllic setting the benefice, at £320 a year, was worth much less than that of Upton Pyne, or even the share of Alphington's £750 a year which John Jane may have received as curate. He does not appear to have been in any position to support his son in London.

A dark period began in Fred T Jane's life. There is little evidence of his work. Recognition for his pen and ink sketches in the press came slowly. Frequently he went hungry. After Jane's death, Cecil Jane wrote of the severe struggles of this part of his brother's life: "which were largely responsible for his extreme readiness in later life to help any lame dogs. He learned that deeper generosity which is known only to such as have themselves faced extreme poverty".[1] At first he lived in an attic in the unsavoury and, at that time, muddy Gray's Inn Road in Holborn, London. A service contemporary described the place in 1916: "It was originally a carpenter's workshop, a rather large absolutely bare place with a big skylight. He fitted it up himself into partitions which he said corresponded to certain parts of a ship — the poop, forecastle, quarter deck, etc — and he used to sleep in the 'owner's cabin'. Here he turned out a lot of work, and once told me that he called every week for 30 consecutive times at the *Illustrated London*

23

Fred T's studio: top of centre building, Gray's Inn Road, London

News and was turned down each time. At the 31st visit he sold a double page drawing, and thenceforward was in it very frequently".[2]

In a move that might appear more typical of a 1960s student, Jane painted large footprints 12 inches across on the floors, The studio was at number 41, at the top of a building shared by a grocer's, and Copas & Co, Wood Engravers. Conveniently, Angelo Campi kept a coffee house next door, while the remainder of the block provided a place of business for pawnbrokers, tailors, engravers, the *Holborn Guardian*, a manufacturer of dairy utensils and, according to Jane, anarchists. Much of the action of his novel, *The Incubated Girl*, is set among the rickety slums and backstreets that characterised the area until the turn of the century, when they were demolished as part of the great redevelopment of Kingsway. The same novel described his own struggles to get "behind the scenes of illustrated journalism".[3] When his aspiring heroine, Stella, made 'the weary round of the illustrated journals: most editors seemed to keep a stout, well-fed, middle-aged person — a sort of buffer — to come between them and importunate artists'.[4] Many editors also had, "tendencies towards 'sweating' or 'cutting' as the artists have it", that is, avoiding ever paying for work. In a piece of vengeful wish fulfilment, the heroine, Stella, horsewhipped the unforthcoming editor of *Potiphar's Budget*.

The extent of Jane's formal training as an artist is unclear, although his naval writing is often illuminated by artistic references. He deprecated the value of drawing lessons at school and had "no kind of interest in the old masters and did not in fact understand them".[5] He preferred what he termed "Pound of tea" pictures, the Impressionist or pre-Raphaelite kind which people hung in their homes. Many of his own pictures would bear out his claim to be a, "strong believer that subject was everything and it did not matter how it was treated".[6] His fiction benefited particularly from the strong visual imagination which allowed him to realise his often fantastic subjects with such clarity. As for *Fighting Ships*, it is difficult to see how anyone lacking a strong artistic talent could have appreciated the visual demands of the subject matter so clearly.

Jane's observations of life in Holborn formed the basis for one of several articles he wrote for the *English Illustrated Magazine*. 'The Small Hours' described the modern Babylon, after the gin

HMS *Nelson* prepares for manoeuvres at Portsmouth

palaces had closed and the street lights had been turned down: "Gradually the less sober wanderers disappear, either with the assistance of policemen, or with the kindly aid of watchful loafers who help them into dark corners and blind alleys, where they remove their valuables, and if their clothes are worth taking, assist them to undress".[7]

Illustrated with wash drawings worthy of Daumier, the article described the moonlight flits of families unable to pay their rent, and the bogus disputes intended, "to get the projected victim to interfere in other people's business, preparatory to interfering with him". There were real fights too, watched with professional interest by cabmen, on the lookout for a fare to the hospital; and a coffee stall which bore the proud legend "Hot Potato Purveyor to the Royal Family" after the Prince of Wales allegedly consumed an "'ot 'tater" there. One would not think, from Jane's account, that in fact the level of urban crime was falling during the period in question.[8]

Only a few examples of Jane's naval work survive from these very early days in London, for example water colours of the ironclad *Belle Isle* and a river gunboat, both executed in 1888.[9] Soon, however, he was producing a constant stream of work.

During the 1885 war scare, the Royal Navy had attempted to mobilise all its ships. The result was a fiasco. Ships needed about

26

40–70 days to complete for sea, compared with the 2 days the French fleet was believed to require. One result of the shambles was regular Naval Manoeuvres.[10] These were held every summer to test mobilisation procedures and the country's naval defences. In 1889 for example, the manoeuvres tested a new signalling system around the British coast. The Post Office's telegraph network was used to transmit news of enemy sightings, linking Coastguard stations with the Admiralty, War Office and naval and army defending units.[11] The manoeuvres were to revive public interest in the Navy. After the soldier's wars, running from the Crimea in the fifties, through to Tel-el-Kebir in 1882, the public had: "yawned prodigiously at the mere mention of the word Navy, and so far as it had any idea on the matter, thought that the Britannia was run by Dr Barnardo . . . as for the Lower Deck, they were believed to be semi-pirates, invariably drunk and likely to cut your throat and throw your body out of the window, if you chanced to be alone in a railway carriage with them".[12]

The negative image was changed by the Admiralty's wise policy of allowing the press on board during the manoeuvres: "Some of the ships only mounted dummy guns but great things took place in Bantry Bay. Every newspaper sent two or three special correspondents . . . on board long before war was declared. These correspondents had to write about something, and they did, columns and columns all about the unknown world in which they found themselves. "Cooks to the Galley" was a poem in prose. The discovery that our tars do not use "shiver my timbers" as an expletive thrilled the nation, and oh! the public excitement when the war came and one stormy night ships broke the blockade and proceeded to "sink, burn and destroy" . . . Towns were bombarded and held to exorbitant ransom. All the shipping in Liverpool was burned despite the heroic defence made by the old *Belle Isle*."

From 1890, Fred T Jane was one of these special correspondents, for his first cruise going on board the old *Northampton*. Built in 1876 for use on foreign stations, she was intended as a compromise warship which could be run economically, while proving a match for any ironclad likely to be met in distant waters. Not surprisingly, the ship was not powerful enough to be used as a battleship and too slow for an armoured cruiser. After refitting, she had been placed in reserve at Sheerness, making annual forays as a third class battleship for the manoeuvres. This could have encouraged a dangerous belief in her capabilities, in the event of real hostilities. In Jane's first novel, *Blake and the Rattlesnake*, the gun detachments of *Northampton*'s unprotected 9 inch guns are all cut down by Russian machine gun fire during a fictitious attack on Khronstadt.

There is some confusion about when Jane first went to sea. Francis McMurtrie claimed this was in 1889, when the Kaiser reviewed the fleet before the manoeuvres, while other sources cite the 1890s. Jane in fact missed the Kaiser. His first shipboard

HMS *Northampton* during a recruiting cruise

sketches appeared in *Pictorial World* in July 1890: a full page illustration of the 'New Channel Squadron', four of the new Admiral class battleships including the ill-fated *Camperdown*, which in 1883 rammed and sank HMS *Victoria* in a training accident, drowning Admiral Sir George Tryon and 321 of his crew. There followed a perfect flood of sketches and wash drawings bearing Jane's name for the next two months. These were something quite out of the ordinary. Not only do Jane's ships appear to lie in the water as ships really do, heeling slightly over, but he drew everything that happened by day or night. Other artists drew manoeuvres as interminable ships' evolutions. Jane's drawings, on the other hand, provide a remarkably complete record of the *Northampton*'s cruise to the Azores, starting in Tor Bay with what became Jane's trademark: a display of the new electric searchlights. The scheme was that: "for a period of about a week the 'Hostile Fleet' will do its best to isolate this country from its supplies, by fastening on and crippling the great trade route of approach to these islands".[13]

It is not clear from Jane's almost schoolboyish account[14] that much can have been learned of strategic value, as only one trading vessel was met during the three week cruise. However the voyage was not without incident. *Northampton*'s steering gear broke down during a terrifyingly depicted gale in the Bay of Biscay, and in the fog she was nearly run down, leading to a sketch entitled, in a masterpiece of under-statement: 'At Sea in Bad Weather: the Iron Duke too near to be pleasant'. At the Azores, the Portuguese authorities were: "so taken aback by the unexpected naval demonstration that they came to the natural conclusion that the capture of their island was the object of the fleet".

Jane sketched a tongue in cheek cartoon of the 'surrender' by Britain's oldest ally. However, on the way home, there was a grim reminder of the cost of naval preparedness: "a third class seaman fell through a port in Iron Duke. All the ships lowered their boats, which rowed to the two life-buoys . . . cast into the water at the cry 'Man Overboard' but the missing man was never seen".

Though the tactical lessons of the exercise were limited, there was plenty of practise in keeping ships at sea. Apart from the *Northampton*'s defective steering, two of the second class cruisers had to be towed to conserve coal, while one of them: "was worse than useless, for . . . she signalled that she was leaking, and in answer to the question 'Where?' made the piteous reply, 'Everywhere'".

In addition to these tests of seamanship, the squadron was coaled at sea, then an almost unheard of achievement. Jane commented: "It is easy to sit at home and devise paper schemes for sea coaling, but the actual thing presents all sorts of practical difficulties that are no nearer a solution than they were ten years ago. Coaling is one of the most disagreeable features of sea life, though with the Jack Tar it is luckily extremely popular, owing to the relaxed discipline on such occasions".

On his return Jane found himself unable to pay his mess bill, instead decorating the ward room with murals in part payment. This worked to his advantage, as the ship's captain, Sir Leicester Keppel, liked them so much that he commissioned a painting of HMS *Constance*, the third class cruiser he had commanded on the China station until the previous year.[15] This picture, "a charming water colour" remained the property of the editor of *Fighting Ships* until 1947.

The cruise of the *Northampton* proved a success in other ways. Jane made valuable contacts which proved useful in the future and gave an indication of his character. Into the first category fell Commander Charles Napier Robinson RN (retd), and William Laird Clowes: "one of the most capable and influential naval writers, of the period".[16] Clowes was the (London) *Times'* naval correspondent, but his wider interests included naval and social history, fiction and poetry. A contributor to the long-established *Brassey's Naval Annual*, Clowes was an early proponent of depth charges and listening devices in anti-submarine warfare.[17] Robinson was another contributor to *Brassey's*, eventually becoming editor during the 1930s. At the time of the cruise, he was naval correspondent on the *Standard* newspaper, a post later held by Jane himself from 1907. Robinson was also interested in the social aspects of naval history. Jane provided illustrations for Robinson's *British Fleet*, and placed a bogus advertisement in his own spoof *Naval Annual of 1895: Per Mare Number 1*: "The British Tar by Commander CN Bobbleson RN – the Daily Liar says: In this painstaking volume Commander Bobbleson has traced the history of tar from its earliest infancy down to its ultimate fate as it bubbles up through the seams in hot weather..."

Both these men placed their systematic knowledge of the world's navies at Jane's disposal for the early issues of *Fighting Ships*.[18] Clowes may even have introduced Jane to Richard Marston, a director of Sampson Low Marston and Co which, besides publishing *Fighting Ships*, also published Clowes' seven volume history of the Royal Navy. In the shorter term, Clowes provided Jane with work, illustrating his war story *The Captain of the Mary Rose*, and, the following year, a lightweight piece on *The New Navies*, which drew on Jane's growing portfolio of warship illustrations.[19]

The other type of contact Jane made was represented by Fleet Engineer David Grant. In modern terms a Commander(E), Grant's service dated from before the launching of HMS *Warrior*. He retired in 1891 as an Inspector of Machinery. On joining *Northampton* at Portsmouth, Jane struck up a close friendship with him, gaining much useful information about the different ships in which he had served.[20] It is typical of Jane's approach to life that he made no bones about mixing with engineering officers, who were then looked down on by executive branch officers. Later his disregard for naval class distinctions led him to become interested in lower deck politics, and provided the source of invaluable comments in *Fighting Ships*, along the lines of "very fast for short spurts, but cannot maintain speed well in a seaway. At full power the vibration is very great."[21] These were not just personal opinions, but were: "aggregated from the opinions of those who have served in or with the ship in question".[22]

Jane evidently harboured warm feelings towards the old ironclad which was the vehicle for this crucial turn in his career. She appeared as the frontispiece to *Per Mare Number 1*, while in the first issue of *Fighting Ships*, the block for *Northampton* carries the additional legend: 'Thanks'.[23] After the 1890 manoeuvres Jane's name was seldom absent for long from the pages of the press. Many of his sketches were of manoeuvres, covered in 1892 and 1893 for the prestigious *Illustrated London News*, and in 1894 for *Black and White*. Increasingly, however, he seems to have developed a niche for himself as the man who could provide reliable, or at any rate timely, illustrations of ships involved either in disasters at sea, or in the war scares which punctuated the nineties. The first of these to be published was that of the leaky cruiser of the 1890 manoeuvres, HMS *Serpent*, wrecked at Cap Villao.[24] Significantly, Jane did not only cover British ships: in March 1895 the *Illustrated London News* carried a dramatic illustration of the Spanish cruiser *Reina Regente*, lost off Gibraltar.[25] As early as 1891 he had drawn the US ships mobilised at San Francisco with a view to intimidating pugnacious British sealers in the Bering Strait. The *Pictorial World* commented with an assurance, typical of the period, that these were: "more formidable in quantity than quality . . . excepting two of them any one of the British gunboats could probably tackle the lot".[26]

Later that year, Jane's expertise in drawing foreign ships was put to use during the Chilean Revolutionary War, a development that provided the basis for the longest running hoax of Jane's life. Chilean President Balmaceda had annoyed his Congress by ruling without them. The Congressionalists eventually won a war which lasted from January to September 1891 and one of the lessons learned was the value of torpedo boats – a theme of crucial importance in *Blake of the Rattlesnake*. So effective were Jane's sketches of the naval bombardments at Iquique and Coquimbo,[27] and later of the torpedo attack on the rebel cruiser *Blanco Encalada*, that many were convinced that he had really taken part in the fighting as a war correspondent. Jane himself was always non-committal about the details, beyond bloodcurdling hints about an enemy who lit fires on the chests of their prisoners.

The wreck of the Spanish cruiser *Reina Regente*

He claimed that he could not remember much about the sinking of the *Blanco Encalada* because he was seasick at the time. However, the dates he published sketches during the period of the war (March to September 1891) leaves little time for the lengthy sea passage to Chile and back. He was at the Easter Volunteer manoeuvres, covering assault landings on Hayling Island by the Royal Marines, and in May was sketching the preparations for the Royal Naval exhibition, at the Royal Hospital Chelsea in London. In August he was in Portsmouth again, drawing the visiting French fleet. The most telling blow to the Chilean legend, however, came from Cecil Jane, who revealed after his brother's death that the drawings: "were actually made in the seclusion of Devonshire".[28]

* * *

Jane's invented adventures as a war correspondent show an important feature of his personality. Although he purported to

The sinking of the *Blanco Encalada* in 1891

33

have had terrifying adventures and spent much time away at sea, he enjoyed his home-life. In his *Hampshire Telegraph* columns he wrote appreciatively of the beer and tobacco with which he relaxed at home, and endorsed Miss Weston's provision of an opportunity for sailors to enjoy the comforts of home in her Sailor's Rests, away from the pressures of either the mission hall, or the public house.

It is a pity therefore that more is not known about his first wife, Alice. Although their marriage certificate describes her as an artist, there is no supporting evidence for this. The 1891 Census return, on the other hand, describes her as a 'General Servant Domestic'. She had been born in London, probably in 1870, and worked for a clergyman who taught mathematics. Her marriage certificate identified her father as Charles Beattie (deceased), a civil engineer, but as her birth escaped registration this is not certain. Although Jane would later claim she was 'daughter of the late Hamilton Beattie of Surbiton',[29] this smacks of wishful thinking. Hamilton Beattie was indeed a civil engineer, and a well-to-do resident of Surbiton. He had helped build the London and South Western Railway, receiving a piece of commemorative silver plate for his services. However, Hamilton Beattie died at the age of 63 in 1871, when Alice would have been one year old. His interminable will makes no mention of Alice or Charles among his numerous legacies, and his first name was Joseph. He does not seem likely to have left a daughter to be reduced to domestic service. It is typical of Jane's insensitivity to the convention of the English class system that he should have been happy with a wife from humbler origins than his own: their marriage lasted 16 years, through bad times and good, and was only ended by her death, which left him devastated. However, it is also indicative of contemporary class pressures that he felt a need to represent Alice's origins as grander than perhaps they were, if only to be taken seriously himself.

We do not know how Jane met his future wife, although her address at 13 Surrendale Place, Maida Vale was not very distant from his own quarters in the Gray's Inn Road. She may even have met him through a shared interest in drawing. They married in Holy Trinity Church, Holborn, on 17 September 1892. Fred was 27, and Alice 22. She seems to have been a good foil to Jane's fiery and untidy personality. She attempted to cure his schoolboy habit of wiping his paintbrush on his handkerchiefs by embroidering them with a stern warning not to use them as a paint rag. There were compensations though, for the wife of a naval artist. Alice and Jane's sister, Helen, paid a visit to HMS *Grasshopper* during the 1893 manoeuvres: "After some minutes struggling — for the ship was rolling a good deal — they managed to get aboard, and as each roll sent their chairs sliding along the deck, they alluded to it as 'a pleasant dreamy motion', a phrase that caught on with us a day or two later when all the wardroom furniture and our duff night dinners were upset by the violence of the waves".[30]

She accompanied him during the election campaign of 1906, at a time when many felt that women were not suited to the hurly-burly of political agitation. Despite a quip in *A Royal Bluejacket* that, "it is useless to expect sentiment from a married man",[31] he would pay loyal tribute at the end of her life to the support she had given him.[32] If the alliance did represent downwards social mobility for Jane, his family do not seem to have resented it. He frequently visited Devon, dedicating books to both his parents, and collaborating with his brother Cecil. Following his marriage, Jane moved out to the developing suburbs of West London. This does not necessarily indicate that he had improved his economic position very much. During the 1890s the London suburbs became increasingly the home of families existing on relatively low incomes of £100–£300 a year.[33] The type of accommodation they originally occupied may have supplied the original of the studios in *The Incubated Girl*: "built in pairs, each being self-contained, each consisting of studio, bedroom, bathroom, and a common kitchen in the basement".[34]

From a bed-sit (one-room apartment) in Shepherd's Bush the Janes moved to the basement of a large house at 12a Edith Terrace, Chelsea, in 1894. They shared the address with a well-established painter, Robert Abraham, who exhibited subjects set in rural Burgundy, far from his native Stoke-on-Trent. Jane took over from another painter, Herbert Percy, a member of the Royal Society of British Artists, with such titles as 'A Rill from a Mountain Tarn' to his name. Perhaps these artistic associations encouraged Jane to exhibit some of his own, very different, work at the Royal Academy: 'The Frankenstein of the East' in 1894, and in 1896, 'The Roman Galleys of Today'. (Groves vol IV, p 237). They do not seem to have attracted critical comment, a contemporary writing of the: "melancholy journey around the water colour room and the black and white room".[35]

Towards the end of 1895 the Janes moved again to more spacious accommodation at 18 Chesilton Road, Fulham. On the south-west side of the road, this was part of a long straight terrace of substantial three-storey houses, with a balcony, bay windows, and a great deal of iron railings, around steps down to a separate basement area. The rateable value, which would have reflected the annual rent, was £31. This is towards the bottom end of the market, rents for suburban London terraces ranging from £28 to £40 a year.[36] However, this should be compared with the 5–7 shillings a week, that is about £15 a year, paid by labourers for sharing smaller houses. The Janes were evidently on their way upwards, if not very quickly. This was just as well, for on 14 November 1896 a daughter was born there: Stella Dorothy Alice. She was named jointly after the heroine of his novel, *The Incubated Girl*, written in the year of the real Stella's birth, and Jane's wife, to whom the book was dedicated, but appears to have been known as Dorothy. As a child, she appears to have resembled her father closely, with a small bright face, and sharp nose.[37] Although Jane came from a large family, Dorothy would be an only child. Middle class families in general were beginning to limit the size of their families at this time, but in the Janes' case, Jane's novels reveal a concern, bordering on obsession, with the perils of childbirth that may provide the explanation of Dorothy's singularity.[38] Certainly puerperal fever, a form of septic poisoning often carried unknowingly by doctors, had reached epidemic levels in the 1870s, persisting at a somewhat reduced level into the 1890s.[39] Although there is no evidence that anyone close to Jane had died from this disease, something of the kind must lie behind his repeated attacks on "medical etiquette" and the heartless incompetence that he felt lay behind it.

Dorothy Jane's birth certificate shows her father's occupation as 'Author and Artist (Painter)', so at this time he evidently still saw himself as something of both. Indeed throughout his life he used his artistic training as a source of metaphors. Trying to convey the extraordinary nature of the revolutionary battleship, HMS *Dreadnought*, he defended her ugliness as being that, "of one of Brangwyn's best pictures alongside the oleographic effort of the conventional RA".[40] During his early years with Alice, however, Jane's art was still a vital matter of bread and butter. During the 1880s fiction replaced theology as the most common form of book published. Novels were no longer expected to be 'improving', indeed the more sensational the better, as a relief perhaps from the humdrum existence of the new reading public. There emerged a whole new class of popular novel, published in one volume. Many of the 'six shilling' novels which replaced the old 'three deckers' required illustrations easily met with Jane's talents. The runaway success of Colonel George Chesney's *Battle of Dorking* in 1871 had led to an apparently unending stream of imitation war stories.[41] These fed off the intense public anxiety set off by the rapid development of new military technologies. This was especially felt in Britain, which since the battle of Trafalgar in 1805 had believed itself immune from foreign attack. Britain reacted to the new threat in much the same way that the US reacted to Sputnik, and the missile gap of the early 1960s. The 1880s and '90s saw frequent war scares, and as these persistently came to nothing, writers alert to market opportunity produced their own versions of what might have happened. Sometimes, the subject was handled realistically, with an obvious political relevance, and sometimes it spilled over into fantasy and what would eventually come to be called science-fiction.

Laird Clowes' admonitory tale *The Captain of the Mary Rose* was an example of the first type of *guerre imaginaire*. Originally it had been illustrated by the distinguished marine artist the Chevalier Eduardo de Martino, who had sketched the real Paraguayan War of the 1860s for the Emperor of Brazil. However, more pictures were required when the *Mary Rose* was serialised in *The Engineer*, by which time the Chevalier had been recalled to South America. Laird Clowes turned to the young artist he had met during the 1890 manoeuvres, who provided a series of wash drawings quite different to the pen and ink sketches of Martino. Generally the war artists of the time pursued a limited realism, concentrating on exact technical detail but neglecting the cost of victory. The work of such artists as Edouard Detaille, the doyen of French military painters, spectacular though it is, provides a distinctly sanitised view of the effects of combat. Jane's sombre half tones, on the other hand, document the new reality of naval warfare, with its torpedoes and searchlights, the choking fumes of the new high explosives, and ships reduced to splinters by quick-firing guns.

Laird Clowes' alternative future was rooted quite firmly in the possibilities of his day: the *Mary Rose* was based on an actual ship built for the Chilean Navy in 1890, the *Capitano Prat*. However,

Guesses at Futurity – Home life in the year 2000

Guesses at Futurity – Sun radiators

Guesses at Futurity – Courtyard to mansion

Guesses at Futurity – Housetop garden

the Tower Publishing Company also dealt in other, more imaginative, alternative futures. George C Griffiths was the successful author of literally dozens of novels in the 1890s, and early 1900s. The first one illustrated by Jane, *The Angel of the Revolution – A Tale of the Coming Terror*, ran into nine editions between 1893 and 1895. A publisher's blurb for this, at the back of William Le Queux's *The Great War in England 1897*, another bestseller for Tower, described how: "In this Romance of Love, War and Revolution, the action takes place ten years hence and turns upon the solution of the problem of aerial navigation, which enables a vast Secret Society to decide the issue of the coming world war . . . Aerial navies engage armies and fleets and fortresses . . . in an unsparing warfare which has as its prize the empire of the world".

Some indication of the lacklustre quality of the writing can be gained from the captions to Jane's illustrations: "'Good God, that is awful'", is the only remark of two characters in flat caps and military overcoats as they demolish a fort at Khronstadt with a single round from their compressed air gun. However, Jane's efforts may be judged successful, as he also illustrated Griffiths' *Olga Romanov — the Syren of the Skies*, a sequel to *The Angel of the Revolution*. Although the subject was aerial warfare, the details of Jane's aircraft show a remarkable resemblance to ships, with armoured conning towers, ram bows, and open gun decks. These features also appeared in his illustrations of Douglas Fawcett's *Hartmann the Anarchist Or, the Doom of the Great City*, which first appeared in the *English Illustrated Magazine* in 1892–93. In later years Jane was: "inclined to think Hartmann the Anarchist was one of the best futurist stories ever written".[42] For a modern reader, the interest of the story is secondary to that of the illustrations, particularly of the aeronef, Attila, whether in flight or attacking an Admiral class battleship with dynamite bombs. Recently Anthony Frewin republished some of the crowd scenes, including the destruction of Big Ben, a subject which must have appealed to Jane, believing as he did that, "every party politician was a damned rogue". Unfortunately these appeared in a greatly reduced form, which hardly does them justice.[43]

Further expression was given to Jane's "wide-ranging visual sense of things to come",[44] in a series of pictorial representations of life in the year 2000. These appeared in the *Pall Mall Magazine* between October 1894 and May 1895. This was an extravagantly produced monthly, "conducted by gentlemen for gentlemen". It had been started by the US millionaire William Waldorf Astoria to publish his own articles as these were regularly turned down by the editor of the *Pall Mall Gazette*, which he also owned.[45] Jane's seven black and white illustrations depicted space craft, television and solar heating in readily recognisable terms, although 'The First Magnetiscope' bears an uncanny resemblance to an early Holland submarine supported by electro-magnets. The architecture and clothing derive from Renaissance or Islamic themes, but more futuristic predictions include gold mining on the moon and buildings not dissimilar to modern indoor shopping malls.[46]

* * *

While Jane was developing his career as an illustrator, he also continued his observations of the Royal Navy. Commander Robinson commented in *The British Fleet*: "Mr F T Jane, who makes a speciality of torpedo boat experiences, has sent me a sketch (p.304) made on board one of these craft during a night attack".[47]

His drawings of torpedo boats, especially at night, broke new ground, or perhaps water. The one published by Robinson, 'A Torpedo Boat Attacking an Ironclad', is in a class quite different from a rather sanitised sketch of 'HRH Prince George in Command of Torpedo Boat No.69', contributed by W H Overend to the same book.[48] Overend's figures are technically superior to Jane's but they are stiff and stereotyped. His clear sunlit lines convey nothing of the atmosphere of torpedo operations, unlike Jane's murky night attack against a monstrous battleship that looms horribly overhead. The future King George V is loyally presented in spotless attire, as if on the royal yacht. Appropriately for a sailor-king he is quite oblivious of the mountainous seas around his strangely level craft, unlike Jane's insignificant figures clinging on to their torpedo tubes for dear life.

In an age when artists often worked from their imaginations, in the studio, Jane's approach to reporting manoeuvres was quite distinctive, trying: "to set out what may be called the social side of torpedo craft, the life as I have seen, experienced and enjoyed it.

All the illustrations of naval manoeuvres and so forth are reproductions of actual sketches made at sea on board the ships with which they deal: the pencil is the best descriptive medium for many of these things ... the attempt has been in each to illustrate the thing as it appeared, not to produce merely a 'picture' of it – events do not invariably suit themselves to 'artistic requirements'".[49]

This concern for actual appearances, rather than artistic convention or photographic effect, would be of crucial importance when he came to produce *Fighting Ships*. As the above quotation shows, however, Jane was not only interested in the hardware. *The Torpedo in Peace and War* breathes with his enthusiasm for "the long sea picnic of the annual manoeuvres", which evidently appealed to some schoolboyish streak in him: "despite the work, filth and discomfort ... no-one ever washes or removes clothing in a torpedo boat unless during a harbour spell ... despite all these inconveniences the life has a charm about it that appeals to officers and men alike. There is a freedom from restraint, an easiness in little matters of discipline, such as smoking and so forth, all of which go to make the life a fairly happy one for the sailor".[50]

The discomforts were real enough. Sleeping was like, "trying to lie still during a series of railway collisions". Sweepstakes were held, "as to who would first be victim to Neptune". Perversely, Jane: "took a certain amount of pride in that the most spirited bidding was for myself and felt quite proud when knocked down for 25 shillings and sixpence".[51] Even when seasickness was absent, food was a problem, despite the meat safe next to the grimy white ensign astern: "A delicate and particular palate is an inconvenient thing to take to sea in a torpedo boat; the staple content of its larder ... being pate de foie gras, plum pudding and sardines, particularly sardines".[52]

In bad weather food was out of the question: "Seas swept the Grasshopper from stem to stern, tons of water fell upon the fokes'le and spurting high upon the fore bridge, fell in a solid sheet upon the funnels. Everything broke loose and banged about as it listed; we were all drenched to the skin. Meals we had none, nor was there a prospect of any till we should get into Milford Haven. Ahead of us firm as a rock ... was the *Thunderer*, the steadiest ship in the navy; and standing in a sheltered position on top of her after turret, a pitying smile on his face, stood a man in evening dress waiting to descend to the creature comforts in the wardroom below".[53]

The Torpedo in Peace and War was a compilation of Jane's journalistic accounts of naval manoeuvres from 1892 to 1894, previously published in Cassell's Magazine, *Good Words*, and the *English Illustrated*. Each was preceded by a technical discussion of the type of boat he had been in that year, the whole rounded off with shorter essays on topics of contemporary relevance, such as a trip in a submarine or aerial torpedoes, and discussions of the torpedo's role in the naval wars of the 1890s. Like many of his later books, the whole does not live up to the promise of a strong beginning, but in this case it matters little. The vigour of the writing, and the quality of the illustrations compensate for the lack of a major theme consistently developed throughout the book.

Another product of Jane's early naval contacts is now among the rarest pieces of Jane's collectables, *Per Mare Number 1: A Serio-Comic Naval Annual*. This appeared in July 1895, at one shilling a copy, or ten shillings and sixpence for the artistically hand-coloured version. It is a fascinating hotch-potch of articles, sketches, cartoons and bad jokes. Jane produced most of it, masquerading in a wide variety of artistic styles, but several naval friends also contributed. The preface, "inserted where it will probably be read by accident, like a patent medicine advert", hoped the annual would become a quarterly affair. However, there is little sign of this. *The Torpedo in Peace and War* referred to a publication, "strangled in the birth through private reasons on the part of the publisher". If he meant *Per Mare No. 1*, perhaps Tower Publications did not altogether approve of Jane's satirical references to Lord Coppery, editor of another naval annual, and such august bodies as the Gravy League: "started to induce the country to impress upon the Admiralty by Constitutional Means the Advisability of supplying better Gravy to Salt Pork".

Perhaps the prime minister, lampooned as Lord Raspberry, took steps to prevent further embarrassing revelations of such projected government measures as the "Brilliant and Economical Scheme to make the Navy self-financing", by selling advertising space on ships' sails, and placing Admirals' pay on a commission basis. Whatever the case, such fascinating naval secrets as "the chemical formula of Marsala as issued in HM Wardrooms" or "The Hatching Ground for Naval Experts" were never to be revealed.

"Every gun on our starboard side was discharged" (Blake of the Rattlesnake)

A more successful venture than *Per Mare No.1* was Jane's first attempt at a sustained piece of writing which appeared in the same year. With his experience of working with Griffiths and Clowes, it is not surprising that Jane should have turned in 1895 to creating his own novel of future warfare. *Blake of the Rattlesnake Or, the Man Who Saved England* was, however, firmly based on his own experiences at sea. Inscribed to "All old shipmates in Catchers and Torpedo Boats" it was particularly dedicated to Lieutenant Arthur Barry RN, who had commanded the various torpedo craft in which Jane had spent the summer manoeuvres of 1892 to 1894: Torpedo Boat No.65, HMS *Grasshopper*, and HMS *Seagull*. Barry had also contributed some more than competent sketches, to *Per Mare No.1*: 'Torpedo Practice during the Late Severe Weather', and 'Floating out the Majestic'. In 1898 he went into the Coast Guard service, retiring as a commander in 1904.

The eponymous hero of the book was partly based on Barry, and partly on the future Admiral Sir Lewis Bayly, who commanded the real HMS *Rattlesnake* in 1892, and later the Channel Squadron in 1914 until the loss of HMS *Formidable*.[54] Despite the claims of friendship, Jane evidently chose the latter's ship as providing a more stirring title than Blake of the Grasshopper would have done. Jane's fictional hero, Blake, is reputedly typical of the executive officer of the period: "devoted heart and soul to his profession . . . Looking on politicians of both parties as knaves alike, contemptuous of civilian control of the fleet, callous to all amusements, and interested in nothing save as it touched his profession".[55]

Blake turns the course of the war through his singleminded devotion to duty, and by his surprise torpedo attack on a hostile squadron moored in Spithead, between Portsmouth and the Isle of Wight. Sir Lewis Bayly's memoirs contain his account of leading five torpedo boats into Spithead at night, HMS *Rattlesnake* and most of her crew covered with black lead, to escape detection.[56] However melodramatic Jane's fictional *denouement* may have been, the episode is clearly based upon practical experience in which he may even have shared.

In many ways, *Blake of the Rattlesnake* is a typical first book. The energy with which it is executed considerably exceeds the skill. It is an uneven piece of work. Jane tries to make too many points at once, destroying the coherence of dialogue and narrative. The plot is developed spasmodically and the characters often seem wooden. The humour is not sufficient to enliven the whole book, but does serve to weaken its serious purpose. This is a pity because, despite these limitations, *Blake of the Rattlesnake* is a good yarn. It was ahead of its rivals in many ways. Jane's war was not, as so often the case in war novels, lost or won overnight. In his account of a war almost lost through political weakness and a paralysing coal strike, he was nearer to the truth of how wars would be ended in the 20th century than the advocates of magical new weapons or surprise attacks. His sea-fights are convincingly chaotic and hard fought, unlike Laird Clowes' neatly choreographed affairs, or Griffiths' one-sided massacres from the air. As one might expect, Jane's night actions are particularly effective. Much of the technical detail is well done, such as the use of searchlights and mines. Plans go wrong, and fire discipline is not what it might be. On more than one occasion ships fire on their own side: "This sort of mistake we had most of us met in manoeuvres, but then everybody considered it a good joke...".[57]

Jane also showed a keen appreciation of the disastrous possibilities of freedom of the press in wartime. A crucial convoy

HMS Seagull firing torpedoes (Torpedo in Peace & War)

of colliers is intercepted by enemy cruisers, because full details of their departure is printed in the English newspapers. Some features of the book are, as with other such tales of the period, at odds with modern attitudes, but serve to show how far matters have changed since the 1890s. Jane saw his purpose as being to: "convince the present and rising generation that scientific advance has not yet eliminated the romance that, let peace-faddists say what they will, clings and has ever clung around war and that man — the vir — is not yet supplanted by man — the homo".[58]

The First World War battles of the Somme and Verdun would show that scientific advance had indeed eliminated the romance from war, but, for a while, Jane and his contemporaries remained secure in the Victorian dream of constant progress.[59]

* * *

The Victorian belief in progress was not just based upon

HMS Grasshopper: torpedo boat crews slept where they could (Torpedo in Peace & War)

innocence, however. The astonishing scientific advances of the 19th century must have seemed good enough reason for optimism. Science provided useful things such as the steam engine and telegraph, as well as compelling explanations of the natural world such as Darwin's Theory of Evolution, or more prosaically the Law of Conservation of Energy. It is not surprising that by the 1890s writers were beginning to use such ideas as the starting point for stories. Jules Verne had written tales inspired by 19th century technological marvels in the 1860s and 1870s. The genre came of age in the 1890s. Before then, tales of the fantastic, such as Mary Shelley's *Frankenstein*, had lacked any recognisable scientific foundation. By the end of the 1890s science-fiction could be viewed, depending on one's humour, as a more or less

Fred T's HMS Rattlesnake (Blake of the Rattlesnake)

serious vehicle for discussing the infinite possibilities of an infinite universe.

Jane's own science-fiction traced a course between these two points. Stella Zadara, the heroine of *The Incubated Girl*, beautiful and intelligent though she may be, is very much the descendant of Frankenstein's monster, her creation owing more to H Rider Haggard's novels than any scientific process. *The Violet Flame*, Jane's last venture in the field, clearly shows familiarity with scientific developments. These had started by demonstrating the interchangeability of energy's different forms of electricity, heat, light, and sound, and culminated by the turn of the century in the discovery of the electron, and hence the structure of matter.

The main function of science in such literature, however, is to allow the author to develop ideas outside the limits of normality. Over the same short period, 1896–99, Jane and his contemporary H G Wells covered all the themes that would make up the science-fiction canon. In some ways, Jane's work covered a wider field than Wells' classics, although they are less well known. Jane began in 1896, in *The Incubated Girl*, with an exploration of society's interaction with a young woman with special powers. These are only hinted at as her creator, the amoral Professor Zadara, destroys the final paragraph of the ancient Egyptian papyrus originally found with the egg from which she hatches. Most of her power over people derives not from any paranormal capabilities, but from her contempt for social convention, having been brought up in isolation in a moral vacuum. Like his real contemporary, Pavlov with his dogs, Zadara uses Stella to study inherited and acquired behaviour. As with Wells' *Invisible Man*, published a year later, much of the interest derives from Stella's effect on other people.

The following year, 1897, Jane produced *To Venus in Five Seconds, An Account of the Disappearance of Thomas Plummer, Pillmaker*, perhaps the most enjoyable of all his fiction, dealing with space travel in a highly satirical vein. Venus has the advantage over Mars that its surface cannot be seen, leaving more scope for its imaginative development. Unlike H G Wells' Martians who followed Jules Verne's lead in firing themselves out of a giant gun, Jane's Venusians used "a queer kind of summerhouse down at the end of the garden". By varying the specific gravity of this vehicle and its occupants it is possible to travel almost instantaneously between giant pyramidal structures in Egypt,

Mexico and Venus: a great step forward from Verne's method, with the added advantage of not reducing the passengers to jelly as they accelerate up the gun barrel. Where Wells' *First Men in the Moon*, published in 1901, used an imaginary metal Cavorite to overcome gravity, Jane's Egypto-Venusians or Sutenraa use an imaginary property of the real gas argon, recently discovered in 1894. Jane also invented ethnic Venusians, or Thotheen, originally assumed, by Thomas Plummer to be hallucinations: "a sort of compound of elephant, mosquito and flea, a thing seven feet high or more with shining scales upon its sides, with great folded gossamer wings, with antennae and a hairy flexible trunk capable of almost endless extension set on top of its head, with eyes capable of *expression*".[60]

Despite their unpromising appearance, these creatures are as far ahead of the Sutenraa as the latter are ahead of Earth scientists. Having discarded language for telepathy, and with electricity as a weapon, they live in: "a vast lamplit dome . . . with misty galleries hanging in mid-air up which went crawling creeping things; dark passages plunging deep into the bowels of the earth; a stream of Thotheen riding upon strange and gigantic machines and here

(left) "The rocket flew blazing into the sky" (Blake of the Rattlesnake).
(right) "The attempt to undermine the Beast's headquarters" (The Violet Flame)

52

and there among them the semi-nude men and women ... with solemn eager faces marked and warped all over with an expression of passionate thirst for knowledge".[61]

To *Venus in Five Seconds* is the shortest of Jane's novels and possibly the most successful. Science fiction often works best in the shorter forms, which maintain the force of the initial idea and end while the reader's suspension of disbelief is still complete. Jane's ideas are always interesting and unusual, but he often fails to sustain them. This is not only true of his fiction, where the action sometimes loses direction, but also his critical work on contemporary naval theory, *Heresies of Sea Power*. His shorter pieces, even the early essays in *The Torpedo in Peace and War*, are always vigorously and tightly written.

Jane's final work of science fiction, *The Violet Flame*, was published in 1899. Here we are close to the catastrophic stories of later writers such as John Wyndham, with terrifyingly realistic details of the likely results of a near collision with a comet: tidal waves, earthquakes, and a hail of meteorites. The almost total annihilation that follows results, however, from the *Violet Flame* itself which rearranges and compacts the hydrogen which

Listening to the Earth's thoughts (The Violet Flame)

provides the basic building blocks of matter. After the disaster, the survivors' children play in what was once Hyde Park with the thousands of little stone dolls which lie everywhere, never guessing what, or rather who, their dolls once were.[62] There is a lot more to *The Violet Flame*, "a book that has everything",[63] than a simple tale of the end of the world brought about by a death ray inspired by discoveries of X-rays and radium. Behind the disaster lies the concept of the solar system as a macrocosmic life form, where planets can think, and the death of millions is of no more significance cosmically than the chemical changes in the synapses of the human mind. Like Jane's other science fiction, the tale involves a mad scientist, Professor Mirzarbeau, who initially uses the Violet Flame to become the Beast of Revelations, and devises a machine rather like an inverted phonograph for listening to the world's thoughts. Given the contemporary belief in the benign progress of human affairs, it is quite striking that by the mid-1890s writers were already beginning to question the moral consequences of the unrestrained pursuit of scientific knowledge. Like H G Wells' Dr Moreau, the evil Professor Zadara was a vivisectionist, although the full significance of this is not obvious until the last few horrific pages of the book. So too were the Sutenraa with their, 'solemn eager faces marked and warped all over with an expression of passionate thirst for knowledge'. The medical student narrator, who cuts lectures because he lacks the "natural craving to see pain and smell blood that every born doctor has", finds himself carried off in the summerhouse for the purposes of medical research. "A splendid physique", murmurs his lady friend as she pulls the levers, "a thousand pities it should be lost to science . . . enjoy yourself while there is time".[64] While Zadara is plainly evil, however, a character in *To Venus in Five Seconds* realises that there is a wider moral dimension to the issue: "we are just like the wretched victims of some earthly vivisector, the people individually may feel pity but collectively they are callous and do nothing — they feel sorry but they have a dim idea that it is for their own good that the animals suffer and then they try to forget all about it as an unpleasant thing".[65]

Jane himself was fond of animals. In later life he kept collie dogs to see off tramps and Prime Minister Lloyd George's land tax inspectors. The theme of cruelty to animals runs through *The Incubated Girl*, surfacing when the vegetarian Stella horsewhips the driver of an omnibus for mistreating his animals. However, it was not the bus-drivers that were to blame: "no, it is the fat, greasy, comfortable shareholders of the companies who suck their dividends out of the sufferings of the wretched beasts; the lazy thoughtless women, who will never trouble to alight when the conveyance stops within ten yards of their destination".[66]

Commercial pressures lay behind another social evil featured in *The Incubated Girl*, which, although centred upon the transcendental Stella, documents the troubles of two other women: Suzie, a waitress and artist's model, and Dora, who becomes something rather worse than an artist's model. Like many a lady's companion she is seduced by a member of her employer's family, and disappears into the Victorian underworld. Unusually Jane did not condemn the women: "The pay of a waitress is never much; in Suzie's case it had been seven shillings a week and what she could earn by tips, and a woman must be virtuous indeed to be content to try and exist on seven shillings a week in London... Political economy shows us that it is the proper thing to avail ourselves of the law of supply and demand; if the girls are: 'no better than they should be', it brings more custom to the restaurant... Dividends are higher... and the supply of street women is kept up".[67]

Jane himself had worked with artist's models, including one of the painter Holman Hunt's angels. One wonders whether he himself ever took advantage of the fact that: "between artists and their models of the gentler sex there often exists a feeling that some call 'camaraderie', others a less pleasant name".[68]

There was a superfluity of women in Victorian society a theme to which Jane returned in *To Venus in Five Seconds*. The constant drain of men to the colonies and the system of late marriages for middle class men left a third of Victorian women unmarried at any time.[69] One victim of this was the girl with whom Plummer falls in love on Venus. Phyllis had: "earned a miserable pittance as governess to the children of some rich tradesman and unable to support that life any longer, she answered an advertisement for a travelling companion... and so fell into the clutches of these Sutenraa",[70] becoming a victim of an inter-planetary version of the white slave trade. The dark view of life implicit in Jane's handling of such issues reflects contemporary attitudes. There was a fashionable *fin-de-siecle* pessimism, possibly born of the same scientific discoveries that fed eschatological stories such as *The Violet Flame*, or H G Wells' prediction of rather less immediate

doom in *The Time Machine*. There were also worries about the
stability of the new urban, democratic society which had emerged
by the 1880s. It is no coincidence that in *The Violet Flame* the last
violent confrontation between the forces of order and anarchy
occurs in Trafalgar Square. In February 1886, the West End of
London really had been 'in the hands of the mob' for several hours
after a demonstration in Trafalgar Square. Unemployed labourers
had smashed club windows in Pall Mall and looted department
stores in Piccadilly. The following year a similar demonstration
had been forcibly prevented by police and troops, becoming
known in socialist circles as Bloody Sunday.[71]

The darkness of the times was enlivened by Jane's black sense of
humour. In all his novels, the narrators are cast in an anti-heroic
mould, being generally quite dim, unlike his female characters.
Despite his scornful view of the 'new woman', Jane had no
illusions about the superior faculties of the original model. Jane's
first Devonshire novel *His Lordship, the Passen, and We*, was
written in the same year as *To Venus in Five Seconds*. The village
tailor, always a focus for village radicalism, takes in hand the
education of the sexton's daughter who, when she adds boxing to
her other skills, literally wipes the floor with her male
competitors. On the other hand, as Thomas Plummer is
kidnapped to Venus, he thinks over his achievements in life: "a
man who never won but a single game of billiards in his life, and
then when he was three parts drunk; who only spotted a winner
in a horse race when he put on the horse he didn't mean to; who
once kissed a lady doctor...".[72]

This type of humour runs through all three books, particularly
To Venus in Five Seconds, despite the horrific situation of the
protagonists. Stella of *The Incubated Girl* causes chaos by riding
an elephant through Hyde Park, after failing to come to terms with
the bicycle more fashionably ridden there. A naval officer worries
about his promotion, as he oversees an attempt to undermine
Mirzarbeau's house, an enterprise so hazardous that the convict
labourers go mad with fear of the annihilating death ray.
Ironically the eventual catastrophe is itself set off unknowingly by
our heroes, when they destroy Mirzarbeau's apparatus that has
kept the comet away. For a long time Thomas Plummer, equipped
with dark glasses against the blazing Venusian sun, fails to
understand where he has gone, and for what purpose, "looking
round, trying to find the house or the neighbours' washing".[73] This

mundaneness adds to the credibility of Jane's characters and the unlikely situations in which they find themselves. In general, this group of novels showed a marked technical improvement over *Blake of the Rattlesnake*, in the use of language, and the handling of character. A major achievement in this direction is the way in which Jane develops sympathy for Stella, despite her often atrocious behaviour. Jane's contribution to science fiction deserves to be better remembered, both for its development of the classic themes of the genre, including social comment, and for its value as entertainment. It may be regretted that Jane abandoned his thrillers as, despite their literary weakness, they contained far more original ideas than the copious output of George Griffiths.[74]

CHAPTER III

BREAKING THE LINE: FIGHTING SHIPS

ALTHOUGH the first issue of *Fighting Ships* did not appear until 1898, its roots went back almost 20 years. In July 1882, the British Mediterranean Fleet bombarded Alexandria, in response to an Egyptian nationalist movement led by Arabi Pasha. The illustrated magazines of the day covered the event in detail, inspiring the teenage son of a West Country clergyman to make rough sketches of the ships involved.[1] From the limited beginning of eight battleships, five gunboats and a despatch boat, Jane went on to put together a bulky sketch book, which he called *Ironclads of the World*. At that time such an undertaking presented difficulties that can only be guessed at today. Photography was in its infancy and the only naval reference work was the unillustrated *Navy List*. The Admiralty itself did not begin collecting photographs of warships until the mid-1880s, and these were confidential, although such commercial pioneers as Long and Symonds at Plymouth and Portsmouth were already at work on the collections now in the Imperial War Museum.[2] Problems caused by the lack of pictorial identification is shown by the example of the Turkish turret ship, *Hufzi-ul-Rahman*. According to one account of the Russo-Turkish war, this ship was torpedoed on 25/26 May 1877, but in fact she survived to appear in the first issue of *Fighting Ships* in 1898. In the absence of a comprehensive reference work it was all too easy to confuse the identity of ships, in this case with the light river gunboat, *Seife*.[3]

Jane's sketch book survived into the 1940s in the possession of Francis McMurtrie, then editor of *Fighting Ships*. The drawings were: "mostly pen and ink outlines, filled in with flat colour wash, the earlier ones being stiff and elementary, with a disproportionate amount of care lavished on rig and similar details. In the later sketches, dated 1889, Jane had acquired the technique of body colour. Here there first emerges the distinctive style which became such a feature in later years".[4]

The album also included hand-written notes of the dimensions and armament of each ship and occasionally comments on the deficiencies of the type, the forerunners of the foot-notes in *Fighting Ships*. Jane was able to draw on two sources for this technical information. In 1882, *The Ships of the Royal Navy 1872-1880* was published in an elegant royal blue cover decorated with gold. The front cover featured HMS *Active*, a training ship that Fred T Jane later drew for the *Illustrated London News*.[5] Responsible for the earlier work was, W F Mitchell, a successful marine artist, who was practically a deaf-mute. Living as a recluse on the Isle of Wight, he illustrated several books about the Royal Navy between the 1880s and early 1900s. Today the colour plates are often to be found individually, in shops selling naval prints. *Ships of the Royal Navy* also featured an anonymous foreword, attributed to Sir Francis Elgar,[6] a Portsmouth-born naval architect who had worked his way up from dockyard apprentice to Director of HM Dockyards, at the Admiralty. Among other duties, he had prepared evidence for the court martial held after the loss of HMS *Captain* in 1871. Many of the issues covered in Elgar's foreword would continue to fuel debate through Jane's professional life: the effects of the Whitehead torpedo, the role of fast merchant cruisers and the imminent demise of the capital ship. It is indicative of the pace of change in the 1870s that a single previous volume of lithographs had sufficed to cover the period 1765 to 1872, while the next eight years required a volume to themselves. Apart from the book's significance as a source of information about particular ships, it provides a pointer to how Jane would tackle his own album. Although Mitchell provided only 25 plates, they covered all types of ship: from the battleships, *Inflexible*, *Alexandra* and *Temeraire* which took part in the Egyptian bombardment, to the cruiser *Shah*, seen engaging the Peruvian *Huascar*, down to a Torpedo Boat 2nd Class, with its depot ship, the *Hecla*. Equally significant, the information about each ship was helpfully presented in a standardised manner on the page following the appropriate illustration. The same items of data, such as length or displacement, were shown clearly and separately for each ship, not hidden away somewhere in a mass of text. However, the style of illustration was still artistic, rather than utilitarian: HMS *Neptune* is depicted behind a cloud of smoke, which does not suggest the book was intended for ship recognition.

Jane's other source was the new *Naval Annual*, which first appeared in July 1886. It was produced by the Civil Lord of the Admiralty in William Ewart Gladstone's Liberal Government of the early 1880s. In his first issue, Lord Brassey announced his intention to produce a yearly consolidation of the: "large amount of information on naval subjects which has hitherto been obtainable only by consulting numerous publications, and chiefly from foreign sources".[7]

A major part of the *Naval Annual* consisted of essays on naval matters of the day, such as the defence of coaling stations, manning the navy, or a description of the action of HMS *Shah* and *Amethyst* against the *Huascar*. Although the editor claimed to pursue an impartial, non-party line, many of the chapters, for example those discussing Admiralty reform, appear highly political. For the accountant and the prurient respectively, there were appendices detailing the naval Estimates of the Powers, and the ill-effects of the non-enforcement of the Contagious Diseases Act. Only a small proportion of its pages provided technical data about ships. This fell into two parts: a section on Armour and Ordnance, and another describing British and Foreign, Armoured and Unarmoured ships. Although far better than in any previous analysis, these were discursive and inconsistently presented. Different types of information were given for British and foreign ships, making comparisons difficult. Furthermore, the technical details were tabulated separately from the 95 plates. These provided plans of 217 ships, mostly elevations, to a variety of scales. It was these, and some old service journals, on which the majority of Jane's early sketches were based.[8]

By the mid-1890s the *Naval Annual* had consolidated its position as the collective organ of the naval establishment under the eponymous title of Brassey's, still a significant name in defence publishing. It carried contributions from such politically significant figures as Sir George Clarke, later the first secretary of the Committee of Imperial Defence, as well as from naval journalists such as William Laird Clowes, and Commander Robinson, who had helped Jane at the turning point of his career during the 1890 manoeuvres. The number of illustrations had increased, from four to 11, Mitchell's ship portraits being described by a reviewer as "most excellent and artistic".[9] However, the 255 ship's plans were still drawn in different scales, varying between 1/500 and 1/750, and by the end of the century the Journal of the Royal United Services Institute (RUSI) was grumbling that there was, "room for improvement in many of the plates".[10] Technical data was still tabulated separately from the plans, while tables purporting to compare the relative strengths of the rival navies listed battleships in date order, and cruisers by speed, variables which may relate to fighting value, but not as closely as the weight of guns or armour carried.

From 1895, Jane's associate, William Laird Clowes, had been addressing the naval user's need for a reference source which was rather more manageable than the *Naval Annual*. His *Naval Pocket Book* generally met with approval, containing a: "vast amount of very useful information condensed in a very small amount of space. The classification of the ships is good and fuller details about armour, armament etc are to be found than in Brassey's or any other of its rivals".[11]

The *Naval Pocket Book* still classified ships by displacement and separated the illustrations from the technical detail, making cross reference tedious. Not all ships were illustrated, especially the older and smaller ones. However, as Jane would point out, it was precisely these vessels of little intrinsic value that would play a leading part in any naval war, as they could be risked where a battleship could not.[12] Also, although Clowes' little book was evidently intended for use on board ship, its format never answered the problem of ship recognition. Again the RUSI's reviewer felt that: "As with Brassey's, the plans of ships are rather a weak point".[13]

Clowes did, however, witness developments that would lead to a solution of the problem which had baffled both his and Lord Brassey's annuals. In an article on 'The New Navies', in the *English Illustrated Magazine*, he used illustrations from an imaginary naval chaplain's portfolio of sketches, which were in fact drawn by Fred T Jane. These showed Jane's usual cosmopolitan choice of material, drawn in an increasingly confident style. In addition,

Clowes gave a significant indication of how Jane worked, the chaplain acknowledging of the USS *Indiana*, that she was "not from life but adapted from a photograph".[14] It was Jane's access in 1896 to what was "probably the finest collection of warship photographs then in existence" which enabled him to carry out his grand design of illustrating every fighting ship in the world.[15] This set of a "dozen big albums" belonged to "the merchant banker William Bieber",[16] who later contributed an index of merchant liners to *Fighting Ships*. In one of his novels, Jane paid tribute to Bieber's collection: "everyone knows, our Admiralty has a collection of sorts of war-ship photos, but the book is so sacred and confidential that hardly anyone under a flag captain may get a squint at it. And I very much doubt if 'tis a patch on what young Ransome had got together".[17]

With typical generosity, Jane always acknowledged the role which others played in the success of his venture. Besides Clowes and Robinson, the first issue of *All the World's Fighting Ships* credited a trio which symbolises Jane's ability to make useful friends: Commander H H Campbell RN, of HMS *Majestic*, flagship of the Channel Fleet; the naval expert H W Wilson; and Major (later Colonel) Cyril Fields, Royal Marine Light Infantry (RMLI), himself an accomplished artist. He had illustrated William Le Queux's *The Great War in England 1897*, and later produced *Britain's Sea Soldiers*, an illustrated history of the Royal Marines.[18]

* * *

If Jane owed much of his basic information to others, the use he made of it was distinctively his own. The 500 pen and ink sketches which he drew from Bieber's collection during 1896–97, about half the total needed for *All the World's Fighting Ships*, were fitted into a logical framework that was quite unique. There were two elements in this. One was the manner in which the individual ship's details were presented, and the second was the provision of several distinct paths into the book, speeding up the process of finding information about any particular ship.

The illustrations and technical information appeared together, so that it was no longer necessary to look at two separate pages to appreciate the layout of a ship's guns and their calibre. This might appear obvious now but it was a concept which had eluded both established reference works. The other obvious idea that nobody had thought of was: "to collect into a convenient form illustrations showing the general appearance of all the fighting ships of the world at sea, with sufficient clearness to lead to their identification at several miles distance".[19] This was achieved through a mixture of sketches and silhouettes. The early issues of *Fighting Ships* deliberately excluded photographs. This was not because Jane was ignorant of photography: he had taken quarter plate photographs of his converted workshop in Holborn. *Fighting Ships* did not use photographs: "because in photographs directly reproduced essential detail is so often obscured by non-essential".[20]

In addition, he contended that the cameras of the day exaggerated the length of ship's hulls. The style of his drawings allowed him to eliminate unnecessary detail, and lent itself to slight accentuation of the salient and characteristic features of a ship's appearance, facilitating prompt recognition. This was consistent with his view, expressed in a lecture 'Every Man His Own Artist' that: "It is to grasp the idea that makes the true artist ... good technique just puts one on the level of a coach painter".[21] The disadvantage of sketches was the effort required to produce them. Late in 1897, Jane was working an 18 hour day to complete the illustrations for *Fighting Ships*, which stretched some 400 feet laid end to end.

To allow each sketch to appear with the appropriate technical detail, Jane pursued a system: "of absolute simplicity combined with practical utility. Guns and armour were referred to by an alphabetical notation expressing their comparative values. For instance a "D" gun (which might be either an old 10 inch or 9.4 inch, or a modern 6 inch) would be capable of piercing armour of "D" or less thickness, whether iron, compound or thin steel".[22] The value assigned to a particular gun depended on its muzzle energy in foot tons, from the most powerful "A" class at 20,000 foot tons, down to "E" class at 2,000 to 800. Armour classifications related: "approximately to what the gun correspondingly lettered may be expected to penetrate at close range in actual practice".[23]

The system provided an immediate comparison of different ships' fighting value, despite the bewildering variety of weapons and protective measures which characterised late 19th century fleets. To know that a ship mounted a particular calibre of gun did not help very much, unless it was also known who made it, and when. As a later review of Brassey's annual commented: "Who is to know that a 3.4 inch German gun is a 15 pounder, or a 2.2 inch in a French ship is a 3 pounder and so on? For the non-expert to have to hunt up what all these small calibre guns are must be a hopelessly confusing business".[24]

Jane's approach to the speed of ships was similarly practical. His willingness to mix with naval personnel regardless of their branch or rank gave him an understanding of practical engineering issues shared by few other commentators of the day. Usually the figures that he quotes are several knots less than those given in other authorities, his reasoning being: "none of the speeds given in tabulated lists of ships is reliable. These speeds are made under the most favourable conditions with picked coal, picked stokers, and in smooth water. The more rough and ready conditions at sea reduce a ship's speed by two to four knots; the fouling of the bottom by seaweed and barnacles, and the gradual ageing of machinery, compels a still greater reduction in time".[25]

One of the most glaring over-statements of ships' speeds was for the Turkish fleet. The Sultan, fearing a naval coup d'etat, had critical parts of the engines removed from his ships and sometimes the propellers. However, the *Naval Annual* continued, without comment, to quote the quite respectable speeds that these sabotaged vessels had achieved on completion in the 1860s.[26]

The second innovation of *All the World's Fighting Ships*, was the way in which it led the user into the illustrations with a page of silhouettes near the start of the book: "drawn as the vessels appeared at extreme horizon distance, with the slight distortion that this view often produces".[27]

The silhouettes were arranged in order of the number of funnels and masts carried, distinguishing between their different types. Facing these was a list of pages on which ships corresponding to each silhouette could be found. It was thus possible to go more or less directly to the correct page simply from the ship's appearance. With some idea of the nationality of a ship it was possible to use the primary sequence of the book, turning directly to the pages for the navy in question. Within each navy ships were arranged in a sequence according to the number of funnels and masts carried. A normal index allowed ships to be looked up by name. However, unlike the compilers of previous naval directories, Jane did not expect the user to know what ship he was looking at before finding it in the directory. The silhouette index lasted in various forms until the late 1980s, by which time ships were identified by their radar characteristics rather than funnels. Perhaps the most remarkable success of silhouettes was their adoption by the successor to Brassey's *Naval Annual*. This eventually replaced its ship diagrams with silhouettes, which it used until 1949 when it ceased to compete as a naval directory.

All the World's Fighting Ships was originally intended for publication at Christmas 1897, its preface being datelined London, November 1897. In fact its prospectus appeared in January 1898, and shortly afterwards the book was on sale in capitals across the world. The British publishers were Sampson Low Marston and Co, of Fetter Lane in the City, a well known maritime publisher. They were new associates for Jane, as his

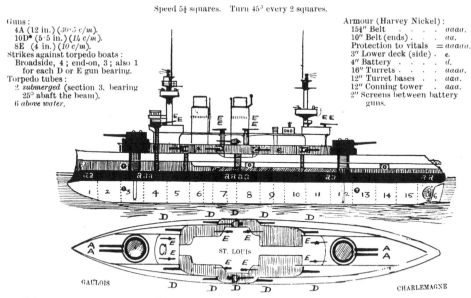

CHARLEMAGNE, ST. LOUIS & GAULOIS. 11,260 tons. Complement 631.
(May also be used for *Iéna*, 12,052 tons.)

Speed 5¼ squares. Turn 45° every 2 squares.

Guns :
4A (12 in.) (*30·5 c/m*).
10D* (5·5 in.) (*14 c/m*).
8E (4 in.) (*10 c/m*).
Strikes against torpedo boats :
Broadside, 4 ; end-on, 3 ; also 1
for each D or E gun bearing.
Torpedo tubes :
2 *submerged* (section 3, bearing
25° abaft the beam).
6 *above water*.

Armour (Harvey Nickel) :
15¾" Belt . . . . *aaaa*.
10" Belt (ends) . . . *aa*.
Protection to vitals = *aaaaa*.
3" Lower deck (side) . *ε*.
4" Battery . . . . *d*.
16" Turrets . . . . *aaaa*.
12" Turret bases . . *aaa*.
12" Conning tower . *aaa*.
2" Screens between battery
guns.

This scorer may also be used for *Iéna* (see "All the World's Fighting Ships" for data). Fire the four 4-inch guns as one 6-inch till three are out of action, then cease fire for all.

The Jane Naval War Game (Naval Kriegspiel). *Copyright*, 1903.

Jane's integrated presentation of warship data

previous naval work had been handled by William Thacker. However, he already published Laird Clowes' *Naval Pocket Book*, and perhaps believed one naval directory was enough. Jane may have been introduced to his new publishers by Laird Clowes, whose seven volume history of the Royal Navy owed much to Richard Marston, one of Sampson Low's directors.

The British price of the new album was ten shillings and sixpence, compared with twelve and six for the *Naval Annual*, and seven and six for the *Naval Pocket Book*. The worldwide sales were indicative of the avowed cosmopolitan approach which characterised the work from its inception. The preface to the first two issues was printed in French, German, and Italian as well as English. In 1900 these were done away with, on the grounds that: "Nearly everybody these days is able to read English sufficiently well to be able to gather the meaning".[28]

However, the title page was still in eight languages, including Russian, Japanese, Spanish, and Swedish, while a multilingual glossary continued for some time. In addition the schematic style in which the information was presented, especially the alphabetic Gun/Armour notation, bypassed many of the linguistic problems of textual descriptions. It is not clear how far the cosmopolitan nature of *Fighting Ships* was the result of the mind-broadening effects of foreign travel, although Jane did claim to have "knocked about in my time" when discussing his method of learning any foreign language using only a dictionary and a Bible.[29] Unfortunately, Jane's anecdotes about Cockney pickpockets at Berlin railway station, or meeting the Kaiser are hopelessly compromised by his admittedly mendacious claims to have been a war-correspondent in South America.

An indication of the international appeal of *Fighting Ships* came from Prince Henry of Prussia, who expressed his interest in the book when Jane met him at Portsmouth in December 1897. Jane usually referred to the Prince as 'Maily Fist', alluding to the blood-curdling speeches made as the Prince's squadron left Wilhelmshaven to assert German interests in the Far East. The German cruisers, *Deutschland* and *Gefion*, put into Portsmouth Harbour for coal, the weather making it unsafe for the lighters to go alongside out in Spithead [30]. This provided an opportunity for the Prince to go up to London to visit his grandmother, Queen Victoria, and for Fred T Jane to go onboard with an acquaintance from the Royal Marines. In more troubled times, not long after the

British defeat at Coronel at the hands of the German Navy, whose commerce raiders in the Pacific surprised and destroyed two old Royal Navy cruisers in November 1914, Jane recalled the fine, thick candelabra of the *Deutschland's* wardroom, and how: "We laughed at both Maily Fist and his ships. I don't think at that time . . . anybody would have believed it possible that the Germans could ever become a great naval power".[31] In an irreverent moment they had tried on the Prince's hat: "more or less impolite but I suppose it indicates how little a few years ago anyone could take the German Navy seriously. And now..."

The German visit to Portsmouth came as Jane decided to move away from London permanently. In the summer of 1897 he had arranged the reception of Sir William Ingram, principal proprietor of the *Illustrated London News*, when he visited Southsea for the Diamond Jubilee Review.[32] British commentators described this as the: 'greatest demonstration in favour of peace that the world has seen".[33] One hundred and sixty-five of the Royal Navy's 451 ships were on display in Spithead. Many of the ships were recently built, forming a modern, homogeneous fleet, in

Some ships from *Fighting Ships* 1898: two Majestics and *Sans Pareil*

contrast with the Review of 1887, when there had been: "scarcely two ships alike in the assembled fleet, and only three of the battleships armed with breech-loading guns".[34]

The Naval Commander in Chief at Portsmouth issued special instructions to prevent accidents arising from the great number of vessels: mail ships were to enter the Solent via the Needles, steamers were to burn only the best Welsh coal to reduce smoke levels, and all private boats were to keep away from the warships during the illuminations to avoid being damaged by the salutes.[35]

However, Jane did not move down to Southsea for good until early 1898, when he was approaching 33 years old. He settled his family in one of the area's duller streets, developed in the 1860s and 1870s, to the west of the prosperous middle class shopping centre of Palmerston Road.[36] Although subsequent issues of *Fighting Ships* were grandiloquently dated 'Tressillian House, Southsea', the street directories reveal that this was otherwise known as 17 Elphinstone Road, a substantial three-storey semi-detached house, with steps up to a grand porch. Like most householders, Jane rented his house. The municipal rating authorities estimated this cost him £55 a year. He was evidently prospering as the rateable value of his new home showed a 50 percent increase over the house he left in Chesilton Road, from £31 to £46-10s.[37] The winding tree-lined streets of Southsea and the Common with its easy access to the beach must have been more congenial than the monotonous 'Bye-Law' streets of Fulham. Perhaps the grandiloquence of 'Tressillian House', named after a village near Truro on the road to Bodmin, was intended to underline Jane's escape from the vulgar drudgery of his London life, to a lifestyle more in keeping with his origins, and his aspirations. It must have been quieter too. Before leaving Fulham he had written, presumably in sarcastic vein, of his preference for working to the strains of a barrel organ, one of the recognised scourges of the London street scene. Apart from the boarding houses associated with a seaside resort, in one of which Jane had stayed in December 1897, the houses in Elphinstone Road were occupied by professional and service personnel. These included a retired admiral, a naval doctor, several colonels, and Captain Pitcairn Jones RN, who would command the Naval Brigade at Colenso, during the Boer War. These neighbours represented a distinct social shift from the rate-collectors and dressmakers of Chelsea, an indication of the success Jane counted on *Fighting*

Jane's house at 17 Elphinstone Road, Southsea

A reminder of Fred T's later connection with the Scout Movement

Ships to bring him. More direct evidence comes from the reviews, which soon recognised that the new directory was unique, standing on a different footing from previous naval reference books: "When we say that illustrations are given of every type of warship in all the navies of the world, special pains being taken to point out any peculiarities of funnels, masts, etc which may assist towards identification, it will be seen what amount of labour and love Mr Jane must have thrown into his book".[38]

The *Times*, referring to; "Mr Jane the well known naval artist", appreciated immediately the value of the distinct and characteristic drawings, "which enable the practised eye to distinguish between vessels of the same general type".[39] Although Mr Jane himself deprecated the artistic value of his drawings, the *Times* felt these were: "not mere diagrams but genuine portraits of ships and considerable skill is displayed in attaining a certain measure of artistic variety of treatment without sacrificing utilitarian distinctness".

The *Times* also provided some pointers to future developments with comments that the technical details could be expanded to use the plentiful blank spaces around the drawings, which in the case of ironclads should also be accompanied by a diagram of their armour. Although *Fighting Ships* did provide armour diagrams in 1898, these were at the back of the book, forming an exception to Jane's usually integrated presentation of information. *The Thunderer* was on less sure ground, however, when it opined that the book: "would probably be found more attractive by the intelligent landsman desirous of studying the evolution of the modern warship than by practical seamen". *The Naval Warrant Officer's Journal*, presenting the view of the professional "bone and muscle of the service", flatly disagreed: "We can only repeat our previous advice to our readers – but more especially to the signal boatswains – viz: Get it at once . . . It should form part of the outfit of every chart-house and be within reach of the signal-man and officer on watch on the bridge".[40]

The following year, the same journal described *Fighting Ships* as "more indispensable than ever",[41] and made a plea for the Admiralty to place a copy within reach of all naval personnel. Whatever the critics, navy-blue or otherwise, may have written, the first issue of *Fighting Ships* enjoyed sufficient commercial success to require a second edition within a few months [42]. Apart from its intrinsic merits, the book owed its success to the readiness of the market for such ventures. It satisfied the Victorian craze for directories, their: "passion for blue books . . . the John Bull belief that whatever can be labelled is safe, and the national belief that facts and figures act as a counter-charm to sentiment and revolution".[43] The rationalist urge for systematisation that, at a philosophical level produced Marx and Darwin, led at a more mundane level to *Kelly's Street Directories*, and Sherlock Holmes' standby, *Bradshaw's Railway Guide*. Jane can be seen as one of the great synthesists of the 19th century, even if one does not necessarily agree with his view, propounded in a debate about suffragettes, that *all* questions are naval questions.[44]

The year 1897 was a particularly good one to launch a naval directory. Apart from the excitement of the Diamond Jubilee, there had been a high level of international instability, always good for sales: "No year since the Naval Annual was first published has been so full of anxiety for those at the helm of the British Empire, in no year has there been such imminent danger of war".[45]

In the same issue of Brassey's annual, attention was drawn to "the vastly increased interest taken by Englishmen in questions of naval defence". Twenty-five years before, when Jane was a schoolboy, periodicals had betrayed "scarcely a trace of any movement of opinion on the matter". Since then: "a great body of public opinion has been formed, and on the occasion of the discussion of naval needs, a sound knowledge of essential facts and principles is often displayed".[46] This body of public opinion was ascribed largely to a number of influential naval writers, military men, and journalists, leading to the foundation in the 1890s of such very different groups as the Navy League and the Navy Records Society. The market largely developed itself, as rising levels of education led to greater awareness of Britain's position in the world, and the threats to that position posed by the rise of other maritime and industrial powers. Be that as it may, if Brassey's list, which included Robinson, Sir George Clarke, and H W Wilson had been compiled a year or two later, it would also have had to include the editor of *Fighting Ships*, as a major purveyor of those 'essential facts'.

* * *

For the editor of *Fighting Ships* the next few years were a time of continuous evolution, and experiment, as he reacted to his critics and developed his own plans: "Thanks to the kindness of readers and users of this book in all parts of the world, the ideal of making it a thoroughly cosmopolitan Annual for all navies seems in a fair way towards realisation. The reception accorded to the first issue was so far favourable that this the second year's issue is able to proceed on the lines of expansion embodied in the original idea . . . The idea is to give everything likely to be of practical utility and to steadily avoid anything else".[47]

The demands of Jane's correspondents for more detail increased the scope of the information provided for each ship. By 1901, detailed gun and armour data was listed on either side of the plans provided for all significant ships, the Engineering notes appearing below. However, Jane defended his alphabetic notation system as the most convenient way of providing a common denominator for all types of armour. It was, he argued, quite impossible to calculate armour penetration quickly: there were simply too many types of armour in existence [48]. He also defended his differentiation of ships by their rig, and steam pipes against those who argued, like the *Times'* critic, that these were easily changed in war, and were therefore unreliable. In fact, it is not so easy to alter such things. The first that Admiral von Spee knew of the arrival of British battlecruisers in the South Atlantic in November 1914 were the tripod masts of HMS *Invincible* and *Inflexible*, above the harbour at Port Stanley. As we have seen, Jane also defended his non-use of photographs, although in 1899 all illustrations had been compared with the: "unique collection of warship photographs owned by Lieutenant the Marquis de Balincourt, author of Les Flottes de Combat".[49]

However, even in the 1899 issue, a single photograph of a French torpedo boat found its way onto page 124, a precursor of things to come. In general the publishing industry had been slow to print photographs, although the first half-tone photographic block had appeared in the *Daily Graphic* in New York in 1880. Until the 1890s, publishers were content to use photographs, as Jane used them, as the authoritative source for engravings made on wood blocks. Then in 1897, the *New York Tribune* became the first newspaper to print half-tone reproductions on high speed presses using the now familiar matrix of thousands of tiny dots. By the end of the century high class magazines were using half-tone reproductions for many of their illustrations.[50] Jane was among the leaders of the industry when, in 1900, he substituted photographs for most of his sketches, conceding that: "should this new departure meet with favour, it will be extended to the remainder of the illustrations".[51]

Such a step could only have been taken at the end of the 1890s, as cameras became available on a sufficiently wide scale to ensure coverage of all the world's ships. The Boer War, which coincided with *Fighting Ship's* migration to the new technology, was among the first to be recorded by cameras held by actual combatants. Similarly Jane's commitment to photography depended on the numerous correspondents: "who have sent corrections and photographs ... For the information of others who may be disposed to place their cameras at the disposal of *Fighting Ships*, I may mention that quarter plate photos are a quite convenient size. The views should be broadside ... not taken from too near. They should be as sharp as possible and the less pictorial and artistic effect the better".[52]

The following year, Jane wrote that every marine photographer of standing was a contributor to his pages.[53] Meanwhile, the appearance of *Fighting Ships* varied dramatically as the book emerged from what Jane termed its "chrysalis stage". There was little uniformity between the individual ship's entries in the 1900 issue. Most had a photograph, supported by a muddle of plans, silhouettes and text, although only the most significant, such as HMS *Majestic* had all three forms of illustration. By 1901 *Fighting Ships* had achieved its mature form with some 3,000 illustrations. In principle this has hardly altered since, although it has grown in size. Jane himself felt that at last he had: "nearly achieved the ideal result for which five years of steady labour have been expended".[54] All the information for any major unit appeared on one page, with a diagram in uniform 1/1200th scale, and at least one photograph: "The fourth Annual Issue of Mr Fred T. Jane's *All the World's Fighting Ships* ... is in many ways an improvement upon its predecessors".[55]

The introduction of photographs, in particular, was seen as "a guarantee of accuracy". The last change introduced was to resequence the ship illustrations by fighting value, that is into the classes in which they would be met in wartime. For recognition purposes, the silhouette indexes were improved, each navy now having its own: "This is an exceedingly useful addition, for in time of war a man seeing a ship come out clear against the horizon does not want to hunt through a list of warships of various nationalities before he can identify her. And the silhouette is all he can see; the minor details are not capable of being distinguished at such a distance".[56]

The cost of these changes, which led to most of the book being reset, was partly borne by price increases, and partly by means of advertisements. In 1899 the price went up to twelve shillings and sixpence, and in 1901 to 15, due to the "enormous cost of production". However, like a good salesman Jane argued that the book was really cheaper, as the: "scope of the book is immensely increased, and the projected Ship Silhouette Book is practically included".[57]

He himself received eight shillings and fourpence for each copy sold of the 1900 issue.[58] Advertisements first appeared in 1899, a mere two pages, mostly devoted to books published by Sampson Low Marston and Co, but also to Siebe and Gorman's Diving Apparatus, and appropriately to Symonds and Co, Marine Photographers. The next year, there were ten pages, and Jane was able to write to his agent that he felt: "ads are going to turn out trumps. I've got one 20-pounder". He was also sufficiently confident to turn down a "£60 ad gold letter on back of cover for a hotel, on grounds that it isn't classy looking and would lower the book's tone".[59]

By this time, early in 1900, Jane was about to take more direct responsibility for production of *Fighting Ships*. He formed a partnership with Henry Western Hutchinson, a civil engineer by trade, not a publisher. They called themselves The Naval Syndicate, with an office at 8 Marmion Buildings, Southsea, five minutes' walk from Jane's home in Elphinstone Road. Early in

March 1900, they bought the title, *Fighting Ships*, from Sampson Low Marston and Co, for £75, together with: "all blocks, electros, all rights in standing type, all exchange blocks from Messrs Thacker . . . together with all other rights and goodwill and stock of every description".[60]

Hutchinson provided the money for this, sending a cheque directly to Marston.[61] In future The Naval Syndicate would allow Sampson Low Marston and Co to: "publish the work in the UK for 10 per cent commission provided that it is delivered to them ready for publication and to do their best to push the same subject".[62]

A later agreement clarified that while The Naval Syndicate was responsible for "producing the work ready for circulation in the printer's hands", Sampson Low Marston and Co should, "bear all other costs incidental to proper advertisement carriage delivery office and otherwise".[63] Other arrangements were included for the return of out-of-date issues, previously sold to the trade, the indemnification of the publishers against legal actions arising from material of a "scandalous or libellous character", and payment by the publishers to The Naval Syndicate quarterly, Jane wanting "no nonsense about 18 months credit".[64] Other publishers handled foreign sales: in France, the magazine *Le Yacht*, and in the United States, Harper Bros of New York.[65]

It is not clear why Jane broke with his original publishers in this way. He was obviously dissatisfied with them as, to begin with, he attempted to issue *Fighting Ships* through another marine publisher, Simpkin, Marshall and Co in London. The obvious alternative, Griffin's at the Hard in Portsmouth, could not take up the book, as they already published the Naval Annual, and Lord Brassey might object. Perhaps the nature of *Fighting Ships* made necessary a closer relationship between author and printer than was usual. Hutchinson, who "has lots of money and doesn't care a rap re F. Ships so long as he doesn't lose on it", was prepared to let Jane get on with the technical side of the book, while he dealt with the administration. It was Hutchinson's name that was specified as the authorised signature of The Naval Syndicate, until he sold his share in 1908. The constant revision of content and layout evidently made *Fighting Ships* a different proposition from the rest of Sampson Low Marston and Co's business. Certainly Jane felt that his work was in a peculiar channel, sails having to be trimmed accordingly.[66] His penchant for plain speaking may not have made him the easiest of authors to work with. His letters to his literary agent, William Colles, exude impatience with the administrative niceties that prevented him forging ahead. When a row loomed with Marston over the Jane Naval Wargame, Jane noted with satisfaction that: "the agreement was drawn up by me & therefore involved & the rest of it (as you have often said) but like all my agreements it'll bear arguing any construction I like to put on it".[67]

It seems, however, that he was generally dissatisfied with his success, or otherwise, as an author. During the early years of *Fighting Ships*, Jane wrote two novels, *The Port Guard Ship*, and *Ever Mohun*. These effectively marked the end of his novel writing, until he returned to the form in 1908 with *A Royal Bluejacket*. Like the later work, *The Port Guard Ship* was concerned primarily with that standby of the English novel, the workings of the class system. Our hero is a naval warrant officer who with the usual obtuseness of Jane's heroes, falls in love with a lady, generally regarded as beyond his station. Even winning the Victoria Cross does not help; a commission, which would make him a gentleman, is beyond his reach. Subsequently the novel was, "understood to have influenced the Admiralty decision to open commissioned rank to warrant officers",[68] although it is not clear to which Admiralty measure this claim refers. It is most likely that McMurtrie meant Admiral Fisher's establishment in 1903 of the rank of lieutenant for a small percentage of chief warrant officers for, "long and meritorious service". However, this only applied to WOs about to retire, and it was only in the Second World War that WOs commonly came to receive commissions. In the meantime, they were victims of the hardening arteries of English society. Only four ratings had been commissioned between 1818 and 1902,[69] reflecting a decline in social mobility, in the navy and in the country as a whole.[70]

It seems unlikely that Jane's novel did in fact cause a change in Admiralty policy. It would take decades of social change, including two world wars, to do that. Even Winston Churchill's 'Mate Scheme' of 1912 had limited effect. Paradoxically this was partly because of opposition from the man to whom Fred T Jane had dedicated *The Port Guard Ship*: Prince Louis of Battenberg, who as First Sea Lord took a dim view of ranker officers.[71] Prince Louis would appear more substantially in Jane's last novel, *A Royal Bluejacket*, as "a princeling of no particular importance", who: "had been put at a tender age into a British naval gunroom and left to shift for himself . . . He had stuck to the sea thereafter because he loved it; and beyond being called Prince instead of by his surname he had lived and had his being just as his fellow officers. There were strange stories at Court in his day as to his disrespect for the usual Court conventions . . .".[72]

The real significance of *The Port Guard Ship* is that it provides the first evidence of Jane's interest in the social reform of the navy. This led to Jane's political adventures, foreshadowed in the novel by a splendid free-fight at an imaginary election address.[73] As a work of literature *The Port Guard Ship* contains some tedious passages not entirely compensated for by the well observed descriptions of naval life in a typical home port, before Admiral Fisher's reforms did away with the system of stationing elderly battleships around the coast in various odd creeks. Strangely Jane did not illustrate the story, although he did consider buying it back from its publisher in order to do so.

Ever Mohun, on the other hand, was a light romance, although as Dr Watson might have said, it cost one man his life, and another his reason. Like Jane's other Devonian tale, *His Lordship, the Passen, and We*, *Ever Mohun* made subtle use of dialect, with plenty of local colour, including a dig at the length of Jane's father's sermons. Dedicated to his mother, the story is again largely concerned with the dysfunctional nature of the class system. Its heroine, a girl called Ever, is like Thomas Hardy's Tess of the d'Urbervilles, from an old rural family fallen on hard times. The family name comes from the 13th century manor of Mohun's Ottery, between Monkton and Upottery, the only (fictional) remains of former grandeur being a pigsty with a Norman arch. Although Ever doesn't suffer the same disastrous fate as Tess, the same general assumption lies behind the story, that only the worst can be expected from a liaison between such a girl and a son of the manor house, even if the squire is only a successful draper knighted for financial services to the Liberal Party. Such was Jane's disillusionment with his prospects as a novelist, that he considered publishing *Ever Mohun* under his wife's name. "The position of my novels is desperate frost – frost – frost. I'm not at all sure 'Ever' hadn't better appear under an assumed name. Mine has no value for it [underlined in original]: send it out under "by Alice Hamilton Beattie" [underlined] & see what comes of it. I don't fancy that its well to do novels and serious literature both under same name".[74]

Certainly science fiction does not seem to have been a very respectable form of writing. Serious writers shied away from it, while H G Wells seems to have been embarrassed by his early successes. By the early 20th century the boom in fantasy writing was largely over. Although it is hard to see how Jane could have followed *The Violet Flame*, so prodigal was it of ideas, even so independent a writer as Jane must have tired of swimming against the tide [75]. In the event, *Ever Mohun* appeared under Jane's own name, but he had reason for complaint on the serious front also: "Nothing definite yet re Admiralty: but there'll be no profit via them this year".[76]

Although the man in the fleet, represented by the *Naval Warrant Officer's Journal* was "utterly unable to understand" why "copies are not distributed throughout the British Navy",[77] the Admiralty never in fact took up *Fighting Ships* officially during Jane's lifetime. Part of the reason may have been the usual Victorian distrust of anything new. An idea put forward to the Admiralty in the 1890s by the young Doveton Sturdee, already a tactical expert, was annotated: "on what authority does this Lieutenant put forward such a proposal?".[78] Ironically when Sturdee was at the Admiralty in 1914, he would be no more ready to delegate authority to subordinates.[79] Another reason for the Admiralty's lack of interest may have been the generally lackadaisical manner in which business was transacted there: "in most departments papers took weeks, even months to deal with and if one had chose not to work there was little incentive to do so".[80] Although the Naval Intelligence Department had been founded in 1887, it had little money to spend, and there was no naval staff at all. In fact, even 20 years later: "officers who made any real study of war from the point of view of staff work were often regarded as cranks or lunatics, hunters of soft jobs".[81]

The net result for Jane was a lack of sales in the very quarter where he might have hoped for support. Even the big shipping lines carried copies of *Fighting Ships* by 1901.[82] The accumulated frustration overflowed in a furious letter that ended his relationship with Colles, at least as far as *Fighting Ships* was concerned: "instead of making the fortune I ought to be making: I'm next door to starving on £500 a year . . . Yet if you asked the ordinary man in the street who were the top men who expounded ships, he'd mention my name before most to a cert. There's no 1st rate in my novels, its true, but they're good 2nd rate. And with it all

I see 3rd raters making more than I do, with half the brains, and a quarter the labour".[83]

By the beginning of the First World War, the average earnings of well-paid professional men were £328 a year, so one may take "next door to starving" with a pinch of salt. However, £500 was below the minimum of £600 a year that one contemporary sociologist thought sufficient to support, "the standard of refined and educated necessities". This bears comparison with the alternative, "standard of simple necessities" which required earnings of 25 shillings a week, a figure that was still more than many labourers achieved.[84] Even if Fred T Jane was not really on the brink of starving, his income did not adequately reflect the professional status to which he aspired. He could not therefore relax his efforts to gain the financial rewards which he felt, with only a little exaggeration, his talents deserved.

CHAPTER IV

HOW TO PLAY THE JANE NAVAL
WARGAME

ANY of the changes made to *Fighting Ships* in its early issues only make sense in the light of Jane's other main interest at that time: the Jane Naval Wargame. In particular, this influenced the style of plans gradually introduced into *Fighting Ships* for all except the most obsolete ships. In 1900 Jane described them as being "uniform wargame plan scale", or 1/1200th. As can be seen from surviving examples, their general layout is identical to the scorer cards used for the game. Such was the interdependence of the book and the game that, when Jane bought *Fighting Ships* back from Sampson Low Marston and Co in March 1900, the contract made specific provision for sharing the blocks used both as scorers and ship illustrations. To a game designer the Gun/ Armour notation system which Jane felt, "worked so satisfactorily in connection with my naval wargame", has every appearance of being a wargame mechanism from the beginning. The Jane Naval Wargame and *Fighting Ships* should therefore be regarded as a single integrated package. In the context of the period, this is less odd than it might now appear. Today, wargaming is frequently considered a hobbyist's pastime. Although defence professionals still use a variety of wargames to simulate different levels of conflict, public knowledge of these is necessarily restricted. They may also use computers, compared with the tin models and cardboard of more homely wargames. At the turn of the century, however, there were good professional reasons for naval officers, often at the forefront of their trade, to use the simple wargaming techniques of the day. As *The Engineer* reminded its readers: "the naval Kriegspiel is a game only in name".[1]

The Jane Naval Wargame had evolved, after the destruction of Fred T Jane's fleet of biscuit-tin-clad models, into something more economical, and perhaps rather safer, involving only the destruction of paper targets. It had then languished in a lumber room until 1897. When he first moved down to Portsmouth the game was dusted off, and taken on board the ships of the Channel Fleet, in particular HMS *Majestic*, where, "it was played . . . very much á la ping pong, 'til one day the captain, Prince Louis of Battenberg, asked about it, and wished to see the rules".[2] Feeling somewhat of a fraud, the inventor: "hastily recast the thing into its original serious mould, plus a variety of improvements that occurred to me, or were suggested by various naval friends".[3]

We will probably never know the exact nature of the original game. However, many of the features of the Jane Naval Wargame show a high degree of continuity with earlier naval wargames. These were a relatively recent development, following the advent

Fred T Jane in his early thirties with the Naval Wargame

of steam-powered battleships. As long as ships were at the mercy of the wind straightforward seamanship was of more account in sea battles than clever tactical manoeuvres which were simply not possible because of the ships' limited mobility. Steamships, on the other hand, appeared to lend themselves only too readily to tactical manoeuvring. Some officers thought the old line of battle was still tactically sound. Others thought that squadrons should form groups of three or four ships, and use the flexibility of movement, under steam, to attack the wings of the enemy fleet, avoiding contact with their main body. What the enemy might do in the meantime was less clear.

The Admiralty certainly offered no guidance, if we may believe Lieutenant William M F Castle RN who presented his fleet manoeuvring game at the RUSI in 1873: "at present no facility whatever for the study of tactical formations is given by the authorities to the officers in charge of ships . . . Another point we are deficient in is the absence of an authorised 'manual of naval tactics' which could be procured by Officers desirous of studying this important subject. We ought to have a tactical naval drill book similar to the Army Light Infantry Drill Book — a book procurable at the nearest stationer's shop".[4]

Much of Castle's game was taken up with mechanical calculations of such elementary manoeuvres as forming line abreast from line ahead. The Admiralty does not appear, at this time, even to have told its officers the size of turning circle required by new ships. It all depended on individual ships' officers conducting the necessary experiments. Castle was himself responsible for the turning circle data used in the game. Several officers present at the meeting commented on the practical value of Castle's tables, even when they doubted that enough data could be collected to produce a rival to the Army's Kriegspiel. However, the purpose of naval wargames was quite different from that of the Kriegspiel: "the wargame amongst military men is not to establish facts; it is to cultivate skill. Your facts are known . . . Under the present conditions, we in the Navy have no facts whatever to go on, and our wargame, for many years to come . . . can only show us not individual skill, but the method in which we are to arm our ships and use them afterwards".[5]

Twenty years later in 1893 HMS *Victoria* was accidentally rammed and sunk by HMS *Camperdown*, a disaster caused by the miscalculation of the courses of two columns of ships turning towards one another. This suggests that some of the facts about steamships were still not as well understood as they might have been, and the Admiralty did begin experiments with turning circles after the tragedy.

Castle's game equipment included a number of pads of paper 16 inches square, marked off in four inch squares. These could be placed together to make a playing surface 64 inches square, representing an area 16 nautical miles across, the effective limit of visibility. The ships were represented by numbered lead markers in the appropriate fleet colour (red or blue). There was no attempt to provide scale models, which at one fifth of an inch in length would have been far too small to handle. Despite Castle's attempts to simplify the game by ignoring differences between ship types, the game suffered from a plethora of tables and an overworked umpire who was expected to provide a mass of background information: "naming the object to be accomplished, the time allowed for the execution of this duty, the place at which coals may be procured, mail met, reinforcements found, ports that have to be closed, those that have to be defended . . . in fact he must supply each player with as much naval intelligence as would probably be communicated to the commander of a squadron..."

However, Castle did achieve his object of stimulating tactical debate amongst his messmates that ultimately had to be resolved by the commander of the ship. Castle had, moreover, introduced a system of command and control that would endure in naval wargames until the First World War. His game required five people: an umpire, and two teams each of a commander, who issued instructions based on the Evolutionary Signal Book, to be carried out by an assistant who actually moved the ships. Invalid instructions were delayed to reflect the resulting confusion. The designer thus ensured that commanders could not acquire sloppy habits, or fudge the results of unclear orders, by moving the ships themselves. Jane's game used a similar system, with admirals using signals to issue instructions to flag captains responsible for moving individual ships.

Castle's game had the serious limitation that it only allowed the players to manoeuvre their ships up to the point of opening fire. This was not because he was uninterested in what happened after that, but because, as a practical man he wanted to build his game in a modular fashion, upon solid foundations. He had deliberately: "only spoken of the elementary but . . . most useful evolutions, avoiding questions of rams, guns, or towing torpedoes, for until this game is accepted in its simpler form, I think it unwise to introduce the consequences of various offensive means which would ... add fresh complications."

However, the 1870s had introduced more complicated forms of battleship, with an emphasis on end-on fire, caused by the craze for ramming tactics. With no practical experience of war, some other means was needed of evaluating the relative fighting power of ironclads. Some placed all their guns on the broadside, as had HMS *Warrior*, while others, such as HMS *Alexandra* launched in 1875, placed them to fire ahead and astern, which reduced the effect of their broadside. Such was the confusion that the Russians even built some circular battleships, which tended to revolve when opening fire. There was no objective means of comparing the tactical value of these different design philosophies. The problem was brought before a meeting of the RUSI in 1879 by Captain, later Vice Admiral, Philip Colomb. He proposed to settle the matter with a wargame, developed from Castle's earlier efforts.[6] Colomb's interests covered such diverse matters as signalling, preventing collisions at sea, machine guns, and the fouling of ships' bottoms. Sir John Fisher, however, distrusted him, writing in 1893 that he was: "not a naval authority and he never comes to the point. He is now called 'a column and a half', in view of the length of his letters".[7]

Certainly, reading Colomb's interventions at RUSI meetings, one can see what Fisher meant. In 1879 Colomb was between commands, having previously commanded HMS *Audacious*, an ironclad, designed for end-on fire. He calculated the effect of gunfire using a points system, which varied with the striking angle and range, which went up to 2,000 yards. Players were allowed to choose the proportion of their guns that could fire ahead or abeam, but other features of the ships were constant. The effect of fire was reduced in proportion to the square of the range, so it was almost ineffective at long range. However, as Fred T Jane noted later, such points systems make no allowance for the lucky hit which inflicts catastrophic damage, like those which sank HMS *Inflexible* and *Invincible* at Jutland (also HMS *Hood* in 1941).[8] Those meeting at the RUSI failed to take up the offer of an immediate trial, ostensibly for lack of an umpire, although one retired admiral commented sadly that: "Many of our evenings are spent on much less interesting subjects than this". Colomb later

RULES
FOR
The Jane Naval War Game

A SEA KRIEGSPIEL SIMULATING ALL THE MOVEMENTS AND EVOLUTIONS OF EVERY
INDIVIDUAL TYPE OF MODERN WARSHIP, AND THE PROPORTIONATE
EFFECT OF EVERY SORT OF GUN AND PROJECTILE

PART I. TACTICAL   PART II. STRATEGICAL

INVENTED BY
FRED T. JANE
Author of "All the World's Fighting Ships," etc., etc.

REVISED AND APPROVED BY CAPTAIN H.I.H. GRAND DUKE ALEXANDER MIHAILOVITCH OF RUSSIA, I.R.N.; CAPTAIN H.S.H.
PRINCE LOUIS OF BATTENBERG, R.N.; CAPTAIN H. J. MAY, R.N.; AND LIEUTENANT R. KAWASHIMA, I.J.N.

LONDON
Sampson Low, Marston and Company
LIMITED
St. Dunstan's House, Fetter Lane, E.C.
1898

Title page of the original Jane Naval Wargame

published his game as 'The Duel', providing a simulation of an action between two single ironclads. The Russian Navy bought it, and used it regularly at their Naval Academy at Khronstadt, but the country for which it had been designed hardly used it at all.[9]

Some of the reasons for this became apparent during a later RUSI meeting. In April 1888, a retired naval lieutenant, Henry Chamberlain, presented his own attempt to provide the Royal Navy with a naval wargame that would be both instructive and playable. Chamberlain had served in HMS *Bellerophon*, with Vice Admiral Sir Edward Inglefield who had himself designed a fleet manoeuvring game, a copy of which is to be found in the National Maritime Museum. Chamberlain's career then seems to have languished somewhat, as he spent seven years at HMS *Vernon*, without apparently qualifying as a torpedo officer. In 1880 he retired from the navy, becoming Secretary of the Royal Naval School at Greenwich. Here he found a game that we can only assume was the Castle/Colomb effort.

The President of the Royal Naval College could not understand it, while the Captain Commanding said it would take him three hours to learn the rules, so what use was it to young officers? This led Chamberlain to the revolutionary discovery that: "for a game to become popular, it is first of all absolutely necessary that it

Wargame equipment: striker, targets, scorers and turning circles

should be simple".[10] This was particularly so in the navy where: "Few places are less adapted for the pursuit of study than the wardroom, gunroom or lower deck, and to expect people in addition to their watches and drills to undertake to play a game

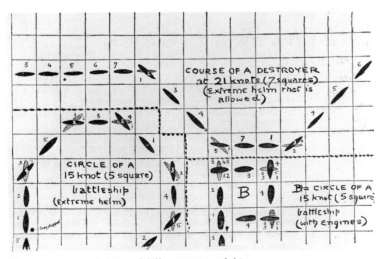

Manoeuvring capabilities of different types of ship

87

which involves a large amount of careful thought would be . . . a thankless task".

His game was therefore deliberately simple. It was played by two players on a two foot square board, divided into one inch squares. A few islands, high enough to block fire, could be rearranged for each game. There were only two ships, one of which was trying to evade a blockade maintained by the other. They moved alternately, at the same speed, one square ahead, or diagonally to port or starboard, without signalling in advance. Stopping or going astern was disallowed on the grounds that it would cause the stokers, down below, to panic. The only difference between the ships was that the blockade runner had a stern chaser, and the other a bow chaser. The effect of a gun firing and rolling 6 on a die, was to disable an opponent for six turns, providing an opportunity for ramming. The whole thing can be set up, played and put away in 15–20 minutes, the sort of time that might be available on board a ship at sea. Like Castle, Chamberlain found that: "before we had been playing more than 20 minutes, we had disputed and argued more about ramming, more about other professional subjects, than those young men had talked of in the last three months".

Young officers had the greater need for such mental exercise, as the passing of sail drastically reduced their opportunities for training on the job: "Twenty years ago, when ships had sails, youngsters were occasionally left in charge of the deck, and allowed to handle the ship under the supervision of the officer of the watch. Now, not only do the boys not get any chance of practice allowed them in handling the ship, but some officers attain the rank of senior Lieutenant, or even Commander, before they are permitted to take entire charge of the vessel".

Colomb, who was present, spoke handsomely, if at length, of the game, praising: "the arrangement of handling the ships on squares . . . because it does give an approximation to the powers which a ship has of turning...", adding ruefully that in his own game, there had been a great deal of medicine, and very little jam. Several officers then attempted to run the blockade. The chairman, Admiral Sir George Elliott, a self-confessed advocate of end-on attack, distinguished himself by ramming and sinking his opponent.

Chamberlain's game was marketed at 12s 6d (72.5p) a set, by a firm in Aldersgate Street, just two blocks to the east of the Gray's

Inn Road, where Jane was living at the time of the lecture. Like his own game, The Game of Naval Blockade broke away from the measuring scales which complicated earlier games, using a grid of small squares to integrate gunnery and movement. Like his game, it was adapted to the physical and mental circumstances of life on board ship, to provide a playable, as well as a useful game. The Jane Naval Wargame was distinguished by its all-embracing, cosmopolitan nature, allowing the players to represent any current warship simply and realistically, thus paving its way to an international success, which for a while rivalled that of *Fighting Ships*.

* * *

The Jane Naval Wargame differed from its predecessors by its generalised equipment and rules. Jane wanted to produce "a thorough sea equivalent to the Army War Game", which allowed any tactical problems to be worked out: "to that end not only each individual type of ship, but also every individual gun and projectile, method of protection, thickness and quality of armour is allowed for".[11]

The key feature was using scale models of every type of warship and the information about their fighting capabilities, now regularly updated in *Fighting Ships*. By 1902 over 100 vessels were available from a list which was regularly updated to keep pace with naval developments.[12] The models were about one and a half inches long, scaled to the blue-painted sea squares, two feet square, representing 2000 yards of water. These were further divided into smaller squares, one and a quarter inches across, each representing 100 yards. Heavier ships were made broader in the beam to make them look more convincing. Players were expected to be able to recognise the ships opposing them from the models. Individual ships were mounted on triangular bases which carried little red and green buoys. These were used to indicate when ships were intending to turn to port or starboard and could be removed when a ship lost its ability to steer.

Each player commanded a single ship which he moved in one minute turns, ostensibly executed in that time, one square per three knots. All first class battleships moved at 15 knots, second class battleships at 12, and cruisers at 18. Slight individual differences of speed appeared not to be of prime importance to Jane, where the evolutions of fleets were in question.[13] Turning circles, which had so troubled the pioneers of naval wargaming, were avoided as an unnecessary complication. In the early versions of Jane's game, the squares were used to provide a matrix for representing turning circles, or rather octagons, an approximation he felt satisfactory for all ordinary purposes. Ships could turn only four points at a time, that is 45 degrees, every other square, thus achieving a turning diameter roughly equal to that achieved by the average ironclad of the day.

The firing system was perhaps the most characteristic part of the game. At one time Jane alluded to a special machine which automatically calculated hit probability, depending on elevation, range and other factors: "This machine not being yet protected, cannot be fully described. It works, however, upon a very simple principle, and estimates the chances according to how the wheel setting the range is put".[14] By the time he published the game, however, a simpler mechanism was in use: "a strip of thin wood about 15 inches long, with an enlarged end, somewhere near the centre of which a short pin point projects. The target being laid flat upon the table, one of the views [of the target ship], according to the range and position of the enemy is struck at; the hole made by the pin point indicates where the shot is supposed to have hit".[15]

Jane admitted that the device had to be used to be appreciated. However, it solved many of the problems of representing the effect of naval gun-fire. It also allowed for chance, and made direction a great deal easier to achieve than elevation: "the variety in aiming power between players gives an equivalent to good or bad gunnery: and finally the thing is so contrived that a very little hesitation or excitement produces wild shooting".[16] The targets were printed on flimsy slips of paper. They provided views of the appropriate warships drawn from ahead and abeam in three sizes for use at 2000, 3000, and 4000 yards. Oblique fire was handled by covering up the defiladed half of the target. In poor visibility, players struck at the back of the targets.

After firing, targets were handed in for inspection by the other side, so that players would not necessarily know what damage they had done. They would therefore be depressed by hits on their own ship, without the moral uplift of knowing what punishment they had inflicted themselves, except when the umpires placed pieces of white or brown paper across the target for explosions or funnel hits. Players marked off the damage suffered by their ships on scorer cards that showed details of the ship's weapons and armour, in the same fashion as in *Fighting Ships*, crossing off guns or shading in sections of the hull which had been destroyed. The scorers were small enough to fit in a player's pocket to prevent their being seen by other players, on either side. The rules originally provided tables of effect for the different types of gun and projectile in use but eventually the strain of keeping up with progress told upon the game's developer, and the damage tables were replaced by the umpire's discretion. Jane defended this step on the grounds that standard damage levels allowed players too much knowledge of the effect of their fire. However, the simplification does not help anyone to play the game who is not a qualified gunnery lieutenant.

The equipment came in a stout wooden box, 29"x11", designed to withstand the hard knocks of naval life. Lined with felt, the box was divided internally into nine pigeon-holes to take the ships and so on, the partitions being sunk below the top of the box to accommodate the sea squares. The boxes had iron carrying handles, and a hinged front. Prices ranged from 4–6 guineas, while special sets ranged up to £40, "containing practically all the warships in the world".[17] An example of a Jane Naval Wargame has survived at the headquarters of Jane's Information Group, Coulsdon, although it lacks the ships and boards. A variety of evidence suggests that this was acquired, in 1906, by Sir Ronald Deane Ross, as a schoolboy. A long-serving Ulster Unionist MP, and spokesman on defence matters, he seems to have been a man after Jane's own heart. After Ross' death in 1958, a London *Times* correspondent wrote of his student days: "even in those days he was greatly interested in arms and armaments. A room in his Irish home was set aside for a complicated naval wargame of his own invention (sic) and he was reported to use his college rooms as a revolver range".[18]

Exactly how the box arrived at Coulsdon is a mystery, although a letter survives at the National Maritime Museum from Francis McMurtrie to Ross written in 1948. Less mysterious is the process by which the Jane Naval Wargame was brought before the public. The year 1897 saw a period of intense testing, partly by the officers of the Channel Fleet, and partly by Japanese officers, whose ship, the *Takasago*, was then at Portsmouth. This was followed by a lecture at the RUSI in June 1898 timed to coincide with publication of the original *Rules for The Jane Naval Wargame*. There was a second session at the RUSI in December 1899 with amended versions of the game appearing in 1902, 1905, and 1912.

One naval officer Captain Henry J May who attended the first RUSI meeting made a particularly significant contribution to the game. A brilliant officer, May took over Admiral Colomb's annual series of lectures at Greenwich in 1895,[19] going on in September 1901 to found the War Course there on his own initiative. Initially his only assistant was his daughter, an indication of the level of official support which he received [20]. While in command of the 3rd class cruiser HMS *Hyacinth* at Esquimault in British Columbia, he had felt the need for some method like Jane's: "In trying to study naval tactics in the Pacific, where although we had lots of space and long sea cruises, we had no ships to manoeuvre with...".[21]

He had therefore written to Jane to enquire about his game, subsequently objecting to some of the complications of the rules which he was sent. A feature of all Jane's wargame books was an openness to "suggestions in the way of increased realism and simplicity".[22] May described how the inventor: "has taken his game on board ships, and down to the wardroom, and has listened to the criticism of the younger officers, and has watched to see the interest which is evoked by playing his game. I have noticed too that he has been ready to change any rules which seem to suggest unreality or to spoil the game as a good game, and I consider he has been wise in steering clear of many fads which people have wished him to adopt".[23]

Although Jane himself frequently denied that the game could teach tactics, May was quick to see the game's potential value for elucidating the tactical questions of the day. Lack of combat experience left such vexed questions as whether one large battleship was better than two small ones, or whether line abreast really was better than line ahead, to be decided more by service politics than by the tactical merits of the issue. In 1906, when HMS *Dreadnought* made every other battleship in the world obsolete, this issue of large battleships against small split the navy. Such officers as Sir Cyprian Bridge objected to the *Dreadnought's* putting too many eggs into one basket, not because they had any real tactical evidence on the matter, but because they were personally at odds with Sir John Fisher, the *Dreadnought's* progenitor. May was closely connected with Fisher, who as commander-in-chief in the Mediterranean, relied on him: "to investigate many strategical and tactical problems for him. Fisher then pursued those investigations afloat on a scale of 12 inches to the foot".[24]

Jane's wargame not only brought him into contact with Fisher's circle of intimates, the Fishpond, but his second presentation at the RUSI in 1900 was chaired by Captain Robert Lowry, who as Lord Charles Beresford's Flag Captain, later attracted Fisher's wrath for mishandling the mooring of his ship in Valletta.[25] As Assistant Director of Naval Intelligence, Lowry was, like several of the officers interested in the wargame, part of the intelligence community responsible for tactical doctrine. Prince Louis of Battenberg himself rose to be Director of Naval Intelligence, while his Commander in *Majestic*, later Captain Henry Campbell, who helped Jane with both the wargame and *Fighting Ships*, also worked in the NID. From 1906 Campbell was responsible for the intelligence analysis that led to the British economic blockade of Germany during the First World War.[26]

Despite the interest of such leading officers of the day, and although there were "game sets in a good many of our ships", the Royal Navy was slow to make official use of the Jane Naval Wargame. Jane originally felt that this was because: "The British Navy as a whole is opposed to anything that seems to smack of 'theory'. I know of only three officers who have gone seriously into the game . . . in each case they requested me to keep quiet as to their interest, 'lest they might get a reputation as theorists, and so find promotion impeded'...".[27] The following year he admitted that the game was slow and too dependent on qualified umpires, of whom "so far there are only three such in existence in the world".[28] Here Jane hit on two serious problems with popularising wargames. In general they take more time to play than the real elapsed time represented. The players have to carry out various mechanical processes which can easily take longer than the time needed for a shell to fly to its target, for example, or for a ship to travel the half mile allotted to it per turn. It is also necessary to educate the players so that they share a common understanding of the game and do not waste time on minutiae. Certainly Jane's gunnery system can be quite slow, unless the players know what they are about. There was obviously a need for something simpler, and Jane was not the only wargame designer at work. Sir John Fisher's chief of staff, Captain George King-Hall, had devised a simple tactical game published in the RUSI Journal in 1900. Fisher liked the game with its little coloured ships and brass turning arcs and ordered 12 sets for the Mediterranean fleet.[29] In 1901, following King-Hall's lead, the Admiralty did provide a simple wargame to all seagoing ships. It combined the movement rules from The Jane Naval Wargame with a points system for gunnery which Jane had originally supplied as an appendix. He derided the resulting arithmetical exercises as of use only to officers wishing to qualify in book-keeping. More seriously, the gradual accumulation of damage left no room for

Portsmouth Naval Wargame Club at the George Hotel 1903

the lucky shot which could decide a battle, such as the shell which killed the Russian Admiral Witgeft during the Battle of the Yellow Sea in August 1904. Jane preferred to keep his strikers, while limiting players to a single stroke per turn, the spot hit being taken as the centre of the area of damage [30]. In the Admiralty's defence it could be argued that almost any game was worthwhile if it made officers think about the problems of handling ships in such a way that they maximised their chances of damaging an enemy squadron. This is not as easy as it seems, even when manoeuvring a few models in the relative safety of one's home. However it seems unlikely that many British naval officers played wargames officially at this time, despite Laird Clowes, Jane's friend from the 1890 manoeuvres, urging in the *Daily Mail* that: "Mr Jane's Naval Wargame, or some modification of it should be played frequently by Naval Officers of the rank of Lieutenant or upwards".[31]

In Portsmouth, Jane was the Secretary of an unofficial naval wargames society, which met regularly at the George Hotel in the High Street, where Nelson had spent his last night on English soil. Admiral Sir John Hopkins was the president: "a great supporter of the wargame",[32] and previously commander-in-chief in the Mediterranean during the Fashoda crisis of 1898, when France and Great Britain came to the brink of war. When the War College moved to Portsmouth in 1907, with Lowry as President, wargaming did form part of the activities, both informally and as part of the course. Lieutenants and more senior officers were invited: "to play tactical games in the War College . . . between the hours of 5 pm and 6.45 pm on Tuesdays and Thursdays. Four officers a side are necessary for a game. The War College will provide umpires".[33]

The time allowed does seem rather more compatible with a normal life-style than the eight hours at a stretch that Jane and his enthusiasts would play. The War College games had moved some distance away from his original concept, although they still used a command system which divided responsibility for issuing orders and carrying them out. The games were played on a smaller scale, about a foot to the mile, which is in fact more practical for larger actions. The gunfire was "assessed by scoring rulers graduated in numbers according to the range, muzzle velocity, armour protection etc". As Jane had commented of the Admiralty's earlier efforts, this arithmetical approach was the more curious as aspiring gunnery officers did in fact study "the theory of areas of armoured and unarmoured parts of ships . . . the very keynote and distinctive feature of the Jane Naval Wargame".[34] Some contemporaries remained unimpressed by the wargame: "It was all very ingenious, but no amount of ingenuity can reproduce the conditions of a fleet action on a tactical board".[35] However, a more cynical participant remarked: "There were ever scoffers at the start of a course, over learning to move ships on a table, but it was

Prince Louis of Battenberg (3rd left) Flag Captain HMS *Majestic*

noted how these were the folk who used up all the club notepaper proving how they had dished up the other fellow".[36]

In *Blake of the Rattlesnake* Jane had lampooned the 'Shouter Gun Fencibles', a subscription force raised by the *Shouter* newspaper for the defence of Sheerness. In ironic contrast to this fictional military incompetence, the War Office in fact took up Jane's game as a means of educating the gunners responsible for coastal defence: "in his last report, Lord Roberts (the last Commander-in-Chief) emphasised the vast difference between those officers who had played the game and those who had not. The former knew the weak points of every enemy; the latter on hearing the name of any ship, could not tell whether she were a battleship or gunboat".[37] Jane even marketed a specific coastal defence version of the game, including, "special coast line models which can now be procured from the publishers", Sampson Low, Marston and Co.[38] These allowed for a variety of terrain types, including railroads, rivers and built up areas, being: "marked into squares upon a special system that takes into account the nature of the ground, and provides automatically for difficulties of this nature".

Jane's ingenuity gradually extended his game to include most features of naval warfare as technology evolved. A special device was available for navigable balloons, allowing them to: "move onward and turn as ships, and rise and fall up the apparatus as well. The speed, turn and rise or fall per minute must depend on the type of flying machine. Special rules are issued with each apparatus".[39] Submariners had an anxious time, only being allowed to view the board directly when surfaced. Otherwise they had to sit with their backs turned, watching the other ships through a mirror, half an inch across, or being shown sketches of the limited view from their periscope.[40] Other changes were introduced to reflect player feedback. Gunnery was made less effective by enlarging the head of the striker to six inches by four and three quarters. Turning circles were introduced for ships with tactical diameters of 600, 800, or 1000 yards (548, 731 or 914 metres), and a scale for moving diagonally across the squares to resolve the distortion otherwise caused. Perhaps the most remarkable development was that of campaigns fought between rival countries, each taking a stretch of British coastline as their base, very much in the same manner as the official manoeuvres. One campaign, played between March and May 1900, involved over 70 players from the Royal Navy, Marines, and Army. An elaborate intelligence system included arrangements: "with a local Portsmouth newspaper, the *Southern Daily Mail*, to print each day just such information as would be common property... Of necessity some of these reports were incorrect — one side indeed devoted a good number of its points to purchasing the right to set about false information".[41]

One lesson of the campaign was that the weaker side's submarines could make their stronger opponents chary of mounting a close blockade: an example of the strategic effects of technological change that, in 1914, the Admiralty would also have to recognise.

* * *

If the British Admiralty was slow to take up either *Fighting Ships* or the Jane Naval Wargame, the same was not true of the Russian Navy. Even before *Fighting Ships* had been published, they had written to Jane, expressing interest in his work. About the same time, late in 1897, the Grand Duke Alexander Mikhailovich, the Tsar's brother-in-law, heard of the wargame. It was then being tested aboard HMS *Majestic*, whose Captain, Prince Louis, was also the cousin of the Grand Duke, who: "with that absence of 'side', so characteristic of the Romanovs, wrote of himself as a naval officer. He had, he told me, himself invented a naval wargame, the strategical part of which was successful, but the tactical not what he had hoped".[42] Such an interest in the theoretical side of his profession recalls the Russian use of Sir Philip Colomb's naval game. In Fred T Jane's case Russian interest would have highly beneficial consequences for his development as: "a well known authority — we do not know whether he would care to be called a 'naval expert' — on warships and naval wargames".[43]

In January 1899, at the invitation of the Grand Duke Jane visited Russian naval installations on the Black Sea and in St Petersburg, where he wrote the preface for that year's issue of *Fighting Ships*. Before going, Jane signed an agreement with William Thacker on 12 January 1899 to publish *The Imperial Russian Navy*. This was evidently not long before he set off, as his Russian Dockyard pass, reproduced in the book, is dated 14 January, according to the Old Style calendar in use there, that is the 27th, New Style. Apart from the more run-of-the-mill naval officials Jane met the Tsar, Nicholas II. Not realising who he was, Jane "frankly told the Emperor that England did not think much of the pacific intentions of Russia", despite the Tsar's sponsorship of the Hague Conference on disarmament to be held later that year.[44] In 1899 Russia was a land of mystery, associated with "plenty of convicts, chains, Siberia and a variety of unpleasant details".[45] Although Jane scouted such views as fallacious, a *Times* review quoted H W Wilson, an admitted naval expert, to the effect that: "even in peacetime we find it difficult enough to ascertain what is going on in the Russian dockyards". On the other hand: "No such difficulty seems to have been encountered by Mr Fred T Jane who gives us an elaborate work on the 'Imperial Russian Navy' almost simultaneously with the book in which the above remark is made".[46]

Jane himself wrote: "Much is written in England and America about the secrecy with which the Russians shroud their dockyards and ships . . . my own experience did not tally with legend; indeed everything was the antithesis, nor were any restrictions of any sort laid upon me as to what I might afterwards write concerning this particular piece of globe trotting".[47] He even visited their naval intelligence department, where he found they had a photograph of himself. After the outbreak of the Russo-Japanese war, however, he revised his estimate of Russian efficiency in this area: "The Japanese Naval Intelligence department is in my opinion the best in the world. In the popular view this is the characteristic of the Russian one, but the Russian Intelligence department hardly lives up to its reputation. For the collection of immaterial facts it is unrivalled, but the little it really gleaned of Japanese war preparation was amply evidenced in February 1904".[48]

The book he wrote from his observations provides an outline of Russian naval history and the development of their naval materiel in a style similar to that used later in *The British Battle Fleet*. He also included the chapters on such frequently neglected aspects of naval strength as personnel, dockyard organisation and building policy: "to include all those side issues which, though not directly naval matters, are yet intimately connected with the Russian sea service".[49] There were 160 illustrations, many taken from *Fighting Ships*, but others sketched inside Russian dockyards or on board their ships. The technique Jane had developed for night actions aboard torpedo craft also served well for the smokeblown battle scenes of the gunpowder era, which he drew to support his survey of Russian naval history.[50] Unfortunately the poorly reproduced illustrations of the otherwise invaluable reprint of 1983 gives little idea of the original quality of these. The historical material was prepared by his youngest brother, L Cecil Jane, to whom Fred dedicated *The Violet Flame*, written the same year. At the time Cecil was reading Modern History at University College Oxford, where he took a second in 1902. He himself became a historical author of some repute, translating Christopher Columbus' journal of his voyages to the new world.[51]

Another, at first sight unlikely, connection between the Imperial Russian Navy and Jane's personal life concerned a pond at Upottery. Here the village blacksmith had assisted, as a boy, with experiments into torpedo warfare. These were carried out by the dashing Hobart Pasha, who rounded off a career of pursuing Brazilian slave traders, and gun-running into the Confederacy, by commanding the Turkish Navy. During the Russo-Turkish War, he foiled the Russian Navy's pioneering attempts at torpedo warfare, perhaps as the result of his researches at Upottery, although Hobart's autobiography does not mention these [52]. It is not particularly surprising that Hobart should have been in Devon, as his father, the Earl of Buckinghamshire, had a country seat at Richmond Lodge, near Sidmouth. Hobart's sister was married there in 1854 and it is quite plausible that later he should have visited the Addingtons, who lived at the manor house in Upottery. The pond is long gone. It was already disappearing in Jane's time. From Jane's sketch in *The Imperial Russian Navy*, however, it must have been down in the water meadows below the vicarage, near the River Ottery, where young *Ever Mohun* courted with the draper-squire's son.

The Russian book received good reviews. *The Daily Chronicle* felt that it filled, "a distinct gap in our naval literature", while the *Daily News* described it as an "up-to-date, well arranged and concise encyclopaedia of the subject" [53]. Although the *Times* referred tartly to, "Mr Jane's rather irritating way of flinging about hasty and ill-considered judgements", it recognised that his book was: "full of information compiled with laudable skill and industry, not the least instructive part of it being that which deals with the personnel of the Russian navy about which the average English reader knows . . . little or nothing"[54].

Jane's work was noticed by other, possibly mightier, authorities than the *Times*: "Greatly impressed by the publicity thus accorded to Russian seapower, the Japanese naval authorities invited Jane to write a similar work on the Imperial Japanese Navy, for which support of a substantial kind was forthcoming".[55] The list of senior Japanese naval officers and constructors which appears in the preface to the book bears out this claim, as does Jane's use of "Japanese drawings and photographs, selected for the book by Japanese officers".[56] Preparation for the book began in 1900, soon after publication of *The Imperial Russian Navy*. It was uniform with the earlier work, covering the same ground, although as Jane did not in fact visit Japan, it lacks his inimitable sketches drawn from personal observation. Instead he had to rely on personal contacts built up during a period when Portsmouth was almost a second home for the Japanese navy: "a Japanese naval officer's (in England) idea of a holiday appears to be to come to Portsmouth, spend the day going over the dockyard, with a visit to my house to play naval wargames into the small hours as a kind of subsequent dissipation and relaxation!".[57]

Many Japanese ships visited Portsmouth. A wargame, in the wardroom, featured during an 'At Home' onboard the *Kasagi* in March 1899: 'Racing game', said one lady; 'how babyish these foreigners are!' 'I don't know, my dear', replied her companion apologetically. 'Perhaps they gamble on it for high stakes.' 'Oh', was the response,'of course that makes a difference'.[58]

Although the Japanese Navy was the youngest of those included among the Great Powers in *Fighting Ships*, it was the only one with much useful combat experience. Although the US Navy had fought the Spanish-American war, Jane felt this had been "disappointing . . . in the matter of adding to our general stock of knowledge".[59] Soon afterwards, the South Americans let everyone down again, despite their interesting ship types: "The prospect of there being no war between Chile and Argentina is probably a disappointment to everyone interested in naval construction".[60]

The Japanese on the other hand had trounced the Chinese at the Yalu and the siege of Wei-Hai-Wei in a most edifying manner, justifying their policy during the 1880s of training their personnel, rather than acquiring materiel beyond their capabilities, as the Chinese had done.[61] In 1899 Jane used the Sino-

Japanese war as background for a serial he wrote for *Sandow's Magazine for Physical Culture*, 'Hazlitt of the Chih Yuen, an ironclad sunk at Wei-Hai-Wei'. Numerous British and US officers had served with the Chinese fleet, much of Jane's own knowledge of the war deriving from them. As he wrote the story for a pot boiler, he assumed it was drivel — at least until he found there was money in it earning two pence in the shilling royalties, a handsome 17 per cent, with illustrations extra (National Maritime Museum uncatalogued manuscript MS75/039). Lest there be any misunderstanding about the nature of the physical culture involved, Mr Sandow was the Charles Atlas of the day, "A Study of the Perfect Type of the Human Form, The marvel of Anatomists, Sculptors, and Artists in the Nude".

For Jane, the outbreak of the Russo-Japanese War provoked conflicting feelings. The fighting engaged his professional interest as a naval analyst, but he had friends on both sides. During the war he received post cards from friends with the beleaguered Russian squadron in Port Arthur, while the cruiser *Takasago*, with whose officers Jane had played many a wargame, was lost to a mine off Port Arthur. In the preface to *The Imperial Japanese Navy*, Jane wrote: "I am neither pro-Japanese nor pro-Russian. As I write, disaster is thick upon the Russian Fleet, and to many close friends in it go these sympathies which, had things been the other way about, would have gone as surely to the Japanese fleet".[62]

Professional necessity also demanded neutrality. In the 1905–6 issue of *Fighting Ships*, he wrote: "Sympathy with one side or the other is totally outside the scope of this book, and the object has been to give each side an impartial hearing".[63] Making use of his wide contacts in both navies, he was able to print the stories of several combatants on each side in that issue and the following year, supplemented by maps and photographs of damaged ships. No amount of professional detachment could conceal the extent of the terrible disasters suffered by the Russian Navy. In the 1906–7 issue of *Fighting Ships*, the stark legend "SUNK" or "NOW JAPANESE" by the photographs of ships lost left no doubt as to Russia's eclipse as a naval power. The war had shown the truth of Jane's prophecy in 1899, that the Russian seizure of Port Arthur after the Sino-Japanese war had been a source of weakness, not strength. The Russians had given a hostage to fortune by splitting their naval strength in the Far East between Port Arthur and Vladivostock. These are almost 1,500 miles apart, practically the steaming radius of some of the Russian ships. As it had turned out, it was impossible for them to effect a junction between the separate squadrons in the face of the Japanese naval base at Nagasaki.[64] In addition, Port Arthur "standing as it does at the extreme end of a narrow peninsula . . . is easily cut off",[65] which it duly was by General Nogi's Third Army. Another prophecy justified by events was Jane's view that Russia's success in the war in the East would depend on "whether the genius of some officers prevailed or whether the dunderheads would be put in command".[66] The loss of two successive Russian admirals in action off Port Arthur would leave the field wide open for the latter. Although Admiral Togo was uncritically hailed as a new Nelson, Jane felt that "like all the officers of his fleet he achieved a modest excellence", his victory at Round Island owing more to the "blue funk" of the Russian second-in-command than to Togo's strategy.[67]

Locally, the war provided Jane with an opportunity to play the role of pundit, as he did on a wider scale during the First World War. In November 1904 he gave one of several lectures on the war to the Portsmouth Literary and Scientific Society, where he was introduced as "that expert of experts on matters naval".[68] During the talk he made his first reference to the 'Yellow Peril', the economic and demographic threat from the Far East, which haunted the Western world: "a real peril because Japanese ability was enough to get control over China and raise a navy, and Chinese bluejackets were the best in the world. They could then build factories and export stuff much below any rate Europe can reach".[69]

Parts of this make better sense than others. The Peril was a live issue at the time, particularly on the West Coast of North America, where an American massacre of Japanese sealers at St Paul Island, in 1907, led to fears of Japanese reprisals against the USA. President Theodore Roosevelt concentrated the US Navy in the Pacific, and sent the appropriately named Great White Fleet to Australia.[70] The Anglo-Saxon alliance that would isolate Japan, and bring about the War in the Pacific, was already forming. Jane would continue his warnings, off and on, to the end of his life. In 1915 he reviewed Homer Lea's *The Valour of Ignorance*, with its 'carefully argued out prophecy that eventually Germany and Japan will divide the world between them'.[71] Homer Lea was a self-proclaimed China specialist from California, with a hunchback and a penchant for wearing Chinese military uniform. In his approval of Homer Lea's book, Jane was in highly dubious company, admired as it was by both the Kaiser and Adolf Hitler.[72]

Jane argued that Russia was "to a large extent fighting for the whole of Europe".[73] Already in 1899, he had pointed out that there were no real reasons for Anglo-Russian hostility, an idea argued previously by Sir George Clarke (later the secretary of the Committee of Imperial Defence) in his book, *Russian Sea Power*.[74] In the drift towards Armageddon, this truth would be borne in upon British policy makers, who would be driven to make common cause with Russia despite their Liberal dislike of the Tsar's autocracy. In the longer term, one aspect of the later 20th century, of which Fred T Jane would undoubtedly have approved, is the end of the Cold War with its ideological exacerbation of Anglo-Russian differences.

CHAPTER V

A PROPHET WITHOUT HONOUR

Y the early years of the 20th century Jane was widely recognised as an authority on naval matters, with *Fighting Ships*, *The Imperial Russian Navy*, and his naval journalism on both sides of the Atlantic in *The Engineer* and *Scientific American*. Despite this he never influenced government policy in any way that can be demonstrated. Not only that, he moved from being a supporter of the Admiralty, as a matter of principle, to appearing as an opponent of their policy, with some very strange bedfellows. In 1907 H W Wilson, in a "carefully written and impartial article", cited Jane, "who has no party politics", with the *Conservative Standard*, the *Liberal Spectator*, and Carlyon Bellairs, a Liberal member of parliament, as the four most severe critics of Admiralty policy.[1] This shift in Jane's attitude towards the naval establishment was a significant turning point in his life, and can be seen as a prelude to his surprisingly low-key role during the First World War. It also demonstrates the deferential and hierarchical nature of Edwardian society. There was a general distrust, on the part of those in positions of authority, of professional expertise, especially of anyone who appeared to pose a threat to accepted opinion. Even if Jane's status as a professional defence analyst had been accepted, he was too independent in his opinions to have fitted neatly into an establishment that felt itself threatened by forces beyond its control. It is possible to look back and see parallels between the stresses that brought about the end of consensus in British politics before 1914, and the strains that, for a while, dissipated any idea of the Royal Navy as a Nelsonian band of brothers.

As the 20th century began the editor of *Fighting Ships* could reasonably have felt pleased with himself. Although he might complain to his literary agent about his lack of financial reward, he had seen his work praised in the service journals and even in the *Times*; he had hobnobbed with royalty, and penetrated the secrets of Khronstadt. However, the provincial grammar school boy soon discovered the limited influence of a civilian writer. The same issue of the *Times* which had dealt favourably with *The Imperial Russian Navy* had remarked about H W Wilson, who had assisted Jane with *Fighting Ships*, that: "he has never grasped the difference between the so-called 'naval expert' of the Press, and the real 'naval expert' of the sea service . . . he takes himself too seriously and fails to understand that wise men do not take much account of the technical criticism of the mere layman".[2].

Fighting Ships during its early years also suffered from this distrust of civilian participation in defence debates. In 1901 Jane solicited the views of a wide range of naval authorities on the best design of battleship, but had to admit the next year that his symposium was "not an unmitigated success". Many of his correspondents gave only the briefest of replies, while the *Army and Navy Gazette* felt the "introduction of such a feature renders the book far too polemical and theoretical".[3] Jane was not the only target for such criticism. Brassey's, the doyen of naval annuals, was attacked for its editorial content: "A volume which aims at being considered a universal work of reference should deal with facts as they are, and statements necessarily of a controversial nature should find no place in it".[4]

Such comment does rather beg the question of where exactly facts end and opinion begins. As late as 1911, Jane omitted articles on general subjects from *Fighting Ships*, feeling that they were: "always somewhat lost . . . [and] in many ways have failed to evoke that attention to which the names of the authors would have entitled them had they seen the light elsewhere".[5]

The most damning evidence of the British establishment's ability to look gift horses in the mouth was the 1909 panic over the German's Dreadnought programme. A popular agitation for the British to lay down eight capital ships instead of four, produced the catchphrase: "We want eight and we won't wait", but Jane felt that no good was likely to come to the Navy from anything so redolent of a music hall ditty: "this catchphrase business is all very well in party political life and 'Winsome Winnie', 'Unalloyed Thief' and 'Mrs Spankhurst' etc etc are right and proper as amusing catchphrases. But the Navy is a serious concern...".[6] Jane was outraged by the slight against his own efficiency when the Foreign Secretary made a speech implying the design of the German ships was not known. This was all: "Fraud – because they DO know what the German Dreadnoughts will carry...As author of *Fighting Ships* I have to run an Intelligence Department and – not having any Winston Churchill or Lloyd George to bother about – my Intelligence Department discovered the real armament of the four ships of the Nassau class. And in case they had drawn blank I sent it up to our Naval Intelligence Department. So they know what the Nassaus are like".[7]

He criticised those who were surprised by the speed of German construction: "Anyone who cared to do so could find out German naval progress without the slightest trouble. The Germans made no secret of it. For years in *Fighting Ships* I have published the number of slips in Germany suitable for building big ships on and the exact rates at which the Germans have turned out warships".[8] In this case, he felt, his expertise was ignored for political reasons: "Everything indicates that the Government's policy is to steer a comfortable middle course between patriots and Little Englanders, with a view to pleasing both. All of which is sound party politics but otherwise despicable".[9]

An illuminating comparison with Jane's fate at the hands of the establishment is provided by the career of Sir Julian Corbett, the naval historian. He was far more of an insider than Jane, corresponding frequently with Fisher, and writing much of the Official History of the War at Sea, but his relationship with the Navy was still an equivocal one. Fisher was happy to use Corbett, when it suited him, but in general naval officers distrusted his sharp legally trained mind. In his lectures at the War Course, Corbett codified strategic doctrine, in much the same way as Fred T Jane codified naval material. However, after his death he would be blamed for the so-called defensive strategy of the Grand Fleet during the 1914–18 war, by officers embarrassed by their self-perceived failure to inflict a decisive defeat on the Germans in the good old style.[10]

Ironically, the political establishment was equally dismissive of its own professional advisers. During wartime Cabinet meetings they were left kicking their heels, while amateur strategists held the floor with specious talk of knocking away Germany's props. Astonishingly Fisher, recalled as First Sea Lord, felt that he and his colleagues were only "the experts who were there to open our mouths when spoken to".[11] Even had the establishment been more open to a parvenu like Fred T Jane, it is doubtful whether he himself would have been prepared to restrain the expression of his views sufficiently to be accepted. He was too much of a free spirit, preferring: "to drift to the gunroom whenever I can and best of all I like to talk to the type of sub who explains how much better he could run the fleet than his admiral".[12]

In 1902 there was an attempt to stimulate debate on naval matters at the RUSI. Admiral Sir John Hopkins, a wargamer and contributor to the battleship symposium, invited Jane to lecture there on 6 June 1902.[13] Jane made a deliberately provocative plea for "Ship's designs to suit our strategic needs" in which he questioned the value of the British battleships of the day. In armour these outclassed the potential opposition, but had little chance of ever catching them. Jane argued that as the Royal Navy had a numerical superiority; its battleships needed superior speed, not better armour. The King Edward VII class: "belongs to the order of the big gooseberry, but in market gardening the wise man does not concentrate all his efforts on a gooseberry to make his neighbours stare, but on a gooseberry for use".

In another homely metaphor, echoing comments made by Fisher about catching the hare before cooking it,[14] Jane suggested that the *King Edward VII* had "excessive means of cooking the hare, and none for catching it", while the new Drake class cruisers had, "too limited cooking appliances". Unfortunately, the audience were no more moved to discussion by Jane's humour than they would be by Corbett's logic during a subsequent RUSI lecture, given at Fisher's instigation in 1907, defending the need for fast battleships.[15]

An entirely more negative reaction followed a lecture, given at the same institution in December 1902, on the protection of commerce in war time. Jane believed that the French, then the most likely opponent, would use not only their cruisers for attacking British commerce, but also their fast battleships, which outpaced the Royal Navy's. He proposed: "taking the bull by the horns, and calling commerce attack piracy . . . make the rule that for every merchant ship pirated they should bombard an unfortified hostile town . . . It was absurd and academical to say that the destruction of private property at sea was legal, while the destruction of property on shore was not".[16]

A succession of naval officers then rose to condemn Jane's proposal. Perhaps the kindest reaction came from Admiral Fremantle who "thought that on this subject he [that is Jane] was not exactly at home". Admiral Henry J May, Jane's old wargaming ally, felt the suggestion was "an extremely wild one". Such was the antipathy to Jane's views that the *RUSI Journal* took the unprecedented step of not publishing an account of the meeting. Not only was he never asked back again, but reviews of *Fighting Ships* did not appear in the *Journal*, although it did review other naval annuals at length. Ironically, the *Times*, which did cover the lecture, also reported a bombardment of the Venezuelan customs house at Puerto Cabella, in response to the recent seizure of a British merchant ship. "No damage was caused to the town", but a German resident and his two servants were killed three miles away by shells from HMS *Charybdis* and SMS *Vineta*.[17] When attacks on merchant ships became a serious strategic concern, in 1914, the remedy adopted was not in fact "to take the bull by the horns" of bloody retribution. More prosaically, the British Government underwrote the insurance risks as suggested in *Heresies of Sea Power*.[18] Jane's next inflammatory venture into naval debate was: "*Heresies of Sea Power* [which] has set the ordinary critics agape with astonishment. That any man should have the effrontery to question the profound wisdom of the school represented by Captain Mahan is more than they can understand or tolerate . . . But there are others . . . who will see in *Heresies of Sea Power* the results of much original thought and deep historical research'.[19]

Alfred Thayer Mahan was a US Navy officer who in the 1890s attempted to show that the rise and fall of empires depended largely on the influence of sea power. In 1890 he published *The Influence of Seapower upon History: 1660–1783*, followed by a similar title dealing with the French Revolutionary and Napoleonic Wars. Based on his lectures at the US Naval War College the first of these ran through fifteen editions by the end of the century, making Mahan a celebrity on both sides of the Atlantic. In 1898 his ideas appeared to be vindicated by the

Spanish-American War, when the US Navy's new ships won victories at Manila Bay and Santiago. Like Karl Marx he based his ideas on history as he saw it, and like Marx he enjoyed a wide and uncritical following, although in rather different circles. At the start of the 20th century, when the role of the capital ship was in question, and the British were forming a continental commitment that would shape their strategic posture for the next century, Mahan's ideas on the primacy of battle and the self-sufficiency of maritime empires were not really very helpful. Jane never had any time for such high flown ideas: "Histories of naval strategy always seem to me like Ruskin's interpretation of the meaning of Turner's pictures — very plausible but always susceptible to some far more commonplace explanation".[20]

He had strong views on the problems posed by historical evidence: "Those who make history — individual combatants — rarely have anything but the haziest impression as to the general facts, as they are seen by subsequent ages. What they desired to do, or hoped to do, is always inextricably mixed with what they actually accomplished [21] ... When versions disagree we have to ask which side had the largest motive for untruthfulness, which had the best and worst reputation that way and so on ... probabilities are the most we can depend on at the best, and probabilities are far removed from absolute facts".[22]

Jane questioned whether anything of contemporary value could be learned from the history of wars between Rome and Carthage, for instance. Given their entirely different historical situations how could it be argued that: "even were the teaching of history a certain recipe for future victory, even were the 'facts' of history unassailable, anything in the history of these sea empires can be of practical value to the two great Island Powers of today?".[23]

Obviously Jane did not deny that victorious nations "happened to make use of the sea in winning": he spent most of his professional life arguing for a stronger navy. What he did object to was the notion that sea power was the only basis for victory. Instead Jane espoused the principle of *Fitness to Win*. Although today this has sinister resonances, it is clear from Jane's words that he saw it as a moral quality that could be acquired, not inherited. It was something broader than the readiness, or otherwise, of a navy. It was more the extent to which the prevailing institutions and attitudes within a society allowed it to mobilise its moral and physical resources effectively. However, his inability to explain the idea properly, and the fragmentation of his book into "a series of detached essays on certain problems of naval warfare", were seized on avidly by hostile reviewers. Describing Mr Jane as "a capable if somewhat wayward writer on naval topics", the *Times Literary Supplement* admitted there were "portions of his perverse volume which are not unworthy of attention".[24] However, it considered it "a very disappointing book", whose "facile dogmatism on some points and its wayward polemic on others might well estrange serious readers". After deriding *Fitness to Win* as "vague, inconsequential and paradoxical", the reviewer concluded: "We have no doubt that Mr Jane could write a good book if he chose, but in this case we are constrained to say that he has not chosen to do so".

The *Army and Navy Gazette* was kinder, although it felt, quite rightly, that the book suffered from "a discursive character", leading to the inclusion of chapters "not quite germane to the matter in hand".[25] Unfortunately many good ideas in the book were lost sight of in the debate. The First World War showed quite clearly that Jane's views on the movement of troops across seas where command was still in dispute were correct, and Mahan's disciples were wrong. Expeditions were mounted against Mesopotamia and East Africa successfully, although German cruisers were still loose in the Indian Ocean.[26] Nobody foresaw that submarines would give the *guerre de course* a new lease of life, but Jane had warned of the risks entailed for the 20th century corsair by the interdependence of trading nations: "commerce war is not what it was and the nation undertaking it on the grand scale will be embarking on an enterprise the limits and dangers of which it can never measure".[27]

Had German leaders heeded this warning, before beginning their unrestricted U-boat offensive, the US might never have entered the First World War. Jane's views on bases were also more in tune with 20th century reality than Mahan's cullings from the age of sail: "in the old days the fleet not the base was the heart of things: today the base is the heart pure and simple and the ships whatever their radius are but arms of the base".[28] It is hard not to think of the Grand Fleet, with its cruiser squadrons and flotillas, spreading out from Scapa Flow, in this context. Aircraft carriers and replenishment at sea have not invalidated the thesis, but rather sent the base to sea. The contemporary, if unwitting, acceptance of Jane's assertion can be seen in the air raids against U-boat and Zeppelin bases, from the earliest days of the First World War.[29]

At the heart of all Jane's heresies was a dynamic view of how strategy develops. Theories drawn from ancient history could have only limited value for modern practice: "It was the Modern idea not the Past that enabled Germany to beat France in 1870–71".[30] The changes of the 19th century in sea warfare were, if anything, far greater than those in land warfare, leading to revolutionary discontinuities in strategy, not a smooth evolution. It was the extent of the changes in naval technique, and their unknown implications, that gave the naval debates of the Edwardian period their peculiar ferocity. This eventually reached such a pitch that Jane described the personal conflicts between the First Sea Lord, Sir John Fisher, and his various detractors and supporters, as a "Naval Civil War".[31]

Although the rumblings of discontent did affect the lower deck of the navy's ships, the crew's agitation for better pay and conditions was as nothing compared with the disputes among the officers. The developments in naval technology not only destroyed the consensus over how fleets should be used, they also threatened the social status quo. Fisher's attempt, known as the Selborne Scheme, to resolve the problem of officer recruitment by eliminating the differences between deck officers and engineers, was bitterly opposed for social, not purely technical, reasons. Jane was clearly aware of the relationship between technology and social behaviour and the traumatic change from sail to steam, and the replacement of old fashioned seamanship by more technical skills. Also, how in: "the bad old days of masted ships... ammunition was thrown overboard because firing made the deck dirty... the custom went with the masts and yards that created it. Even now we hear moans about the old "seaman"... whose ideal of life was to be proficient at everything except warfare".[33]

The advent of mines and submarines was every bit as revolutionary as the change from sail to steam, subverting the old naval trinity of battleships, cruisers and flotillas. The torpedo boat had been successfully integrated with the latter, providing opportunities for talented young officers such as Doveton Sturdee, who went on to command the battlecruisers during the conflict of the Falklands in 1914. The new weapons fought in an entirely different way. Battleship design could not be unaffected by changing circumstances. In 1897, Captain Henry J May had analysed the new tactical conditions, demonstrating the importance of greater speed, as a means of dictating the range of engagement, and longer range guns, as a means of engaging torpedo boats. However, battleship designers continued to pile on more armour and secondary guns, but without increasing their speed or main armament.[34] Jane had spoken of the need for speed at the RUSI, and the following year *Fighting Ships* outlined the design characteristics of a revolutionary warship that outclassed any existing battleship. The Italian naval designer, Colonel Vittorio Cuniberti, was acclaimed for his "intermediate" types combining the qualities of armoured cruisers and battleships. By chance he was a close friend of an English engineer resident in Italy, Charles de Grave Sells, who wrote regularly for *Fighting Ships* on marine engineering.[35]

To oblige de Grave Sells, Jane agreed to publish an article by Cuniberti: 'An Ideal Warship for the British Navy',[36] a type of vessel turned down by the Italian Navy as too expensive: "The immediate result was that I wished I had not, as everybody described the Cuniberti ship as more suitable for the pages of H G Wells than for a serious publication dealing technically with matters naval".[37] How far Cuniberti's article contributed to the building of HMS *Dreadnought*, two years later, is open to argument. There was a key difference between the tactical function of his '*Invincible*' and the real *Dreadnought*, despite their physical similarity: "Cuniberti's high speed ideal ship carried a big 12 inch armament heavily protected so as to bring an overwhelming volume of fire into action at decisive range. Dreadnought was evolved for a totally different method of fighting and in response to the demands of long range gunnery".[38]

Cuniberti's tactical concept did not answer the problem of the close-range torpedo attack, although his big gun armament would allow his battleship to avoid the threat by engaging at longer ranges. In 1903, when Cuniberti was making his proposal, the British Department of Naval Construction was already considering a large, fast battleship, with a uniform armament of 12-inch guns, rather than the usual mixture of calibres. At the time this was rejected as "highly impracticable".[39] However, within a year Sir John Fisher returned from the Mediterranean with "plans for various new warships", including a battleship with 12 12-inch guns [40]. The Admiralty was evidently reaching the same conclusions as Jane, justifying the claim that: "Never before had Jane so clearly attained his ambition of making *Fighting Ships* the mirror of naval progress".[41]

If there was a more direct link between Jane and the Admiralty policy makers, it was through Captain Henry J May and the wargame. Jane had found that his wargames demonstrated the superiority of one large ship over two smaller ones:[42] "history has always shown — except perhaps to the perennial contributors of 'Pleas for Moderate Dimensions', in *Brassey's Naval Annual* — that other things being equal, one big ship is always worth two smaller ones — because of unity of command".[43] He had also tried out May's 'long bowls' tactics with the officers of the *Takasago*; an "object lesson in the power of the big gun: despite all the American experience at Santiago, (where hardly any of the big

Cuniberti's ideal battleship (Fighting Ships 1903)

guns hit anything – author) it is safer to prophesy that the monster gun will crop up again, than that the 12 inch gun is to be the big gun of the future ... Ten years hence we may see the armament of our warships ... 13.5 to 16 inch".[44]

In fact, Jane overestimated the rate of progress very slightly. The *Orion* of 1910–11 was the first British battleship to mount 13.5s, while the next step up was to the 15 inch guns of the *Queen Elizabeth* in 1913. To some extent Henry J May, the "overworked, brilliant and undervalued founder of the War College",[45] was like Jane, a victim of the Edwardian Navy's distrust of the expert. May's tactical articles were read more in the Russian Navy than in his own.[46] However, as we have seen, he was close to Fisher who had hoped May would take the post of Director of Naval Intelligence. Unfortunately May died in 1904 from gastro-enteritis acquired on a bicycling trip, thus removing one of the navy's few original thinkers about tactics, and depriving Jane of an ally. Another of Jane's old associates, Laird Clowes, who had done much to publicise the need for faster, more hard-hitting warships, never saw the ships for which he had prepared the way. He died of consumption in 1905, at the age of 49, before *Dreadnought* was begun.

The ideal battleship as built: HMS *Dreadnought* on trial

Jane, however, was on hand to watch the completed *Dreadnought* setting out for sea trials. His words help us understand the shock she caused a generation used to ships that were traditionally things of beauty: "There is no ship in the world like her nor is there anything on sea or land to compare her to. She is ugly beyond expression in so far as any departure from accepted convention is hideous and inartistic. An enormous mast supported by pillars, like those of Westminster Abbey; two enormous flat sided funnels apparently heaped promiscuously amidship and aft; a stumpy mast and vast erections suggestive of a tin mine; before and behind them many low turrets barely visible, save for the enormous muzzles of the 12 inch guns. Such is the *Dreadnought*".[47]

As she steamed out of Portsmouth harbour in the October sunshine, she had all the appearance of St Paul's cathedral, "moving slowly and irresistibly down Ludgate Hill". With her ten 12 inch guns, maximum speed of 21.6 knots, and up to 11 inches of armour, she rendered every other battleship in existence obsolete, although there were concerns about, "what will happen to the men in the end turrets when the side turrets fire past them".[48] The rapid completion of this revolutionary design showed, that whatever problems the UK may have had in other areas of industry, there was nothing wrong with shipbuilding. Perhaps for the man onboard, however, the most significant feature of the *Dreadnought* was that he could have fresh bread, every day, baked in her "well-equipped bakery".[49]

Shortly after the *Dreadnought*'s sea trials, Jane began "his most characteristic and versatile production";[50] a 'Weekly Causerie' in the *Hampshire Telegraph*. This Portsmouth newspaper included several pages devoted to the *Naval Chronicle*. Dating back to the French Revolution of the 1790s, this was respected both for its coverage of Parliament's naval business, and for its commitment to the social well-being of the fleet [51].

The editor asked Jane: "to start this column on special lines, to use it to comment on what is being said and done in the Navy and about the Navy outside it; and to say what I think without tying myself by the leg to any particular "policy". In this the "H. T." is initiating something new, because the usual newspaper rule is that all views expressed (outside the correspondence column) should be uniform. But here, if the editor takes one view and I another, we shall each say just what we think".[52]

Jane's 'Dreadnought Broadside', quoted earlier, appeared in the *Illustrated London News* alongside a weekly column contributed by G K Chesterton. Apart from Chesterton, H G Wells, Bernard Shaw and others had begun the new fashion – the regular column by named writers in newspapers. Generally Jane's arrangement with the *Hampshire Telegraph* worked well, their moderate views providing a counterpoint to his more highly charged opinions for the next eight years. There was a gap in 1912, after a row with the editor, that ended when the latter rang Jane: "and suggested that our old quarrel had gone on long enough; and since neither of us could remember what the row was about, peace was declared and so I return to the scene of what a sender of anonymous postcards in the old days, used to call 'the scene of my weekly lies'".[53]

The editor must have been happy with the experiment, as he also invited columns from those mutually hostile campaigners upon lower deck issues, Gunner Capper, and Lionel Yexley, to broaden the range of opinions expressed in his pages. From this vantage point in the local press, Jane provided a running commentary on contemporary naval developments. In the early columns these often centred around the controversial figure of Sir John Fisher, the First Sea Lord. Initially Jane had been all in favour of the man he saw "trampling down everything in the cause of naval efficiency: Few have been more consistent Press supporters of Admiral Fisher than I have in the past. I have fought my hardest and would still those who have attacked him on grounds of personal animus. Few indeed are those who have done more for the Navy than he has".[54] Even after the Liberals came to power intent on cutting the Navy: "there is no question he has done the best a man can do with the limited funds at disposal. More, I should say that it is due to him that we have any Navy at all, after the barometer set to Economy".[55]

However, Sir John's autocratic nature made him intolerant of opposition, stifling the expression of naval opinion: "For those on the verge of promotion the Navy today is very little better than was Russia some ten years ago . . . every aspirant to promotion chews his words all day long on certain subjects. It is unsafe for him to hold an opinion as to whether JF is a deity as depicted by Arnold White, or an ordinary mortal liable to error as others, or an old scoundrel as described by his opponents".[56] Fisher met stiff opposition on key issues such as the long overdue reform of officer recruitment, or the scrapping of hundreds of obsolete ironclads and bugtrap gunboats that, like the old *Northampton*, diverted resources from the desperate need to build an effective navy for home defence. In the long run, however, he was "altogether too 'one man' for an institution like the British Navy", Jane summarising the navy's reaction to Fisher's departure as, "thank God he is gone".[57]

Jane put much of the blame for the ill-feeling upon those outside the active ranks of the service, who kept the cauldron boiling. Among these were the Navy League, founded in 1895 to bring the navy's past achievements, and its present needs, before the public eye. Jane is said to have done "a great deal for the Navy League", attempting to galvanise them out of their "habit of dwelling on past glories".[58] However, closer investigation leads one to wonder if his attentions were entirely appreciated. He first got into hot water with the League in October 1903. Introduced, with Carlyon Bellairs, as one of "the two greatest living experts in Naval matters",[59] Jane ungratefully proceeded to "paralyse them with horror by telling them they had 'too much Nelson'". Yexley later suggested that had he ventured to tell a concourse of Muslim pilgrims that they had too much Mohammed, "their horror and indignation would scarcely exceed that of the Navy League, faced with Mr Jane's bombshell".[60] Jane called on the loudly dissenting Navy Leaguers to throw Nelson overboard, echoing Admiral Fisher's words: "the watchword today must be 'Tomorrow, Tomorrow', not 'yesterday'". However, in the Navy the: "legacy of Nelson's days remained today and was seen in the policy of keeping a ship smart more than anything else. Smartness should be a means to an end, and not the end itself. The end of naval matters should be the ship's fighting capacity, and not its appearance. By keeping the old days before the public the League really tended to delay progress".[61]

Jane knew quite well that 'spit and polish' was not entirely pointless: coal burning ships were dirty places and always needed cleaning.[62] The problem was the attitude that resulted in such petty impositions as the daily inspection, first imposed in 1903, of the ratings' knives and forks. On the *Dreadnought* the men continued to use their jack-knives and fingers, returning the cutlery to the Paymaster when the Commander insisted on it being arranged, in a geometrical pattern, around the salt and pepper pots.[63] This "deadweight of tradition" was the more serious as new navies like Germany's , "had no heroic past behind them to obscure modern realities in a sentimental haze".[64] During a subsequent lecture on 'The Navy in The Future', an audience of warrant officers showed that, unlike the civilians at the Navy League, they had not misunderstood Jane's message about the need for change, applauding his predictions that the next naval war would be with Germany not France, and that one day, "there would be 'ranker' captains and commanders, besides numerous other ranker officers on the quarter deck".[65] It was often the fate of the League to be distrusted by those whose interests it was ostensibly formed to promote. In the 1890s a number of naval officers, such as Sir Philip Colomb, had left the League because they felt it was too much like the fat boy in Charles Dickens' novel, *The Pickwick Papers*, always wanting "to make your flesh creep".[66] Jane himself commented on how their "crying wolf" allowed officials to decry agitations based on, "vague generalisations indicating imperfect knowledge of the subject".[67]

More pointed differences arose in 1907, when Jane delivered a 'Message From Portsmouth' during a very lively meeting at the Caxton Hall, emphasising that he was purely there as a spokesman for the service. He remarked later of his audience that it "would be better if there were rather more Navy and rather less League about it:[68] criticism of the Channel Fleet is outside their province. It is not the business of the Navy League to say whether Admiral Fisher is good or bad. The general opinion in the Navy is that he has done very well with the money provided. There is too little money provided. The Navy League's duty is to fight the economists and not to bother about Admiral Fisher (Applause)".[69]

There were noisy exchanges about "dirty little Radical and Socialist faddists" [that is the Government], the spirit of Nelson ("A Voice: 'Are you the spirit of Nelson?' (Loud laughter)", and comparisons between the League's executive and the Lloyd George Liberals who had supported the enemy during the Boer War. Finally the meeting broke up, "amid some commotion", after accusations of ballot rigging by the executive.

* * *

If Jane did not achieve the political influence he may have expected, he was eventually successful enough in financial terms, despite earlier remarks about throat cutting and wandering what authors lived on. One measure of this was that he could afford a car. In fact, over the years he was the owner of "something like 20 motor cars at different times".[70] His name appears on the opening page of the driving licence register for Portsmouth, with licence number 35. It was dated 1 January 1904, immediately after the 1903 Motor Car Registration and Licensing Act came into force. In April that year his wife Alice also took out a driving licence, which she maintained until the year of her death.[71] Motoring at that time was not a pastime for the poor, nor for that matter the faint hearted. The Motor Manufacturing Company's sales literature for their 10 HP model, as used by Jane, quoted prices from £450 to £475, depending on whether the model purchased had a tubular or flitch plate frame.[72] Petrol was only one shilling and threepence a gallon, but mileages varied between five and 15 miles to the gallon, depending whether the objective was efficiency or economy.

It is not at all surprising that Jane should have taken to motor cars. He shared several characteristics with the ebullient Mr Toad hero of the children's classic *The Wind in the Willows*. He also shared that gentleman's enthusiasm for mechanical novelties, especially if they involved rapid, and preferably hazardous, movement. On one occasion he appeared before the magistrates of Newton, Hampshire: "in answer to a charge of furiously driving his motor car to the common danger", by exceeding 50 miles an hour. The police stated that he appeared "like a blue streak" but then, as one contemporary driving magazine remarked, it was hard to know what speed you are doing over 18 miles an hour! In any case, Jane pleaded: "the road was quite straight and entirely deserted . . . he was nearly out of petrol, and therefore had to hurry".[73]

Unlike Mr Toad, however, Jane was not a consistently reckless driver. In this case he was acquitted after one of the magistrates intervened to testify to the consideration shown earlier the same day by the motorist: "on meeting him with a troublesome young horse". The chairman dismissed the case: "to mark their appreciation of the difference between motorists who were a nuisance and danger to others, and those who were a danger only to themselves".

It is not possible to identify the exact model of car involved in the above scrape, the records for Portsmouth registered vehicles having been destroyed. However, it is reasonably certain that he would have been driving one of several MMC vehicles which he owned. These were made by the Motor Manufacturing Company, formerly the Great Horseless Carriage Co Ltd of Holborn. Their vehicles seem to have been good value and Jane even wrote a testimonial letter for them, "I am glad to hear that your Company is continuing to make MMC cars. As I have during the last few years driven nearly every type you have ever made, and covered over 60,000 miles on MMCs, including driving in places where few cars would care to go, and several collisions, I am prepared to give the Company a good testimonial as to the really excellent construction, in their cars".[74]

Autocar had this to say of MMC cars: "The country is flooded with more or less shoddy cars, which are financially a great success, but which bear about the same lasting value compared with MMCs as modern villas do to the Pyramids".[75]

In October 1904, Jane's 10 HP MMC took part in the Naval Motor Club's run from the Granada Road Garage, Southsea, out to South Harting, on the north side of the Downs. Here, the Petersfield-Chichester road crossed the estate of Colonel the Honourable Turnour Featherstonhaugh of Uppark House, where the housekeeper, mother of H G Wells gave Fred the run of the library. The venue situated on the northern side of the Downs Uppark provided a splendid spot for hill trials. The winner was I D Siddeley in a 40 HP Mercedes, taking 1 minute, 5.6 seconds to do the course, which had an average gradient of one in twelve. Jane's MMC, with four passengers, came sixth, taking 3 minutes, 7 seconds to do the course.[76] If Jane really did drive the first car to go through Portsmouth Dockyard, as claimed,[77] one may safely assume that it was an MMC.

As mentioned previously, Edwardian motoring had its dangers. Perhaps the least of these were boys who pursued cars throwing stones and injuring the passengers.[78] Road surfaces were maintained by local authorities, so were variable to say the least. Jane himself fell victim to the tram lines in Portsmouth's North End, which caused him to collide with a tree, smashing the single headlight of his car.[79] A more serious accident occurred at Chideock, in Dorset, on a one in five gradient, between Bridport and Axminster: "The car stopped on a very steep hill, and Mr Jane alighted, when the car suddenly began to run backwards. The sprag was down, but the car overrode it and went violently back. Mr Jane attempted to put on the side brakes but these failed to hold. One wheel passed over his foot, and he was then dragged some 50 yards until the car collided with the hedge where it upset".[80] Fortunately his wife and daughter, Dorothy, had already got out, and Jane himself escaped with only cuts and bruises.

Although speeds were relatively low, speed limits were even lower, and an irregular form of warfare broke out between motorists and the police. A speaker at the Motor Union's 'Emancipation Day' dinner on the 1906 anniversary of the 1896 'Light Locomotives Act' said: "he was not a motorist but a lawyer, he saw many familiar faces around from the courts. He did not like to urge motorists not to break the law, for though they did not profit by it, he did".[81]

Automobile Association Scouts would warn motorists approaching police speed traps. The Motor Union set up a 'Legal and Legislative Defence Fund', appealing "to motorists to place their movement beyond the reach of the village constable and the bucolic JP".[82] Its Sussex branch declared: "there are many who regard the methods of Dick Turpin as far more gentlemanly than those which are designed to thwart the progress of automobilism in Sussex. When he tracked his victims there was a chance of escape; from the trap of the Sussex Police and the fine of the Sussex JP there is none".[83] Fred T Jane commented that catching motorists: "beats big-game hunting any day, as long as you don't mind lying in court as well as in the hedges".[84] In his motoring anecdotes, published in Lord Montague's *CAR Illustrated*, the names of the country towns around Portsmouth are significantly translated into Peelersfield, Catchem, and Avem.

Jane appeared before Sir F Fitzwygram Bart, at the Havant Petty Sessions: "for driving a motor car at a speed greater than 12 mph through Warblington on the Havant Road". Constable Green had timed the defendant's car over a quarter of a mile course, which it had traversed in 38.5 seconds, equivalent to a speed of 23.5 mph. He started his watch on receiving a signal from a constable at the start of the trap who was "standing in a field and held up his handkerchief as the car passed". Their sergeant testified to the accuracy of the arrangements: after all, the watch had been tested within the last three months.

The defendant pleaded that his car was unable to travel faster than 12mph as the carburetor was out of order. He had increased speed to avoid some boys running after the car to catch hold of it and then to pass a motorcycle: "Just then he was stopped by the policeman whose buttons he had seen in the hedge for some distance along the road. He was driving with great care as Mrs Jane, who was one of the occupants, was nervous".[85] However, his chauffeur, travelling as a passenger, estimated their speed to have been 15mph so Jane was fined five shillings with 17 shillings costs. Oddly enough, he did not keep a chauffeur in later years, but preferred to tackle the engine himself, wiping his hands on his coat afterwards.

Unlike ships, to which Jane devoted his serious writing, cars engaged Jane's energies as a humourist. He contributed a series of humorous sketches to *CAR Illustrated* between 1904 and 1911. These appeared originally under the general heading of 'Diary of a Motor Man', and then 'Garage Yarns'.[86] These slight pieces are still amusing enough in small doses. They document the warfare between police and motorists, the numerous dodges of unscrupulous garage owners and mechanics, and the escapades of various of Jane's naval acquaintances. It may be surmised that the Lieutenant 'Iggens of 'HMS *Undeniable*', who attempted to take a taxi to his ship out in Spithead, later rose to be Captain H L Hitchens. It may be wiser not to go too far into such matters, but Lieutenant Henry L Hitchens was undoubtedly at Portsmouth in

The mighty Benz leading the BSAA across Southsea Common, 1910

HMS *Vernon*, qualifying as a torpedo officer, when Jane was writing the stories.

Many of the stories were narrated in excruciating Cockney by the chief mechanic at Fetlock's Garage, "the small establishment which ultimately blossomed into the well known undertaking of Vospers Ltd".[87] Herbert Edward Vosper had been a "pioneer of the internal combustion engine, developing vaporising paraffin engines and crude oil engines. In 1891, he had the first paraffin motor running on the Thames".[88] By 1900 the company had moved from its original home in Greek Street, to 18–36 Broad Street, in Old Portsmouth, near the Camber. Jane went there weekly for his "usual hour's instruction in the theory of the motor car (£2/2s the course, £3/3s private tuition)".[89] Vosper's workshop may also have inspired some unjustly neglected inventions recorded by the 'Yarns': The Stent-Bradden Patent Dust Exterminator, made from an old silencer, and the Stent-Fetlock Sun Engine, which attempted to replace spark plugs with a magnifying glass: "The sun engine ain't ded yet an' it's on'y the shockin' bad weather wot's 'inderin' its progress".

Jane may also have contributed to the *Hampshire Telegraph's*

BENZOLIN BANGS
EXPLANING TO THE COPPER
WHAT A VOITURET IS

" *This is a voiturette.*"

One of the cartoons that accompanied *Garage Yarns*

124

Naval Motoring column, under the pseudonym 'Direct Drive'. The
prose style and very pointed comments about Portsmouth's trams
and the commercial motoring press all tend to support this view.
In 1907 the column reported rumours about the imminent
release of a skit on "Wisdom while you Wait" lines. There was
room for such a book as: "motorists as a class take themselves
more seriously than they need, while a good half of the
Automobile press is only a shade removed from a tradesman's
tout".[90] The literary satire in question was the 'Ought-to-Go': "a
publication devoted to the interests of all vehicles self propelled
or otherwise shoved".[91] It was published anonymously, at one
shilling, and proudly announced on the title page that it was,
"quite useless to motorists".[92] It must be one of the rarest of Jane's
publications, having totally eluded the current author's efforts to
track it down.

A more serious piece of writing appeared in *Autocar* in
November 1912, describing the most powerful, and certainly
most famous vehicle to carry Jane's 'BK 97' number plate. In June
1909 he bought an eight litre Benz 90 HP chain driven racer from
G H Cox and Co Ltd, in St Edwards Road, Southsea, which had
moved on from rollerskates and bicycles, to rather more serious
pieces of machinery. The Benz 90 HP racer had the "unique
distinction of being well placed in two of the hardest races of a
Homeric year in motor racing".[93] In July 1907 it had gained fourth
place at the Ardennes circuit's meeting for Kaiserpreis class cars,
but its finest hour was at Brescia in the Coppa Florio in September
1907, driven by one of the great figures of early motor racing:
"Here she secured the second prize in a field of 42 cars. Héméry
replaced Hanriot as her driver and completed the course in 4h.
49m. 49s., his average speed throughout the period being about
62.5 mph." Its successor, in the racing world, was the famous
'Blitzen Benz' built for the 1908 French Grand Prix, which held
the world land speed record from 1909 to 1924, with speeds
rising from 127.4 mph in 1909 to 141.7 mph in 1911.[94]

Although Jane claimed to "take little interest in speed except on
hills", he soon had to face the magistrates at Avem again, in what
he claimed was "a world record, even for a motor car
prosecution". The case resulted in a £10 fine: "for driving at full
speed through a flock of over 100 sheep! This, the prosecutor
alleged, resulted in one sheep having its foot cut off! The injured
sheep could not be produced: but a witness as to speed was found.

He swore to it that 'the car went so fast that its back wheels were off the ground all the time!'".[95]

With his usual fairness, Jane added that: "to the credit of the local police . . . they were not involved in the prosecution". However, so bizarre was the conviction that Alan Burgoyne MP, also the editor of the *Navy League Annual*, raised a question in Parliament as to the mechanical miracles involved. He asked the Home Secretary of the day, the ubiquitous Winston Churchill: "whether his attention had been called to the conviction of Mr Fred T Jane by the Havant bench on Saturday May 6th for driving a motor car, No. BK 97, to the public danger through a flock of about 170 sheep and subsequently for driving sideways . . . whether he is aware that the defendant stated that he had skidded in his endeavour to avoid a horse and cart which suddenly drew across him, and that according to the prosecuting solicitor the driver of this cart was absent from it at the time; whether the car alleged to have struck a bank at 40 to 50 miles an hour was on the statement of the prosecution got out of the ditch and proceeding uninjured 100 yards further within three minutes".[96]

Mr Churchill promised to look into the matter of remitting the fine, but nothing resulted from it, despite a subsequent appeal against the sentence.

After its part in the electoral battles of 1910, BK 97 had to be "entirely reconstructed externally, from designs by Mrs Jane", to appear as it does in the later *CAR Illustrated* cartoons. There were no rear mud guards: "these were torn off in the final battle and have never been replaced. The front ones are perfectly flat wooden ones, very slightly inclined in the rear and 11in. wide. In this form they offer no wind resistance, can carry a deal of luggage, and make a splendid bench when anything has to be done to the engine".[97]

The stern of the car was rebuilt with a streamlined 'boat shape', incorporating a third seat, where a passenger could sit amid a pile of spare tyres, known as the 'conning tower'. Other changes to the original design of the car included a large Bessemer steel starting handle, to overcome the enormous compression of the engine, and removal of the fan: "The original fan once got adrift. One blade cut a hole in the radiator. Another missed my head by about a quarter of an inch as the bonnet chanced to be open at the time. Repairs were effected (with complete efficiency) by a Devonshire blacksmith, who for 'taking off radiator, soldering several cuts, and replacing same' charged 1 shilling".[98] As this was an astonishingly low bill, even for Edwardian car repairs, Jane kept it framed on the dash.

CHAPTER VI

DAMNATION TO ALL PARTY POLITICIANS

HE interest shown by Jane in the Navy extended beyond questions of material and doctrine, to include the concerns of what was termed the lower deck. In itself this attitude was uncharacteristic of the middle class people of the day, who tended to disparage the working class. Jane's sympathy for the very real grievances of the non-commissioned ranks of the navy probably helped to make him a figure of suspicion within an establishment where poverty was regarded as the result of moral inadequacy rather than low wages. Not surprisingly Jane's professional pride in his own work, and the service he provided through *Fighting Ships*, brought him closest to the long-serving warrant and petty officers, the professional bedrock of the service. Many commissioned officers, it was admitted, owed their promotion to the support of such men.[1] Jane repaid the glowing reviews of *Fighting Ships* in the *Naval Warrant Officers' Journal* not just with the loan of old blocks from *Fighting Ships* for the journal's masthead, but by his whole-hearted espousal of their concerns.

Despite the "tremendous diversity of interests that obtain on the Lower Deck",[2] similar problems affected all ranks. The central grievance was pay which had not changed since 1853, and by the turn of the century had fallen behind civilian wages. A barmaid in Jane's novel, *A Royal Bluejacket*, assumes that a day's pay is five shillings, whereas for a sailor it was more like one and sevenpence, after deductions. From 1900 to 1912 there was 15

Lord Charles Beresford as a Vice Admiral

per cent inflation. For sailors with families this was exacerbated by the concentration of the fleet in home waters, which led to rent increases in the home ports, Portsmouth, Plymouth and Chatham.[3] When Lord Charles Beresford suggested that crack gunlayers of the Channel Fleet were, "worth their weight in diamonds", an expert said it was: "difficult to establish the exact value of a man's weight in diamonds, but an expert says that the remuneration of a Navy marksman is more probably based on his weight in copper".[4]

The great advantage of the Royal Navy as a career was its relative security, but for many senior ratings, such as petty officers, this

Beresford as seen on a cigar box label

131

was diminished by the summary manner in which they could be disrated. Not only could they arbitrarily lose their hard-earned status, but the improved pension which went with it.[5] However in 1912 Churchill, a reforming First Lord of the Admiralty, restricted a captain's powers to disrate, while allowing petty officers the right to court martial, if they preferred that to summary disrating.

The slender pay of the sailor was often further diminished by various forms of corruption. Dress regulations were unnecessarily elaborated by 'uniform strategists', providing ships' corporals with a ready source of income in the form of bribes from sailors anxious to avoid being detected in minor, but expensive, transgressions of the rules. Such malpractices were particularly acute at the RN barracks in home ports, although Commodore Spencer Login, who had introduced Jane's wargame at the Royal Naval College Greenwich, began to attack the clothing abuses at Portsmouth from 1904.[6] Food was another source of grievance. The rations issued were often poor. Soldiers en route to the Boer War in 1899 refused to eat salt beef held in cask onboard HMS *Ramillies* since 1893.[7] Jane himself distrusted food reformers as faddists, feeling that, "one man's meat is another man's poison: The Irish problem is reckoned to be a pretty hard nut to crack — it is one that bowls over every statesman that tries to solve it — but it is a teacupful of water compared to the naval messing problem . . . There are those who — like Mr Yexley — have devoted half a lifetime to it, to find that the utmost they can achieve is a compromise that satisfies a certain percentage only".[8]

Much of the credit for the improvements that were made to messing arrangements can be attributed to Lionel Yexley, formerly known as Petty Officer James Woods. He bought himself out of the Royal Navy in 1898, one year short of pension, in order to pursue his campaigns for better pay, promotion, and food, unfettered by any obligation to the Admiralty. As editor of *The Bluejacket* and then *The Fleet*, he built a personal relationship with Fisher and Churchill, persuading them to accept not only his diagnosis of the navy's social problems, but often his solutions.[9] Jane was never as single-minded about lower deck reform as Yexley, although he was every bit as vocal over individual cases of injustice. They often clashed ferociously, although sometimes their disputes seem to arise more from their incompatible personalities than more objective reasons. Even so, Jane would defend Yexley's honesty: "he has never written anything he does not believe. I like people who do that ... and hence I like Mr Yexley. I like him best when he lays it on thick against me in *The Fleet*: 'music hall patter', 'Boy Scout spurs' etc, etc. He couldn't have got there by humbug writing".[10] Sometimes they made common cause, for instance over Yexley's scheme for a benevolent fund, to take the place, within the navy, of Lloyd George's national insurance: "even in face of his alluding to it as the BF — liable to make people think he is merely expressing fresh views about myself".[11]

They also stood together against the efforts of "faddist teetotallers", to suppress the rum ration: "a healthier drink than many of the so-called T. T. drinks which are unduly full of gas and other chemicals"[12]. Jane would have preferred rum to be replaced by beer: "The trouble is the difficulty of keeping it onboard – there would be hardly room for the guns if ships carried the equivalent of rum in beer".

Jane himself admitted to a liking for a glass of ale, with bread and cheese, after "a hard day's motoring, plenty of scorching, and a few punctures thrown in".[13] He set his face, however, against "the deadly teapot and the poisonous concoctions ... stewed therein on HM ships", which he felt certain would ruin the digestions of anyone drinking it habitually.[14] Given their temperamental differences, however, it was perhaps as well that Yexley resisted Jane's attempt to take over *The Bluejacket*, to further his political ambitions: "when the late Fred T Jane contested Portsmouth as an Independent Naval Candidate, with a special appeal to the Navy – officers and men ... Fred T approached me with object of buying the paper. He wanted it as a permanent propaganda organ, and offered me a contract as editor if he was allowed to buy it. The paper was not for sale on such terms. I was not prepared to be the paid hack of Fred T, or anyone else".[15]

The idea of specifically naval representation in parliament was quite acceptable then, Oxford and Cambridge Universities still having their parliamentary seats. Lord Charles Beresford had made periodic forays into politics, behaving very much as an MP for the navy, leading to the sarcastic suggestion that the Admiralty should allow a rating to stand at Portsmouth, posting him to the Royal Yacht if elected, as had once been done for Charlie Beresford.[16] Direct representation seemed to many to be the only effective way of bringing naval concerns before Parliament, as there were "a good many lower deck questions that could not be properly represented second-hand". At the same time, there were "objections to retired Naval Officers putting up ... [they were] not used to talking and writing about things, and to a certain extent tended to take a one-sided view".[17] When Jane joined the other five parliamentary candidates for Portsmouth in 1903, he told the *Hampshire Telegraph* he "had been approached by a strong body representing the WOs and lower deck, and incidentally other naval interests".[18] Presumably these included Admiral Sir John Hopkins, who endorsed Jane's candidacy during the 1906 General Election.[19] Jane always claimed to be non-political. It was: "not an important matter for Portsmouth whether the town returned a Radical [that is Liberal] or Conservative. What it needed was someone who was well up in Naval matters".[20]

Party loyalties were in any case a recent innovation, developed since Joseph Chamberlain's Caucus, of the 1880s, which Jane's yokels had aped in *His Lordship, the Passen, and We*. Victorian audiences were always greatly relieved when issues turned out to be 'non-party'.[21] Jane's 1903 interview spelled out the issues that he would pursue into the General Election, three years later. It was better, he said, to expand Portsmouth dockyard, rather than open up new facilities on the Firth of Forth in Scotland. The "pay of the service was on antique lines ... [it] paid the ordinary citizen better to live at home at his ease than risk his life for his country". The army and navy were more important than the Education Act, "about which all this fuss was being made".

Although the *Army and Navy Gazette* endorsed Jane's stand, the local Conservatives were less pleased, as he threatened to split their vote in the same way that the Labour candidate, Alderman Sanders, had split the opposition. An attempt to paper over the cracks failed, despite the offer of one Conservative candidate to accept an executive decision against him if his opponent would do likewise, but Mr Jane stood firm: "he was pledged to the Navy Before Party, and though he regretted the necessity of adopting such an uncompromising attitude, he could not allow the question of whether he was standing or not to be decided by the Conservative Association".[22]

When the General Election campaign opened in January 1906 Jane started slowly, being confined to his house by a severe chill. However, this did not stop him giving a short exposition of his views to some of his workers, in characteristic terms: "not being tied by the leg to a party, he was in the happy position of being able to say what he really thought about things — a rare luxury he believed at election times".[23]

In his view the great political issues of the day, Tariff Reform and Irish Home Rule, were irrelevant to Portsmouth, which depended on the Navy for its prosperity. Consequently he "pledged to devote himself entirely to questions affecting the Senior Service", and to abstain from voting on other matters. He even made the sporting offer to take his constituents' opinion after 12 months and resign if they were not satisfied with him.[24] His campaign was prosecuted along "decidedly original lines", with no large meetings or placards saying 'Vote for Jane'. Instead he preferred to "appeal to the convictions of the electors through the medium of the Press", and by driving about Portsmouth, accompanied by his wife and daughter, to hold impromptu: "gatherings at street corners addressed in terse vigorous language from the deck of his 'battle grey' motor car".[25] Although the *Hampshire Telegraph* admitted that "the support given him at the polls may after all be something of a surprise packet", it felt that, while "sporting men will admire him for his pluck . . . probably they would not back him for a place".[26] In general the campaign at Portsmouth was a good natured one, despite the Conservatives being refused a hearing outside the Dockyard, where "remembrance of the recent discharges still rankles".[27]

On election night, some 30,000 people waited in Portsmouth's Guildhall Square until after one o'clock for the result, which was a double victory for Liberalism. In those days Portsmouth returned two members to Parliament, not being split into separate single member constituencies until 1918. Fred T Jane gained only 1,859 votes, from some 28,000 voters, coming bottom of the poll, while Sir John Baker at the top received 10,500 votes. Each voter had two votes, the Liberals receiving 20,736 altogether. Although Jane had fewest votes he compensated by making most noise, in a "Remarkable Speech": "He had tried to run the contest honestly. Many had told him at the outset that success was impossible that way – he now believed it and congratulated his advisers on their knowledge of the Portsmouth electorate (howls) . . . As long as he lived he would stand by the Lower Deck which had stood by him (jeers). If the electors of Portsmouth preferred party (cries of 'We do') they were welcome to it (cheers for Baker and Thomas Bramsdon).

"'Howl away" he said "but in the hour when you are cheering for party and jeering at the Navy that keeps you going, you have seen the birth of a new ideal which has for its watchword 'D to all party politician'" (howls and catcalls and three cheers for the Navy). "A babel of jeers and cries of 'Go Home' followed this call and Mr Jane having shaken his fist at the crowd and asserted his intention to try again, retired up the steps amidst wild confusion".[28]

Later he felt that the cause of direct naval representation had been "defeated not disgraced" and that, "it was worth having . . . stood up and been jeered for it". Meanwhile, as voting in other constituencies had yet to be completed: "Till the General

Electioneering in 1906 with his first wife and daughter, Alice and Dorothy

Election is over the old grey pennant will fly from BK 49 in the streets of Portsmouth and next election it will fly again".[29]

In its post-election analysis the *Hampshire Telegraph* felt that: "Mr Jane would undoubtedly have made a better impression had he worked along more conventional lines".[30] The campaign showed the importance of the newly respectable art of canvassing. Some 4,000 votes had been promised him but not given. Jane lacked helpers, "well versed in electioneering tactics to bring his would-be supporters into the firing line". Despite this failure of organisation it appeared: "worth the while of local Unionists . . . making arrangements for the next campaign to hear what Mr Jane has to say. If he can poll nearly two thousand votes single handed, he is worth considering with an eye to future contingencies".[31] Perhaps the last word on the campaign should be left to the Blue Streak candidate himself. In a later election, when the 'Fighting 1859' supported Beresford, he recalled how: "at a time when both parties were at the 'cutting down the Navy' game . . . in nine days without any organisation, I got 1,859 votes".[32]

Although Jane's attempts to carry the lower deck's concerns into parliament had failed, he did not forget those who had stood by him. Service issues were very much to the fore in the *Hampshire Telegraph* columns which he began the year after his political débâcle. These attacked every type of "economy at Jack's expense", ranging from the Channel Fleet's use of Portland over Christmas, forcing sailors to spend much precious leave time on the railways, instead of at home, to 'hospital stoppages' whereby a man's pay was docked after 30 days in the sick bay, even if his injuries had occurred while working: "free medical attention afloat is of course all humbug: hospital stoppages really resolve themselves into heavy doctor's bills, cash down. And seeing how the Admiralty pays its doctors, I would never swear that it doesn't make a profit on the deal".[33] It took a world war and an unlikely alliance between Lord Beresford and Ben Tillet, leader of the Docker's Union, to redress that grievance.[34]

Jane was nothing if not persistent, however, returning to the social novel, a literary form he had given up eight years before. *A Royal Bluejacket* was more successful than its predecessors, a "new and cheap edition one shilling Net", following the six shillings original. By comparison, *Blake of the Rattlesnake* seems to have been the only other novel of Jane's to appear in a second edition [35]. This may have been because by 1909 the author of *A Royal Bluejacket* could command reviews in the *Army and Navy Gazette*, which saw this "fresh and original sea story", as a tongue in cheek piece of social realism. The style is greatly improved over his earlier novels, with shorter sentences and much effective use of matelot's banter to carry things along: "As we have not ourselves experienced life on the lower deck of a man-of-war we must take Mr Jane's account of it as accurate . . . But the evolution of character is well worked out and the incidents highly dramatic".[36]

As had become customary the main character was quite dense, and more than somewhat a cad, quickly earning a reputation as the: "sea-lawyer of the division, joined the ship when half fuddled with drink, though able to walk straight and appear sober. Shirks his work when he can and is clever enough not to get run in".[37] Young Arthur Smith does have the disadvantage of being a member of the Royal Family, being quite unable to find his way about London, or even order a meal in a restaurant. Prince Arthur enlists as an Ordinary Seaman, in order to impress his beautiful cousin. This allows Jane, besides following his social themes, to develop an almost Shakespearean series of misunderstandings. To some extent, the confusion reflects the nature of Jane's own life. He does seem to have gone from one scrape to another: a brawl at Berlin Central railway station, precipitated by German queuing habits, and another at a pacifist meeting during the Boer War; the indoor hockey match where he roller-skated through a plate glass door at G H Cox's bicycle riding school in Southsea – requiring several stitches in his arm and hand [38]. On another occasion Jane was enlisted, or rather his car was, by the Cosham police to help catch a suspected car thief: "I looked out alright but having failed to get the number properly, chased the wrong car . . . apologies to the unfortunate motorist who was so worried last Sunday by BK 97 making circles round him".[39]

For all its superiority to *The Port Guard Ship* in style and content, *A Royal Bluejacket* is not great literature. Like much of Jane's fictional output it is mainly interesting for its humour and social content, providing a type of historical insight not available elsewhere. This process is assisted by the device of Prince Arthur's incognito, which calls into question the relationship upon the inner worth of the individual and their outward appearance. Like Prince Arthur, modern reader, gradually begins to understand the complex social relationships on board ship. Only the civilians come off badly, moving their deck chairs away when the royal bluejacket sits near them on Southsea Common – an indication of the Edwardian attitude towards the 'handy man' of the navy, reminiscent of Kipling's "making mock of uniforms that guards you while you sleep". In 1909 the patriotic play, *An Englishman's Home*, written about a German invasion of the UK, was performed at the King's Theatre. It was well supported by the 'lower deck', but "some insufferable bounder" thought it: "'rather thick that men in uniform should be allowed in the dress circle – glad to record it was a Naval Officer who promptly stepped rather heavily indeed on the speaker's toes".[40] *A Royal Bluejacket* should be counted, "among the best of Mr Jane's novels".[41] Arthur Smith gains the love of his princess, but the aftermath of a cordite fire, "nothing very serious merely a few bluejackets...", leaves the reader in suspense as to whether it will do him any good.

* * *

On Thursday, 10 December 1908, Jane's wife, Alice Beattie Jane, died after the type of gynaecological procedure that today might follow a miscarriage, but then might have been used to remove a tumour.[42] The remarkable thing is not so much that Alice died from the shock but that such an operation was carried out at home, in Elphinstone Road. It was a cruel irony that Alice should have suffered a similar fate to several of Jane's fictional women.

Alice was only 38 years old. She was buried the following Tuesday at Highland Road Cemetery, in Southsea, in a ceremony marked by features not usually associated with the drab dullness of the characteristic British funeral: "By special desire of the deceased, the ordinary dismal death colours of black and white were avoided ... The coffin was draped in violet with pale pink so as to reproduce the colours of her favourite flowers – violets and pink carnations".[43]

One particularly striking wreath of scarlet geraniums and yellow chrysanthemums came from 'The Friends in the Imperial Japanese Navy'. A single carriage followed the funeral coach covered with "bright coloured wreaths...sent by Mrs Jane's friends in Southsea and the relatives in Devon". Although Jane and his little daughter were the only two official mourners, popular sympathy was expressed by a "considerable attendance" outside the house in Elphinstone Road, while at the cemetery the Navy provided "a party of an officer and about 30 men, including 12 Petty Officers", who: "out of respect for Mr and the late Mrs Jane had volunteered to render such unofficial Naval honours as the regulations would permit. This was specially sanctioned by Admiral Sir John Fisher".[44]

Three officers of the Japanese navy were also present, saluting as the coffin was borne to the grave. A large assemblage listened impressively to the service conducted by the Vicar of Portsmouth, manifesting: "the greatest sympathy for the sad faced winsome motherless child whom the father had to support back to the carriage".[45]

The same issue of the *Hampshire Telegraph* that reported this affecting scene carried a remarkable piece of writing, under the legend: "FROM THE DEAD". Jane apologised for: "allowing his private sorrows to intrude into his professional duties", but he felt that both for him, and for his column, things were different: "an

Alice Beattie's headstone

140

author always lives in the shop. And if his wife takes an interest in his work at all, she gets bound up with it and helps him, in a way that cannot happen, with any other job, and which none can realise until after the great parting has come".[46]

Alice had always taken a particular interest in his column: "From its very beginning she always had a hand in it, suggesting subjects for comment, ideas, revisions, and what not, toning me down when I was too fiery, and sometimes firing me up when the subject was one that she felt strongly about".[47]

Much of the piece was of a rambling and often incoherent nature, which in the circumstances is hardly surprising, but two things stood out. One was the extent to which Jane and his wife had shared the patriotism which characterises, and sometimes detracts from his column; the other, how Jane shared the Victorian need for commemoration, feeling that "to be forgotten is the worst of all ills". He took comfort in words that were to appear, on her headstone: "a sentence that she once thought of: 'The dead who are remembered, still live'." Alice's headstone was an impressive affair of Cornish pink granite, with expensive raised lettering, that would mark not only her final resting place, but Jane's own. Unluckily, the grand gesture was marred in the execution, the masons failing to realise just how much space was needed for 'Remembered', as can be seen to this day. Meanwhile, Jane felt that, without Alice's moderating influence, he was "like a ship without a rudder".

This may possibly account for why, within two months of this terrible blow, Jane embarked on what would become the most famous of his many practical jokes. The kidnapping by car of a Labour MP in January 1909 can either be taken as evidence of Jane's irrepressible nature, or as proof that he was not indulging in conventional rhetoric when he wrote of his rudderless condition. Usually Jane's practical joking expressed itself in harmless leg-pulling, or such suggestions as the idea that officers anxious for quick promotion might take the place of the rats placed on board old ironclads expended as targets to establish the true protective value of armour against modern gunfire.[48] To modern eyes the 'alleged abduction' appears a bizarre episode, beyond the bounds of reasonable behaviour. However, one should beware of applying modern standards of judgement to other historical periods. Political attitudes were much more robust in the Edwardian period, as can clearly be seen from the

The headlines after Jane's most notorious practical joke

hurly-burly of Jane's own electioneering in 1910 when his car was practically demolished around him. Political figures did not command the sort of respect that they seem to expect today. It is worth noting that none of the reports of Mr Grayson's ride offered any criticism of his alleged kidnappers. The only critical note was sounded by an old schoolmate, who deflated Jane with the remark: "Well, at School, of course, you always were a bit off your chump, weren't you".[49]

Attitudes to horseplay in general were more tolerant, perhaps as a reaction to the general stuffiness of Edwardian society. It was an age when Royal Marine officers would leap onto the mantlepiece after RMA mess nights, and Portsmouth crowds cheered drunken sailors as they fought the police in Commercial Road. During one of the 1910 election campaigns in Portsmouth, "some gay sparks collected a huge crowd for a Radical meeting, at the wrong place", blandly offering satisfaction to anyone who felt aggrieved.[50] A similar hoax was played by the landlord of the White Hart Hotel in Harwich. With the aid of some sailors who were mendaciously sporting Airship No 1 on their cap ribbons, he persuaded a large crowd to gather on Harwich pier at five the next morning, hoping to witness the bogus dirigible. Standards of robustness were already slipping however. Jane remembered an admiral once remarking to him how: "the midshipmen of today were a hopelessly inferior breed to what they were in his youth: 'We used to kick each other's heads to see who could hold out the longest'".[51]

One thing is certain: the kidnapping was not a specifically Tory plot. As we have seen, Jane stood against the official Conservative candidates at the 1906 election, and was generally regarded as 'having no party politics'.[52] In 1910, he reserved his electoral support for only one of the Conservative candidates, Lord Charles Beresford. He left voters to make their own choice between the other Conservative and the Labour candidate,[53] reserving his disapprobation for the Liberal candidates. Paradoxically, in spite of his frequently outspoken opinions about Socialism, Jane had quite a positive attitude towards the local Labour Party. In 1906 he had suggested to Alderman Sanders, their candidate, that they form a: "sort of alliance . . . because we had certain points in common and because such of the Labour party workers I came across struck me as square and honest men, not hole and corner politicians. The Alderman replied quite squarely that there were points in his platform that did not tally with some of mine, and there the matter ended except that neither party went in for slanging the other during the contest".[54]

A high level of cross-voting by supporters of Jane and Sanders at the January 1906 poll suggests that the former may have been on to something. One may surmise that the points Jane felt he had in common with Labour related to their social programme. With his personal experiences of poverty in London, and of the rookeries in Portsea, Jane had no quarrel with practical attempts at social reform. His complaint was that London had adopted a more doctrinaire socialism, more akin to the Marxism of the German SPD: "When the Labour Party was first started its object was to look after the interests of all who worked: now all that has been thrown aside in favour of a lot of made-in-Germany fads about the conditions under which our great grandchildren shall exist"[55]

When the Labour Party came to Portsmouth for its conference in January 1909, a struggle was in progress between the pragmatic and the doctrinaire wings of the party.[56] Older party workers remembered how the movement had faltered in the 1890s for lack of money, and wanted to integrate the democratic socialist ILP with the more conservative Labour movement, financed by the Trade Unions. This would, they hoped, provide a more viable organisation, both politically and financially. The move was resisted however by younger, more idealistic elements in the party who looked for leadership to the charismatic Victor Grayson: "the *enfant terrible* of the Labour movement. His temper is vitriolic, his language pungent, his comings and goings meteoric. At the Colne Valley he, a quite unknown young man, staggered all parties, the Labour Party most of all, by running the seat against Liberal and Unionist as an out-and-out champion of Socialism . . . He started a new epoch in English political history by being the first M. P. to enter Parliament as a Socialist owning allegiance to no existent Parliamentary party . . . As a coiner of phrases he outvies Bernard Shaw, and as a creator of 'scenes' he has obtained notoriety at St Stephen's."[57]

The conference at Portsmouth ran from Tuesday 26 January through the following Thursday. Bernard Shaw thought it: "'More dull than a meeting of the National Liberal Federation, and much more respectable'".[58] Grayson was expected to speak against the executive on the Tuesday, but he failed to appear. On the Wednesday: "Speculation as to whether he would appear or not was speedily laid to rest by the man himself walking into the hall wearing his familiar crushed felt hat".[59] Yet again, he missed his chance as he "lounged elegantly against one of the pillars of the hall, and carefully held his peace".[60] His last opportunity would be on the Thursday afternoon, but just before lunch he received an invitation from an admirer to view the sights of Portsmouth from a motor car. Earlier, BK 97 had been obstructed by some Labour delegates outside the Guildhall, and its driver abused as a bloated capitalist. Seeking revenge, Jane may have selected Grayson as his victim because he knew he was planning to speak that day, after failing to do so in the preceding sessions.[61] Accepting the offer, Grayson found himself deceived: "Instead of a short drive round the town, they made along the road into the open country, driving at what I considered to be a dangerous pace. I protested, but my protests were ignored. The driver made no attempt to stop or return to Portsmouth".[62]

As his accomplice in the escapade, Jane had chosen a "Lieutenant Kenneth Wilson, late Indian Army", who stood 6ft 2in tall and was a champion boxer, so he was well able to ignore any protests. The original plan had been to leave Grayson at the roadside ten miles outside Portsmouth. However his company was evidently congenial enough to persuade his kidnappers to take him instead to the Red Lion at Petersfield, 18 miles away, where: "We gave him a jolly good lunch, which he thoroughly enjoyed, and afterwards we sat down and smoked cigarettes and drank liqueurs for some time".[63]

Jane took the precaution of bribing the waiter to serve as slowly as possible, and apologised for eating his rice pudding so slowly: "'Do you know' said Mr Grayson to me, 'that I begin to think this is an arrangement of Keir Hardie and Ramsay Macdonald [of the Independent Labour Party], to get me out of the way'. We laughed till we could hardly stand".[64]

Grayson was known to enjoy good company, and was a lively and humorous companion.[65] His character as a maverick would also have commended him to Jane, as would his untypically patriotic views. Like Jane he had clear views about the threat of German aggression, which appeared weekly in the columns of the "Clarion" published by Robert Blatchford. Jane approved of Blatchford, partly because of his position on defence matters, and partly because he owed allegiance to no party line: "Socialist or not, whether he were an Anarchist or a Peer, or anything whatever in between, if he stood for Parliament for Portsmouth I fancy I should vote for him, and try to get all others of the Navy Before Party to do likewise, because he puts the Country first, and party politics second".[66]

During the return journey, the car appeared to break down, and had to be 'mended'. Eventually Grayson was taken back to Portsmouth, escaping onto a tram bound for the Queen's Hotel, where he was staying. Meanwhile his allies in the Social Democratic Federation had seen their opportunity slip away: "We waited upon tiptoe in the very agony of exuberation for the great man of the day. Time passed. The day came to an end. No Grayson. It was all over. A very promising young leader had lost the chance of his life."[67]

It might have been better for Grayson's reputation if Jane had stuck to his original plan. As it was, Victor was discredited with his supporters, who could see, in the *Daily Mirror*, a photograph of their leader being driven out of the Guild Hall Square, hobnobbing with their class enemy. He lost his seat at the January 1910 General Election, partly as a result of the drinking problems which undermined his health. Wounded at Passchendaele in 1917, he was discharged from the Army suffering from shell shock, to be employed by the War Office making patriotic speeches in support of the war effort, rather as Jane had spent the earlier part of the war. His eventual fate is unknown, as he disappeared in September 1920, after a murky period allegedly blackmailing Maundy Gregory, who sold honours on behalf of the Lloyd George Liberals.[68]

The wider consequences of Grayson's abduction may have been rather greater than Francis McMurtrie knew when he wrote that: "It is to be feared the popularity of that politician never entirely recovered from the shock".[69] Failing to win over the infant Labour Party, the dissidents went on, in 1911, to form the British Socialist Party. This diverted many future Communist Party members away from the Labour Party, helping to make it a more readily elected party, capable of attracting a mass following.[70]

For Fred T Jane the episode confirmed his reputation as "the biggest joker in Portsmouth". There was an immediate outbreak of reported kidnappings: "On Saturday, Lieut. Wilson 'mysteriously disappeared' and is said to have been lured to another town but returned on Sunday evening, very hungry, and hinting at an 'exciting adventure'. It is also stated that on Sunday evening Mr Shaw was invited to take a motor car drive, but declined the honour".[71]

At the Imperial Naval Press Conference the following June an incident occurred which may have led to the claim that a similar attempt against Winston Churchill, when First Lord, was only foiled by a last minute change of travel arrangements. Jane wrote: "Went down to the Dockyard in BK 97. Some unscrupulous practical joker recognised the car, got hold of Mr McKenna [then First Lord of the Admiralty] and told him to beware — that I would invite him to go round the Dockyard in the car and land him at the Red Lion, Petersfield. As a result, the unfortunate McKenna unable to think out a satisfactory reason to refuse the supposed invitation, spent quite a lot of his time at Whale Island — dodging clear of me".[72]

Thus the political head of the most powerful navy in the world was reduced to dodging around Portsmouth naval base to avoid being kidnapped by the country's leading naval journalist.

CHAPTER VII

INTO THE BLUE

LEVEN years after the launch of *Fighting Ships*, 1909 found Jane on the threshold of changes more radical than any he had experienced since the heady days of the late 1890s. He was recently widowed, aged 44, perhaps suffering a mid-life crisis. He appeared from photographs of the time to be putting on weight, compared with the lean figure who addressed the 1906 electorate from the deck of his battle-grey MMC. Within the year, however, he began a second yearbook, by which his name is still known, mobilised the motorists of Portsmouth in support of the new Scouting movement, and found a new wife. In addition he was nearly killed trying to fly.

Perhaps some of Jane's energy came from the need to take his mind off the loss of his first wife. However, he had long been interested in aviation. In the 1890s he had illustrated the aerial fantasies of *The Angel of the Revolution*, and *Hartmann the Anarchist*. Earlier still, before leaving home, he had illustrated stories about aircraft written by one of his brothers.[1] *Fighting Ships* had shown his early awareness of the possible significance of flight for naval warfare. The Swedish Navy is not renowned for its pioneering role in naval aviation, but the 1902 issue included their balloon barge, perhaps the first vessel designed to carry aircraft, and in this case the necessary hydrogen generation equipment.[2] In the same issue, a year and a half before the Wright brothers' first successful flight, Jane predicted that, "only the heavier than air type of flying machine seems likely to have any future at all". He also issued a warning that could apply to many subsequent weapon developments, from the main battle tank to 'Star Wars' high technology: "The military value of an appliance depends not on its sensational possibilities, but on its capacity for practical use . . . The airship analogous to the destroyer is yet far off . . . but the airship that may be as efficient a scout as many small cruisers and destroyers are, is perhaps near at hand".[3]

Within five years, the French were equipping the fortresses on their border with Germany with scouting balloons.[4] Only two years later, Louis Blériot flew the English Channel in a heavier-than-air monoplane, while Jane was already: "burning the midnight oil over a book that will illustrate everyone of them in existence, *Fighting Ships* fashion. I'm a kind of walking encyclopedia on the subject and exude phrases like monoplane, biplane, multiplane, helicopter etc, until the police require me to modify my language".[5]

This appeared in November 1909, as *All the World's Airships*, then a generic term for any machine that flew. There was "a good deal of trepidation and misgivings as to whether it was not a few years ahead of its time". It was "of necessity somewhat chaotic, so far as aeroplanes were concerned, owing to the constant appearance of new types, often to the tune of several a day".[6] Frequently it was impossible to give complete details of every type, "since in a great number of cases the inventors desire to keep certain details secret"[7]. At that time aeroplanes were generally built in a shed somewhere, by a couple of garage mechanics, like the Porte and Pirie Biplane constructed at Gosport for two naval lieutenants.[8] Jane must have witnessed the trial of this particular specimen, as *All the World's Airships 1909* includes a photograph of its gliding trials at Portsmouth in August. Many of the aircraft listed had never flown or reached the stage of being photographed, forcing Jane to apologise for the large number of unillustrated pages. However, even the skeletal book showed the strength of Jane's standardised approach to data collection, as gaps revealed where more information was needed. Jane felt "there are sure to be some readers able to supply the missing details", providing a pre-addressed 'Form for Particulars of New Machines', to help them do so. Readers wishing "to assist in the production of a book crammed as far as possible with every possible detail" were invited to send in their information by the following August.[9] Besides listing the different types of aircraft by nationality, the first issue covered aerial societies, journals, and flying grounds. Admiral Sir Percy Scott, who had revolutionised the Navy's approach to gunnery, contributed an article on aerial warfare. Cecil Jane covered the political aspects of aviation, and the indefatigable Charles de Grave Sells, who wrote similar pieces for *Fighting Ships*, discussed aerial engineering. By 1911 the work was established, the *Times* feeling that it "deserves very high praise": "The amount of information collected is astonishing and all the more creditable because of the constant changes in detail due to the progress of the subject matter. In Great Britain there appears to be six aerial societies; four journals; 21 flying grounds; 56 aero-clubs and about 90 owners of machines. About 600 machines are mentioned in the book, and something like 700 airmen".[10]

The new directory was accepted more quickly than *Fighting Ships* had been. Jane was a well established figure by 1909, and perhaps there were also fewer vested interests in the new field of aviation. The *Daily Mail* headlined a review on its leader page 'The First Flying Directory'.[11] Society itself was changing in the years just before the First World War. There was a greater readiness to accept new ideas, in all sorts of areas, a change in attitude ascribed by Virginia Woolf to December 1910, roughly contemporary with the *Times'* glowing review.[12] Critical acclaim did not add up to financial success, however. In the last issue for which he was personally responsible, Jane apologised for "the slimness of the book in relation to its price", then 21 shillings: "it has entailed a heavy financial loss ever since its first production . . . every fresh issue has entailed the scrapping of whatever may have appeared in the previous year, and the cost of production has been in proportion".[13]

As with *Fighting Ships*, Jane received extensive help from enthusiasts worldwide. These included aviation pioneers like Louis Blériot, A V Roe, and Prince Henry of Prussia, whom Jane had applauded as a prince, "who drives his own car and doesn't mind lying down underneath it when something goes wrong"[14]. Major Baden-Powell, late Scots Guards and brother of the Chief Scout, revised the proofs of the 1910–11 issue. He had invented a man-carrying kite in the 1890s and lectured at the RUSI on the military value of aviation. He also believed infantry should fight from armoured fighting vehicles, having had his watch smashed by a Mauser bullet during the Relief of Mafeking. The contents pages of the (pre-war) issues of *All the World's Aircraft* show the extent of Jane's international contacts, with the more significant national contributions all ascribed to appropriate 'special editors'. By then it had become apparent that the book had to change its name, as 'Airship' had developed the specific connotation of lighter-than-air craft.[15]

Appropriately, the 1914 issue, which appeared early, just after the outbreak of the First World War, noted another change in the flying scene: "except as a war machine — neither the aeroplane nor the dirigible has any immediate utility at the present time ... For all practical purposes aircraft have no more to do with peace than have submarines".[16] For this reason, Jane censored the 1914 issue, blacking out whole sections relating to British equipment and organisation. However, the value of the work's accuracy helped public confidence in wartime by dispelling exaggerated rumours about imminent German air raids: "Germany is shown not to possess anything but the merest nucleus of that fleet of 50 'Zeppelins' which she was reported a few days ago to have ready for an attack on these islands".[17] In fact, the first Zeppelin raid on the UK did not occur until 1915.

In 1909, when Jane was compiling the first issue of *All the World's Airships*, he himself had been one of those "more or less hare-brained inventors", whose passing the 1914 issue had signalled. This cannot have been a cheap venture. Machines cost between £480 and £1,000, plus a premium for prompt delivery, such was the demand. Flying lessons at Wembley airfield cost £100, plus £50 deposit and £10 insurance, in case the pupil "alights on someone's cucumber frame or ploughs his way through a poultry run".[18] The risks were not trivial, Jane commenting, "in its present stage, aviation generally means broken necks or broken legs".[19] Several of his naval friends were killed in flying accidents, and he discovered that "the earth is a good deal harder than I had any conception of".[20] Supporting the proposed use of Langstone Harbour, to the east of Portsmouth, as a base for dirigibles he remarked on how: "the wide reaches of mud are attractive to practical aeroplanists, in the early stages of aviation. Something soft to come down on means a good deal, as most of us who try to fly are now coming to realise".[21]

Soon after this Jane's attempts to conquer the air came to a sudden end, while experimenting on Dartmoor: "Several short flights had been accomplished and Mr Jane was essaying a longer distance when a sudden gust of wind caught the machine sideways causing it to swoop. In doing so it came into contact with a treetop. Mr Jane fell among the upper branches and was quite unhurt, but the machine tumbled to the ground and was smashed to fragments; and the petrol in the engine, by some way igniting, it was also burned".[22]

He took its loss philosophically, merely remarking that "it would be one less to include in the forthcoming work All the World's Airships". At the time he evidently intended to continue his efforts, having ordered a "large monoplane of Italian design". From the *Hampshire Telegraph*'s description, this would appear to be the Miller monoplane. Although this had the advantage of detachable wings, allowing the fuselage to be driven along the road, like an ordinary motor car, the handbook commented laconically: "Has not met with much success".[23] There is no firm evidence that Jane ever took delivery, as although one of his Boy Scouts believed a monoplane was kept at Jane's Bedhampton residence, he never in fact saw it.[24]

Jane was very cautious about the practical value of aircraft, unlike H G Wells, whose *War In The Air* appeared in 1908. As a naval analyst rather than a novelist, Jane had to take a more sober view of "mythical aerial navies of the sweet bye and bye", which he saw as a threat to the navy's hard won *Dreadnought* programme. At first a "firm believer in the early advent of regular aerial navies", he was, after some personal experience, "inclined to think that aerial scouts on fine days are about as far as we are likely to see for a good many years".[25] With the limited aircraft of the day Jane was quite right to minimise the value of aerial bombardment, although he did see ahead to the need for warships with armoured decks and high angle guns to engage aircraft: "The important thing is the utter revolution that aircraft must make in scouting . . . naval strategy of the past was something like a game of poker — aircraft have already made it poker with the cards face up".[26]

He also foresaw the potential tactical uses of aircraft: "as longer flight is secured the aeroplane is going to be invaluable for Naval purposes. It is not an impossible dream that an aeroplane will be the fire control platform of the future. It should be invaluable for spotting . . . Any submarine near will be sighted. And there will be an end to all problems of guessing the enemy's real formation, bearing and so forth".[27] As usual Jane saw the personnel side of the problem: "Properly trained naval aviators are essential otherwise the most misleading information might be brought back". He also saw how: "depot ships . . . could be fitted up to give ample room for any aeroplane to rise from. They might even be built so there would be a fair prospect of the aeroplane being able to return".[28]

Before the war, the Royal Navy did conduct experiments launching aircraft off the turrets of battleships, involving Jane's friend Lieutenant L'Estrange Malone, flying off HMS *London*. During the First World War he commanded seaplanes at Gallipoli, spotting naval gunfire as Jane had predicted.[29] However, at Jutland the Grand Fleet still lacked an effective aircraft carrier.[30] The result was rather more like blindman's buff than poker with the cards face up. However, the equipment was technically still very limited. In 1913, Jane remarked how seaplanes still suffered from the drawback that: "a pilot cannot learn to handle one efficiently without killing himself in the process . . . the voluntarily submersible hydro-aeroplane is yet far to seek, but so much has been done by aviators involuntarily in this direction that provision against it . . . is only a matter of time".[31]

In general, the Edwardian period of 1901–1909 was characterised by a high level of technical innovation which caught the public imagination without necessarily being of immediate practical use. Astonishing inventions appeared in the staid columns of the *Naval Chronicle*, for example the 'anti-warship magnet': "able to draw battleships out of their course and render their huge guns useless. Smaller vessels it is claimed can be sunk entirely by its means".[32] Even anti-gravity devices were taken seriously.[33] After all, such an idea must have appeared no more unlikely than radium or wireless telegraphy had until then. The world was: "on the threshold only as yet of the discoveries . . . to be made. Everyone realises that. Indeed the trouble is that they realise it only too easily".[34]

Professional naval men of Jane's day should be treated with some sympathy if they failed to realise all the implications of the often bizarre equipment with which they were confronted. The later 20th century has not always been distinguished by the intelligent exploitation of technology. Hindsight generally justifies Jane's cautious attitude towards innovation, rather than the naivety of the 'bright soul' who wrote to the daily papers in 1913, predicting an imminent invasion by 70,000 German

The end in Trafalgar Square (The Violet Flame)

airborne troops. Jane calculated that in single file, using the aircraft of the day, the invaders would occupy 2,800 miles, concluding: "fifty or a 100 years hence no one knows what may be possible, but we are living today and must legislate for today".[35]

* * *

Technology was not the only area of change in Edwardian society. People were beginning to look for a less apocalyptic approach to the problems of modern society than blowing the whole thing to bits, like Jane's imaginary anarchists, the Finis Mundi, in *The Violet Flame*. Liberals, such as Lloyd George and Churchill, looked to Trade Boards and National Insurance, but more conservative elements in society were also concerned with the deteriorating physical condition of the British working classes which had forced the army to make: "successive reductions in the standard in order to secure a sufficient number [of recruits] ... and a large number of these prove unfit".[36]

In the 1990s lack of fit recruits is put down to too much television and food plus too little exercise. In Edwardian times the causes adduced included "overcrowding — neglect of proper precautions with regard to milk supply — inadequate attention generally given to physical training". One way of addressing the latter problem was the Boy Scouts movement, founded by Sir Robert Baden-Powell in 1908. This provided an alternative source of moral education to the Sunday Schools, combined with practical activities which took urban children into the countryside, away from football matches. These were deplored as strongly by Fred T Jane as by the Chief Scout, as opportunities for the spectators to catch pneumonia, or, more metaphorically, catch a cold gambling.[37]

Jane's contribution was to organise Field Days which eventually involved hundreds of scouts, dozens of cars and cycles, and, on one occasion, six trams. The general idea was to sharpen the boys' scouting abilities against a force of mechanised 'invaders', played by Jane and his friends, many of them naval officers or ratings, who acted as cyclists and signallers. The scheme had been "evolved long ago by one whose column this once was", that is to say, his dead wife Alice.[38] Although the first occasion in June 1909 was ill-supported by Portsmouth's motorists, the day was saved by the naval cycling clubs, and a green-grocer who turned out with his donkey and cart. To make up for the lack of motor cars, Jane drove up and down the main roads into Cosham, to lure the Boy Scouts out of hiding to be caught by the cyclists, so that soon "Cosham wallowed in metaphorical blood like a miniature Sedan". Many of the younger Scouts: "regarded the whole affair as a glorified 'beano' with Mr Jane as the genial MC. They scampered over Portsdown Hill, facing the invaders with magnificent bravery, only taking cover to eat their lunch.[39] The best part of the day for many must have been the return journey in the 'grey flagship': BK 97 is a two seat car, with a space behind for the spare tyres and the collie dog; but Mr Jane and Miss Jane frequently had eight and ten scouts around them. Three sat astride the radiator, three sat among the indicators, and upon Mr and Miss Jane's feet, and four sat among the dog".[40]

The celebrated Portsmouth photographer, Mr Silk, who had been on hand for the Grayson kidnapping, "wandered round snapshotting the scene . . . got in the way occasionally and I precious nearly ran him over once". His exhibition of pictures brought in numerous volunteers, perhaps the most illustrious being Lord Charles Beresford, who as MP for Portsmouth ran his own Scout Troop, 17th Portsmouth or 'Beresford's Own'. Jane insisted, however, that no-one pulled rank: "all social differences are to be utterly obliterated. If a coster-monger on a donkey shay made out the best programme, and the whole House of Lords turned up in their motor cars, they should be there to help the coster-monger".[41]

So successful was the affair that Field Days became monthly events, the next being a night attack on a Scout camp in the Meon valley. Jane was the "first to be slain", tripping over a cow which stood up as he tried to jump over it. He "recovered to find half a dozen Boy Scouts sitting on top of me asking whether I would surrender or be hit with broomsticks till I did".[42] A naval officer "took cover in a bank of stinging nettles and spent an hour afterwards looking for dock leaves with a box of matches". Perhaps the most elaborate Field Day occurred in January 1910. Lord Charles Beresford commanded an attack on Fareham "assisted by a battery of artillery operating from somewhere near Fort Wallington, to say nothing of a raiding party, who will attempt to land on Fareham Quay, blow up the railway viaduct, and capture the railway station".[43] General Baden-Powell was invited to command the defenders of Fareham, and it was hoped that a dirigible would be available to bombard them with confetti, those struck being honour-bound to retire from the action. In a period with relatively limited leisure activities, the Field Days also provided an opportunity for the general population to join in: "Innocent looking inhabitants of Hayling Island carried in small Scouts hidden behind them on bicycle carriers. Tradesmans vans contained concealed Scouts; sometimes concealed invaders. The

Fred Jane sharing a joke with Lord Charles Beresford during a Scouts field day

defending Scouts got quite used to seeing hatless middle-aged citizens bearing the BSAA white badge spring suddenly upon them out of dust carts or bakers' vans".[44]

During the winter evenings Jane exercised his talents lecturing to Sarah on naval construction since the days of King Alfred, and on aviation: "The lecture was clear, terse and simple, relieved with characteristic boyish humour and quaint drollery, intensified by the lecturer's intentionally amusing though explicit blackboard effects".[45]

Apart from his tireless activity, "advertising the movement and attracting new supporters, and in many cases causing the appointment of fresh Scoutmasters", Jane formed his own troop of 60 Scouts at Bedhampton.[46] They wore green pullovers with blue shorts, and carried water bottles, haversacks and billycans.[47] On Field Days they trapped rabbits and cooked them, engaging in 'wacker fights' with rolled up magazines. Harking back to his own early days, Jane installed a hand press in the Drill Hall with which the Scouts produced a troop magazine. This was illustrated with cartoons by one of their number, and photographs of various Scouting activities, presumably taken by the Scoutmaster, as Jane himself appears in none of the pictures. The Scouts received commercial backing, advertising local businesses, such as Street's the ironmongers, and Davies' the chemist, which still exist in Havant today. Copies were presented to King George V, the Kaiser, and Lloyd George. Starting in November 1913, four issues were produced before the outbreak of war in 1914 brought publication to an abrupt end.[48]

It was then that the training of the Field Days came into practical use. German spies were believed to be everywhere, often disguised as bogus parsons. So active were Jane's Scouts in pursuit of these that he received complaints: "it must be an infernal nuisance to be chased about and spied on by Boy Scouts just because you are a stranger ... But we are in the midst of the biggest war our country has ever been engaged in".[49] Scouts played a variety of roles, carrying messages and manning checkpoints, for example at Number One Post at Hilsea, covering the only land approach to Portsmouth [50]. They even suffered casualties during air raids. Indeed, the closest that Jane ever came to any form of active service was as "Scoutmaster under military orders at Portsmouth".[51]

* * *

Among the participants in the Motor Field Days was a young naval sub-lieutenant, Edward Cambridge Carré, with his 9 HP BAT motorcycle. As a midshipman he had been in HMS *King Edward VII*, flagship of the Channel Fleet, before joining HMS *Mercury*, an old 2nd class cruiser now Depot Ship Submarines, Portsmouth, "for course of instruction in Submarines". Later Fred T Jane sketched Ted Carré on the conning tower of a 'C' class submarine, showing that he still practised his drawing, if only for pleasure.

Carré's mother lived across the road from the Janes, at 20 Elphinstone Road, being "much involved in charitable work among sailors' wives",[52] as befitted the widow of a retired naval officer. Lieutenant Henry Chase Carré had served in the Pacific and East Indies, and was sometimes termed 'Captain', in acknowledgement of his having commanded HMS *Pioneer*, a six gun paddle vessel in West Africa. Unlike the captain of Jane's fictional gunboat, in *The Port Guard Ship*, Henry Chase Carré escaped the perils of West Africa, dying at Weston House, Fareham in 1898, of heart failure, aggravated by cirrhosis of the liver. His entire estate of £82-11s (net) went to his wife, who had then moved her family to Southsea. The terms of her will, dating from this period, suggest that Emilie Carré was a kind, sensible woman, making careful arrangements for her children, against the event of her own death.

Apart from Edward, the submariner, the family included Collings Trenchard Carré, and their elder sister, Edith Frances Muriel. In 1909, aged 27, she was still living at home, having been educated by a governess and at boarding school. Her photographs show a slender, attractive young woman, elegantly dressed in the fashion of the day. Having lived in Elphinstone Road almost as long as the Janes, the Carrés can hardly have been unaware of their exuberant neighbour. They may have taken care of his daughter Dorothy after her mother's sudden death.[53] However the relationship between Jane and Muriel developed, an announcement appeared in the Social and Personal column of the *Portsmouth Times*, towards the end of 1909: "A marriage has been arranged and will shortly take place between Mr Frederick T Jane of Southsea . . . and Edith Frances Muriel only daughter of the late Henry Chase Carré, Lieutenant RN and Mrs Henry Chase Carré".[54]

The wedding followed on 18 December 1909, a little more than 12 months after the death of Alice Jane: "The wedding of Mr Fred T Jane and Miss Muriel Carré took place very quietly at St Jude's on

Saturday morning last . . . The bride who was married in her blue travelling dress was given away by her uncle Lieutenant Colonel Carré RHA (retd)".[55] The marriage certificate was witnessed by Cecil Jane and Collings Trenchard Carré. The author of the *Portsmouth Times'* Scouting column, "received a very nice box of wedding cake from Mr and Mrs Fred T Jane", and added his own good wishes to the "many messages of goodwill", that they had received.[56]

The career of Muriel's uncle George made her father's appear comparatively tame. Apart from commanding the Hazara Mountain Battery on the North West frontier of India and having "assisted in conducting the sap" at Orakau, during the Waikato campaign in New Zealand, he had shot ibex in Tibet and travelled three times around the world.[57] The family could be traced back to a disgraced bishop, whom William the Conqueror had banished to the Channel Islands. However that may be, the Carrés were certainly a well established family from Guernsey, serving as Jurats in the island's elective assembly.[58] There was obviously a considerable disparity in the ages of the newly married couple, Jane being 17 years the senior. He may have felt this himself. A volume of animal portraits by Wilhelm Kuhnert that still survives is dedicated, "To Muriel from her old man Xmas 1913".[59] The book is large and expensively bound in leather, Jane doing nothing by halves. However, such an age difference was not uncommon in middle class marriages of the time, especially in service circles, and as we have seen Fred T Jane did not always act his age. Besides their fondness for animals, the couple seem to have shared an interest in motoring. BK 97 required two to drive it so Mrs Jane acted as mechanic: "looking after petrol pressure, lubrication, auxiliary third brake. etc., etc., and is an adept at shifting rims, and for that matter tyres also, single-handed".[60] Like Alice, the second Mrs Jane took out a driving licence, although later in life she developed a profound dislike of cars, preferring a pony and trap.[61] Perhaps Jane's propensity for 'scorching' had unnerved her, although in his will, written in 1912, he left her his motor cars among the more conventional household effects.

In the first quarter of 1911 the Janes moved out of Portsmouth to Hill House, in Bedhampton Hill Road, the old main road from Havant to Cosham. Hill House was a large detached 'villa', on the same site as an earlier Prospect Cottage. It commanded a fine view of Langstone Harbour across open fields, lying just to the south-

Muriel Carré: Jane's second wife

Barbara: Jane's second daughter

east of the chalk pit between Bedhampton Hill and Portsdown
Hill Roads. Jane's letter headings referred to his new abode as "Cat
and Fiddle House", the name of the public house and erstwhile
haunt of smugglers from which it had been converted. There had
once been caves below the pub with a tunnel running down to
the marshes below. Horse drawn waggons, carrying false name
boards, would draw up at the inn for refreshment, and drop kegs
of brandy into the tunnel through the false bottoms of their
vehicles.[62]

Why the Janes moved is not clear. Perhaps they wanted more
room for the pedigree Airedales they bred,[63] or else Jane wanted
quicker access to the country roads than that provided by
Portsmouth's Commercial Road, "the worst street to drive in, in
England".[64] Perhaps he did not wish to remain in Southsea with its
memories. To keep in touch with his naval and other associates,
Jane had the telephone, Havant 115, and a telegraphic address:
JANE Bedhampton.

In April 1911 Mrs Carré died, Jane appearing as the informant
on the death certificate. Under the terms of her mother's will,
Muriel would have inherited a third of her estate of £1877-11s-9d.
The following July, Jane and Muriel's only child, a daughter, was
born at Bedhampton. Barbara Jane was baptised by her recently
ordained uncle Colin, at St Thomas' Church, in September that
year. Barbara is remembered as being very pretty, "the dead spit of
her father", but also as "a very headstrong girl with a quick
temper", with no great concern for her appearance.[65] She may
have inherited more than her looks from her father.

* * *

Before leaving the scenes of his earlier exploits, Jane made his
final excursion into political life. This time he did not take the
leading part himself. Instead he threw the Navy Before Party
behind that 'Great Showman of the Navy', and quondam 'Member
for the Navy', Lord Charles Beresford. All too often Beresford is
made to appear as a comic turn, like some demon king
threatening the attempts of the good fairy, Sir John Fisher, to
change the naval pumpkin into something more suited to 20th
century warfare, in time for the German Emperor's ball. To some

extent Beresford's reputation has suffered from his mixed career as politician and sailor: "In the Navy we knew he was not a sailor but thought that he was a politician; in the House of Commons they knew he was not a politician but thought he was a sailor".[66] He had a distinguished service career commanding HMS *Condor* during the bombardment of Alexandria in 1882 and leading the Naval Brigade during the Gordon Relief Expedition three years later.

Beresford has been neglected by historians. His papers have never been subjected to the same scholarly analysis as those of his great opponents, Fisher and Churchill, who by winning the political arguments of the day, pre-empted historical debate. Fisher's cruel characterisation of Beresford as "The great dirigible: the biggest of all recorded gasbags", should be set against his earlier praise of Beresford as a "First class officer afloat, no better exists in my opinion".[67] Fisher's change of tune has to be put down to his fears of Beresford as a rival, and his inability to see him as a successor, capable of continuing his own work.[68] Jane had been neutral, objecting to the "utter rot" appearing about Lord Beresford in the *Daily Mail*, and deprecating his row with Fisher: "two distinguished officers have no more right to or reason to impart their personal relations into naval affairs than have two ordinary seamen who have a squabble on the mess deck".[69]

Much of the blame for this state of affairs he placed on the "inkslingers . . . who after all are the folk who have kept the fishpot boiling".[70] However, by the summer of 1909, Jane was defending Beresford against the Liberal press, which objected to his denunciations of "economy at all costs". In the Radical view it was "apparently an unpardonable sin for an Admiral to think at all".[71] Apart from their converging views on the material needs of the Royal Navy, Beresford and Jane had similar views on its social needs. Despite his patrician origins, Beresford had usually run a happy ship, and was known for his liberality over such matters as leave.[72]

Jane and Beresford also shared a similarly robust sense of humour. In his younger days, Beresford had driven a water cart down Rotten Row in London's Hyde Park, spraying passers-by; and used a hansom cab to remove a particularly well-secured doorknob in Berkeley Square, which had defied the efforts of less forthright 'knocker-wrenchers'. During an earlier spell in the House of Commons, he had stolen the boot of a gouty old MP snoozing, in his socks, behind the Speaker's chair. At division (voting) time, the victim perforce hopped into the lobby, to the cheers of those members in the secret.[73]

Beresford had hauled down his flag for the last time in March 1909, receiving a hero's send-off from the crowds assembled on Portsmouth Hard.[74] In November he was adopted as Conservative candidate, to stand at the by-election following the death of Sir John Baker MP, Jane's successful rival in 1906. When the candidacy was announced Jane immediately telegraphed the Navy Before Party's endorsement for Beresford's stand, signing himself, 'President and ex-candidate': "WOs, POs and men of the lower deck who form the committee of the Navy Before Party request you to be our candidate in the coming election in conjunction with your candidature for the Conservative and Unionist parties . . . We the Navy Before Party were only 1,859 at the last election but we are a fighting 1,859 and have increased since then and we mean to fight for you for all we are worth".[75]

Jane's intervention also took a more direct form. At an "immensely enthusiastic meeting" of the Portsmouth Labour Party he invited them to endorse Beresford, for the sake of the country: "At this stage everything was drowned in shouting. There were cries of, 'We have no country'. From the gallery more sportive people yelled, 'What about Victor Grayson' and the Chairman motioned to Mr Jane to sit down".[76] The Labour candidate refused to stand down, being pledged "to fight a great cause", but his reference to the Conservative candidate as the 'Great Showman of the British Empire': "brought Mr Jane to his feet again with some unprintable words about traitors. He then left the hall amidst considerable uproar, making some rather heated remarks to the audience".[77]

The surprising thing is not that he was thrown out but that some of the audience followed him. In the event the by-election never took place. In January 1910 local politics were caught up in the national crisis provoked by the House of Lords' rejection of Lloyd George's budget. There was a General Election instead, with both of Portsmouth's two seats at stake. This allowed Jane to repeat his advice that voters should give one vote to the Navy, that is Beresford, and one to their own party.

George Bernard Shaw gives us a glimpse of Jane canvassing in his chaff about a "Boy Scout on the other side of the square advocating the claims of Admiral Beresford with a flood of passionate eloquence".[78] Greater notoriety arose from Jane's reaction to the claim that no Conservative had ever dared speak outside the Unicorn Gate of the Dockyard. He drove down there in BK 97 heavily decked out with Union Jacks, to provoke, "one of the most extraordinary election scenes ever witnessed in Portsmouth".[79] For an hour and a half pandemonium reigned while a crowd "some 2000 strong" booed, cheered and sang 'Tell me the Old, Old Story', the Dockyard men sat on the wall eating their dinners, and Jane, unable to make himself heard, smiled on the crowd: "Just before bell-ringing matters looked very grave. The crowd surged around the car in great waves. Once the vehicle was heaved up and Mr Jane was thrown off balance, but the car was stopped from going over by a tree. Repeatedly Mr Jane attempted to start away, but the crowd pushed in the other direction ... Then Constable Blunden came to the rescue and was pushed about around the vehicle".[80]

Eventually some bluejackets lent a hand, and the car drove off, "amid a volley of jeers and some cheering". Although it had suffered £15 worth of damage, and everything portable was stolen, its running was unimpaired. Jane "threw fuel on the flames by driving her around Portsmouth in her wrecked condition, flying the tatters of her one remaining Union Jack". The car was photographed outside the rebuilt Queen's Hotel, bearing the

The mighty Benze after the battle of Unicorn Gate

167

hand drawn legend: "This is the result of trusting Portsmouth Radicals to be sportsmen. Vote for Beresford".[81] On the election night, "asking for trouble produced its natural reward". The car was boarded and the last Union Jack removed. Unfortunately for the boarders there were bluejackets about: "There ensued a free fight which beggared description. It ended in some ten sailors of HMS *Jupiter* jumping on board the car with what was recaptured of the flag. Others fought a way free for it, and it crawled home nearly red-hot,its tyres cut to pieces and little but the chassis left'.[82]

After Beresford's victory, BK 97 retired from public life, and so to a large extent did its owner. Perhaps he, or his wife, realised just how close he had come to serious personal injury. There was a second general election in 1910 when Jane was: "only in for 'transport duty' but we can't all be top sawyer. The thing is to take the job that comes along".[83] But then there was no longer the same need for a Navy Before Party candidate. With Beresford in Parliament, Fisher and Churchill were anxious not to lose any credit for naval reforms, so began to implement Lionel Yexley's well thought-out schemes.[84] On the material side: "During the present year the Liberals have undoubtedly toed the line on the Navy question and no voters felt that their return to power would mean big Naval reductions".[85]

The old antipathy to party politics persisted: "Party politics are probably played out. The House of Commons as we have it now is probably on its last legs. In ten years time as like as not there'll be no House of Commons. Quite likely . . . we'll have something in which all the conflicting interests in the country are properly represented, with a Referendum when they don't agree and permanent officials to carry on the government".[86]

So far this has not been one of Fred T Jane's more successful prophecies.

* * *

While at Hill House, Jane produced his last new major piece of work, *The British Battle Fleet*, a "history of warship design from earliest times".[87] However, there was a lot more than that to a book which in many ways summed up Jane's career and opinions. It was "not intended to be a history of the British Navy in the generally accepted sense of the word",[88] although "improvements in naval construction all through the centuries necessarily include a naval history". The slant of the work can be detected from its dedication to "Those who in all ages built the ships of the Royal Navy and to the unknown men who have worked those ships and so made possible the fame of many admirals".[89] The significance of the battle of Trafalgar from this perspective is not the "tremendous strategical questions involved", but rather the improvements to British ship design which followed subsequent inspection of HMS *Victory's* much damaged forward bulkhead. Superior ventilation of ships' bilges was deemed to be as significant a factor as the skill of admirals, or the courage of their crews, although these provide more exciting reading.[90]

First appearing as one volume in 1912, there was a second edition in two volumes in 1915. Both were illustrated from William Bieber's photographic collection, with original artwork by the distinguished maritime painter W L Wyllie, who: "translated into vivid pictorial obviousness a number of details which old prints of an architectural nature entirely fail to convey".[91] Regrettably the 1990 reprint was unable to reproduce these splendid colour plates. The most enduring parts of the book are naturally those that deal with developments within Jane's own lifetime. In particular: "his chapters on the Dreadnought period, on submarines and aerial navigation contain such a mass of information that The British Battle Fleet may well be regarded as a text book".[92]

However, the earlier chapters are characterised by the same down-to-earth attitude towards evidence that lay beneath the irreverence of *Heresies of Sea Power*. This can be seen both in Jane's salutary debunking of the notion that King Alfred "was seized with the whole modern theory of 'Sea Power' as a sudden inspiration"[93] and his rejection of the idea that the bad living conditions that caused the naval mutinies of 1797 were commonplace. If they had been, "the men would have been too used to the conditions to find in them a special cause of complaint".[94]

This type of historical imagination also underpins Jane's analysis of the technical side of his subject, for instance his cyclical view of changes in ship design, with the constant dialectic between speed and weight, and between gun-power and protection. Consequently, Jane was generally sympathetic to naval constructors, such as Sir Nathaniel Barnaby, whose ideas about warship design had become unfashionable. One may even detect a sense of personal resentment in his comments upon episodes where the experts were condemned or overridden, for instance the popular attitude towards the retirement of Sir William White, designer of the *Majestic* and King Edward VII class of battleships.[95] There are the usual humorous touches upon such little known aspects of naval construction as the fireproof wood used in the Aboukir class cruisers which, "deteriorated the gold lace of the uniforms stored in drawers made of it",[96] or the sideways funnels of HMS *Neptune* (1874), the first ship in the Navy to have a bathroom.[97]

All the time that Jane was involved in his other projects, politics, and so on, he continued to produce regular annual issues of the book which had made his name. From 1905 this was known by the shorter title of *Fighting Ships*. To be editor was evidently no sinecure, most years producing some such comment as: "revolution is thick upon the naval world and there never has been an edition of this book in which so many alterations have had to be made".[98] In the years leading up to the First World War the pace of naval change quickened, requiring constant updates of detail, and sometimes wholesale reorganisation, such as when Russia went from being the third naval power to the eighth after the Russo-Japanese War.[99] The same issue was reordered into the sequence still in use. Ships now appeared in reverse date order within type, reflecting their modernity rather than an "arbitrary judgement as to relative power".[100]

Photographs and silhouettes needed constant replacement, "the principle of this book being to show in elevation the ship rigged as she actually is, and not as she was originally contemplated".[101] In 1909 Jane replaced all photos of German ships, reflecting the worldwide attention focused upon their navy. The following year 500 new photographs were needed to keep up with changes, "so extensive that last year's edition is hopelessly out of date".[102] In 1911 Jane had viewed the previous edition with complacency and thought that few changes would be required, only to find "changes in existing ships more prolific than ever".[103] Silhouettes were always a problem as they needed: "to express the ship not only as she actually is but also the ship as she strikes the ordinary observer who is mentally comparing her with other vessels. This necessitates some slight accentuation of peculiarities ... A suitable silhouette has therefore to be a slight caricature, and it is not always possible to hit off the likeness first time".[104]

The scope of *Fighting Ships* continually widened, both geographically and technically. New navies were added, such as Mexico and Peru in 1907. In 1903 naval flags appeared for the first time, a recently revived feature of *Jane's Fighting Ships*. Jane's often stated belief that "no war vessel is too insignificant to include and the less she is known the greater the need for her inclusion"[105] reflected his belief that future naval wars would depend as much on small ships manned by a handful of regular bluejackets, under the command of a warrant officer: "Attention in *Fighting Ships* is always specially concentrated on such craft because while photographs of capital ships continually appear everywhere, *Fighting Ships* is the only publication in the world which gives pictures of auxiliaries and those other small craft which are never heard of unless a war is in progress".[106]

Jane frequently acknowledged that his success in illustrating such obscure ships depended upon: "the now almost innumerable army of readers, and users of this book , who in every clime have placed their cameras at my disposal. They range from a judge in the Sandwich Islands to a German lady in Siam".[107]

There were complaints about "the ever-increasing size of this book".[108] As a result "certain preliminary pages which have outlived their usefulness" were done away with, and margins reduced to pack in 20 per cent more material. However, a comparison of the 875 double sized pages of the current *Jane's Fighting Ships*, with the 460 pages of the 1908 issue shows that, like naval vessels of any particular type, naval directories have an inbuilt tendency to grow in size and price. Today *Fighting Ships* includes details of some 15,000 ships, costing £250 a copy, compared with 1,000 ships covered by the first issue of 1898, at 10/6d.

From 1912 the proofs of the ship pages were officially revised by the appropriate Admiralties which "has occasionally tended to curtail the information given as to ships yet unlaunched". However: "Where details of prospective warships are officially secret, the elaborating of speculative data about them does not appear to serve any particularly useful purpose. Reliable facts about existing ships seem of more solid utility".[109]

Besides the pages that formed its core, *Fighting Ships* always

included supporting material. Sometimes these were in response
to concerns of the day, such as the analysis of dreadnoughts, built
or building.[110] Others were more general articles, such as the
annual survey of developments in marine engineering,
contributed by Charles de Grave Sells. Some of these articles were
by acknowledged international experts. From 1909, William
Hovgaard, Professor of Naval Construction at the Massachusetts
Institute of Technology, dealt with "whatever constructional
problem is most to the fore".[111] Other articles were by personal
friends such as Lieutenant Arthur Rice RN who, while training in
wireless at HMS *Vernon*, proposed, 'A Reserve of Electrical Power
in Warships', to run lights and communications equipment in an
emergency. A participant in the Motor Field Days, Rice was
nominated guardian of Jane's elder daughter Dorothy in his will of
1912. Before his horrific death in a seaplane disaster off the Isle of
Wight in June 1914, Rice made a further contribution to *Fighting
Ships* with a new crisper silhouette system.[112] Before Jane moved
to Bedhampton, *Fighting Ships* had already begun to fulfil his
promise to his erstwhile literary agent that, "if things run as now —
there will be a tidy profit out of F Ships". When Western
Hutchinson sold out his interest in October 1908, he had done
very well out of the £50 which he had paid for it in 1901. His price
was £900 plus half the expected profits from the 1908 issue, his
share being estimated at £800.[113] Hutchinson, by now resident at
Crabwood, Upper Shirley, Southampton, had been responsible
for managing the business side of *The Naval Syndicate*. It is not
surprising therefore that before long Jane was forging closer links
with his publishers that allowed him to concentrate on the
technical aspects of running *Fighting Ships*. In December that
year, a bare week after becoming a widower, Jane agreed to sell a
quarter share in *Fighting Ships* to Sampson Low and Co. He
recouped much of the cost of buying out Hutchinson's share,
receiving £1,100, £600 in cash. The agreement carefully laid out
the responsibilities of the two parties. It provides fascinating
insights into the running of *Fighting Ships* at this time, and
explains why the book survived Jane's own death, while Laird
Clowes' *Naval Pocket Book* did not long outlast its creator. Jane's
agreement was not terminated by his death, as he undertook: "to
edit and prepare the book for publication . . . and to make proper
arrangements for the conduct of the book in the event of his death
or disablement".[114]

Without written consent from both parties, no serious changes could be made in the form or composition of the book, which was to appear as soon after 1 May as possible, as it has continued to do. Each side had the first option of buying the other's share, if they wished to sell. The arrangements between the publishers and Naval Syndicate must have been satisfactory as Sampson Low continued publication on the existing basis, although there was obviously less trust than there had been between Hutchinson and Jane, as cheques for sums over £50 had to be signed by both Jane and the publishers.

On the other hand, Jane was given an annual budget of £900 a year within which he had: "a free hand in the said production which shall include composition paper printing binding blocks contributions photographs fees prospectuses".[115] Furthermore he was recognised as responsible for all dealings with printers, engravers, advertising agents and contributors. There were three of the latter mentioned specifically: Charles de Grave Sells, Professor Hovgaard and William Bieber. The agreement also mentioned the advertising agents who had first been employed by Hutchinson. They had sole responsibility for all advertisements, and were expected to generate £300 revenue a year by 1911. Jane was evidently still concerned to maintain the appropriate image for *Fighting Ships*, as the agents were only to collect: "advertisements of a character suitable to the contents of the publication and The Naval Syndicate shall have the right to refuse any advertisements they may deem harmful to the publication".[116]

After Jane's remarriage, the following year, further steps were taken to ensure continuity of publication. Under his marriage settlement of December 1909 an interest in half of Jane's remaining share was assigned to his wife's trustees. However, these had "no power to interfere in the management of the said book".[117] The value of *Fighting Ships*, reflected in the careful arrangements for its production, was increasingly recognised by 1914. It obviously irked Jane that more account was not taken of his work in earlier years, as can be seen from a comment in 1907, apropos his projections of the comparative naval strength of the Great Powers: "In the agitation now proceeding as to the relative superiority of the British Fleet it is somewhat curious that the points here tabulated have been little discussed".[118]

However, a review of August 1914 in the *Times Literary Supplement*, the same publication which had shredded *Heresies of Sea Power*, demonstrated the extent of Jane's acceptance. Appearing the day before the cruiser action in the Heligoland Bight the review referred to the "very general demand for fuller information . . . at a time like the present". It went on to discuss "two publications, both well known to and well appreciated by all students of naval affairs from which such information may be obtained in a convenient and authoritative form".[119] The first was of course *Brassey's Naval Annual*, while the other was *Fighting Ships*: "founded 17 years ago by Mr Fred T Jane, and still edited by that esteemed writer on naval topics".[120]

The TLS recognised that the distinctive feature of Brassey's was the large share of its pages devoted to original papers, but gave pre-eminence to Jane's book in the matter of diagrams and other illustrations: "since he not only gives innumerable photos of British and foreign warships side by side with diagrams indicating the nature of their armour, armament and other salient features, but furnishes also silhouettes of the same ships so accurately drawn as to enable the mariner at sea . . . to identify either the ship itself or its type as it passes. This is the salient feature of Mr Jane's undertaking, and it is manifestly a very valuable feature".[121]

Recognition of the crucial features of his work, from such a quarter, must have been sweet reading, but the war put at risk everything Jane valued, personally and professionally. Despite his attacks on 'Little Englanders' and 'peace faddists' Jane had few illusions about the probable effects of war: "we don't want war. War would ruin this country whether we won or lost. "Peace at any Price" is the motto . . . the price of peace is preparedness for war".[122] Jane had hoped that the uncertainty of the pre-war arms race would be a deterrent: "International beggar my neighbour is a foolish thing enough. But as Lord Charles Beresford once observed, "Battleships are cheaper than war". There is nothing like a Knockout ship to keep the peace – provided that people see and believe that it is Knockout".[123]

However there remained the danger that one side might incorrectly believe the odds to be in its favour: "So we are likely to tumble into a presumed finality, and with it the General War which may be the end of all things".

CHAPTER VIII

THE SPECTATOR WHO SAW MORE OF THE GAME

N general the outbreak of the First World War took the British by surprise. Neither Jane nor Yexley, the *Hampshire Telegraph's* regular naval columnists, appeared in the first wartime issue with its headline: 'EUROPEAN BLAZE – SEVEN NATIONS AT WAR'.[1]

The week before, Jane had reviewed David Hannay's study of Naval Courts Martial and their role in the Great Mutinies of 1797. His column in the *Evening Standard* had been even further removed from all too present reality. He had discussed the origins of the title Grand Fleet, quoting Farewell and Adieu to you Spanish Ladies: "one of the oldest real naval songs from the pre-Nelson era ... now falling into disuse but 20 or 30 years ago there was never a wardroom or gunroom sing-song but the historical chorus was heard".[2]

Although he had long forecast an Anglo-German war, Jane's first reaction to the invasion of Belgium was that the Germans had simply gone mad. His reflexes as a naval analyst, however, were sure, denying that it was unfair of the Germans to lay mines off the east coast, and quashing hopes of a swift decision at sea: "people are disappointed that we have not had a Trafalgar or a Tsushima. Events of that sort make very fine reading and also fine pieces for picture palaces, but they are not modern warfare".[3]

British naval officers had long been expecting to fight the rapidly growing German Navy. The wargames at the Portsmouth War Course were openly directed at Germany, an over-excited

British player taunting an opponent who quite reasonably lurked in harbour with "you sausage eater, come out and fight".[4] Jane had attracted the wrath of Portsmouth's Esperanto enthusiasts by suggesting that German would be a more useful language to learn, if only for interrogating prisoners.[5] Ordinarily, however, not much notice was taken of the warnings of military men, or the handful of defence journalists, all too easily seen as trying to feather their own nests. Most people would probably have agreed with George Bernard Shaw that the German scare of 1909, "was intolerably stale by this time". Compared with the furore caused in 1871 by the fictional Battle of Dorking the "present one was not really a proper scare at all".[6] In all fairness, many of the attempts to arouse public interest in the external threat must have appeared less than convincing. Colonel Lonsdale Hale, a student of German methods in the Franco-Prussian War of 1870, produced several pamphlets with such titles as, 'Arise Ye Britishers To Your Peril From Over the Way, And Hasten To Meet It'. The *RUSI Journal* found his works "uncomfortably enlightening", but feared that most recipients of his mail shot would throw it in the waste paper bin.[7] Perhaps there was insufficient distinction between real threats and the imaginary. The usually sober *Army and Navy Gazette* reviewed, "a grand romance of aircraft warfare between France and Germany", called *War in Space* and featuring "a diabolical plot developed by the Imperial Chancellor Prince Battmann 'the great German Macchiavelli'".[8] Jane's own wartime pot-boiler *Warships At A Glance* advertised a confusing mixture of boys' fiction and Mahan's 'Famous Sea-Power Works'.

The shock, to a complacent and uninformed public opinion, of Germany's attack on Belgium reacted upon an undercurrent of xenophobia that had been gathering strength well before the war. From 1906 legislation restricted entry to the UK, its first victims including 17 French onion sellers from Roscoff, refused permission to land at Plymouth until special instructions were telegraphed from the Home Office.[9] By 1913, the Home Office was compiling a Register of Aliens.[10] Jane had treated such chauvinism with some scepticism. He claimed to have known anarchists in Holborn, and believed that once in Britain such people kept their heads down. He was more concerned about such international criminals as the Cockney who had once picked his pocket at Berlin railway station.[11]

Jane was also sceptical about intelligence gathering despite, or perhaps because of, his own links with members of the Naval Intelligence Department. This organisation was believed to refund the postage to officers sending in valuable information, but nobody had ever earned the stamps.[12] In 1899 Jane had written a series of tales on 'The Naval Secret Service' for *Stories*, a truly dreadful penny-paper, but in more sober vein he wrote: "The bulk of the work done by any Intelligence department is with scissors and paste, and spies live mostly in the pages of fiction".[13]

However, at some point he began to believe in the presence of more substantial German spies, although he usually put his own twist upon the more ridiculous spy stories. When an alleged spy was arrested near Fort Widley, which overlooks Portsmouth Harbour, he derided newspaper claims that this could possibly be 'one of the first objectives in a hostile raid on the South coast': "Seeing that this fort is absolutely obsolete and photographs of it can be bought for a penny, it is difficult to imagine any German officer . . . being fool enough to take the trouble to make sketches of it".[14] Jane could only conclude that the affair was a bluff, to draw attention away from the real area of German interest, probably the ill-surveyed roads, north of Portsdown Hill. In fact Lieutenant Siegried Helms of the 21st Nassau Pioneers was quite fool enough to have been caught sketching Portsmouth's antiquated defences, openly viewing the Spithead forts through the City Council's telescopes on the Esplanade.[15]

As with warnings of Germany's aggressive intentions, spy stories from this pre-war period were a mare's nest of claims and hoaxes. To the claim that 50,000 Mauser rifles were stored within a quarter of a mile of Charing Cross, Jane added a story of his own about a local arms cache, hushed up to avoid international repercussions. He was able, however, to dismiss the giant airship which had recently troubled the minds of his readers, having been: "assured by a man the other day that the whole thing was a practical joke – a big kite towed behind a friend of his on a motor cycle".[16]

Unfortunately the real spy-catchers could not always recognise the bogus nature of much of their 'intelligence'. Their lack of professional expertise must be placed against a background of cheeseparing economy. Before the war beginning in South Africa in 1899, the British Army's intelligence budget to cover the entire Empire was less than that of the Boer Republics. When Lieutenant-Colonel James Edmonds became head of the Army's counter-intelligence section in 1906 he had a budget of £200 a year, and a number of highly imaginative friends. These included William Le Queux, originator of numerous imaginary invasions, and Fred T Jane. The latter was: "on the lookout for spies, [and] kidnapped a Portsmouth German in his car and deposited him in the Duke of Bedford's animal park at Woburn".[17]

The resulting publicity produced a flood of letters from members of the public, detailing the suspicious behaviour of German visitors. Edmonds, who was later responsible for the Official History of the Great War, used this information to convince Haldane, the quite properly sceptical Secretary of State for War. Originally Haldane thought that what Edmonds had "unearthed was the apparatus of the white slave traffic",[18] but he was converted by the weight if not the quality of the evidence. In 1910 the Government brought in a Defence of the Realm Act (DORA), which passed the House of Commons on a Friday afternoon, with only 117 MPs present.[19] DORA generated any number of more or less bizarre cases. Examples included a Gosport motorist whose headlights carelessly illuminated Portsmouth Hard, and an old soldier shockingly alleged to have supplied a sailor with beer. The motorist was fined two pounds, and the old soldier given the benefit of the doubt.[20] A Portsea printer was less lucky, being fined ten pounds for publishing leaflets that revealed naval dispositions under the guise of advertising trips to the Isle of Wight.[21]

Although a handful of real German spies were rounded up on 4 August 1914[22], the outbreak of war saw a great deal of unofficial harassment of Germans and other foreigners. In Portsmouth these included Russian bakers, Britian's theoretical allies, who got their windows smashed,[23] and in Fratton, a barber called Jacobovitz was arrested for boasting about his service with the Austro-Hungarian Army. The magistrates found he was in fact a Russian-Pole, not Austrian, and let him off with a caution.[24]

Jane himself argued that it was necessary to "put a heap of aliens behind barbed wire", but had enough residual sense of fair play to realise that most of them would be "innocent souls paying for the odd one". Even after the sinking of the *Lusitania*, and the introduction of internment for all enemy aliens, he felt, "there is something horrible in the idea that one harmless alien in our midst should suffer for the machinations of some other...". In any case, it was far too obvious for the real spies to be Germans. The authorities would do better to investigate English people in the hands of money-lenders.[25] Not content with verbally encouraging spy mania, Jane took a personal hand in rounding up suspected spies, although he had the grace to appear embarrassed by the exigencies of patriotism: "It is of course all against the grain. I have done a little of the mill. Some time back an Army officer and I sent an awful pretty girl to limbo. Having done it we asked each other — Don't you feel an awful swine".[26] Certainly a girl was arrested in Pelham Road, Southsea, soon after the outbreak of war, who may have been Jane's victim.[27]

Spy mania must be regarded as one of those irrational panics that seize populations in times of extreme stress. There was no clear lead from a government unable to trust its own supporters,[28] and "music hall nonsense about British 'eroes' and 'skulking German cowards'"[29] was no preparation for the reality of war, with its steady toll of ships and men. Despite his observation: "there is no sport in war",[30] Jane complained that none of the British ships sunk by November 1914 had been lost "clean-handed". When three old cruisers were torpedoed in the North Sea, he echoed Beresford's claim that the ships' movements had been betrayed.[31] He even gave credence to claims that U-boats in the Irish Sea were operating from remote corners of North Wales, where supplies had been smuggled ashore. Jane suggested Boy Scouts should be used to search the coastline.[32] Where the supposed experts led it is no surprise that ordinary people followed. However, events had appeared to prove the experts right about the threat of war, and people thought perhaps they were now right about the threat from German agents: "A few years ago if you wrote about matters of this sort you were reckoned a lunatic . . . Any number of people still laugh at Lord Charles Beresford for the fuss he is making about German spies. They laughed at him in the old days when he talked of our being at war with Germany. They have since had good reason to stop laughing on that score".[33]

But amidst all the wild talk and injustice there were cases that suggest that not everyone had lost their heads. A musician named Euler, at Southsea's King's Theatre had the nerve to proclaim his German birth, and suggest that had the need arose the British would themselves have sunk the *Lusitania*. Appearing in the Police Court after the inevitable fracas he was simply discharged with the suggestion that he leave town.[34]

* * *

It may be doubted whether Fred T Jane profited from the First World War to the extent that the professional pundit might expect to do in the late 20th century. In the short term hostilities brought the opportunity to recycle material from *Fighting Ships* into cheaper formats to meet a popular need for information about the ships which featured daily in the newspapers. Several of this type of publication appeared by the end of 1914, with titles such as *Warships at a Glance*, and *Silhouettes of British Fighting Ships*. There was also *Your Navy as a Fighting Machine*, written simply but informatively: "an entirely non-technical hand book for the use of those, who until the Great War came along, did not interest themselves in naval matters".[35]

With remarkable promptness, a weekly commentary on the war, *Land and Water*, was started under the auspices of the *Times'* advertising manager on 22 August 1914, achieving a circulation of 100,000.[36] By the end of the year, demand was such that early numbers had to be reprinted.[37] Jane collaborated in this with Hilaire Belloc, who is better remembered for his *Cautionary Tales* for children. Like Jane, Belloc was too old, and probably too untidy, for a commission. He derived a considerable income from *Land and Water*, although his expertise was often mocked. A popular volume in the army entitled, 'What I Know About The War, by Blare Hilloc', was filled with blank pages.[38] However, Jane's views on the nature of the war were a lot less optimist than his collaborator's, which the *Daily Mail* described as 'Belloc's Fables'. Other contributors included John Buchan, who wrote *Greenmantle* and the *Thirty-Nine Steps*, and Arthur Pollen, inventor of a naval gunnery control system superior to the Dreyer tables used by the navy.

For *Fighting Ships* the war was a disaster. Although the German Navy was presumably well equipped with pre-war copies, the Admiralty originally refused to allow any information at all about the Royal Navy to appear in the 1915 issue. After this had been published they relented, allowing another, more complete edition: "In this issue the Admiralty authorities will allow the names of British ships and information regarding them to stand; only the plans, photos and identifying marks will be omitted. The first edition, which is without the entire British section, will be withdrawn".[39]

There was yet another, fully illustrated, edition available to the British and Allied forces. 'Business as usual' was evidently expected to resume shortly: "When the war is over any civilian purchasers of this edition will be supplied gratis with the missing pages, by sending to the publishers the annexed coupon".[40]

Apart from increased production costs, information became scarce: "As regards the enemy, a great deal of money has been expended in an effort to secure odd items of information . . . It has unfortunately not been possible to obtain exact information on the entire progress of the German navy since the outbreak of the war...".[41]

As costs rose revenue fell, as there were no advertisements in the 1915 issue. Strangely the Admiralty did not object to the photographs in *The World's Warships*, which first appeared in 1915: "using in a somewhat enlarged form the most up-to-date photographs available of the more important and interesting warships of the principal powers".[42]

Although these omitted the latest 'R' class battleships, the book did feature HMS *Queen Elizabeth*, completed in January 1915. Had the Portsmouth police noticed this indiscretion, Jane could have been in court along with several local tobacconists prosecuted for retailing cigarette cards showing details of HMS *Queen Mary*, which had appeared, with HMS *Queen Elizabeth*, in the 1914 *Fighting Ships*.[43]

Jane's newspaper work also suffered, although he professed not to mind as he was paid whether published or not, but: "what with censors, sub-censors and editors, trying to fathom their requirements, I am a bit hipped at writing anything at all".[44]

Twice he fell victim to the "perfervid patriotism of the editor or the Censor", for comments on the thrift campaign and conditions in the trenches which, "might have stopped some mealy mouthed youth from joining up".[45] One is left, however, with a question mark over the sincerity of Jane's defence of the censorship, as "entirely and completely right".[46] The Admiralty had invited him in to discuss the matter: "I told them that if they saw fit that was good enough. But they said that they would rather tell. I came away with an all-abiding faith in the censorship and a conviction that the sillier it may appear to be, the wiser and saner and all important it probably is".[47]

In the opening months of the war however, Jane had been more sceptical about censorship as a means of keeping the Germans in the dark: "Personally I don't believe it for a moment – any more than I believe that we have cleared out of the Portsmouth area many a spy that matters".[48]

Earlier in his career he had objected to the "growing official tendency to shroud everything under the mask of 'strictly confidential'",[49] describing secrecy as a "splendid cloak for incompetence". It also contributed to the Royal Navy's ignorance of foreign warships as the Admiralty "cannot send round a photograph without labelling it 'confidential'".[50] More seriously, Jane was convinced that, "Victory by Press Laws can never be achieved". Modern wars are won by "the fitness of the nation rather than by the fitness of individuals; and a nation that is bored over its war news is not well in the way to exhibit those staying qualities so necessary for the successful conduct of a great war".[51]

This was the crux of the whole question, constituting Jane's "main heresy against conventionally accepted axioms of Sea Power", which placed the role of the individual man or service before that of the people as a whole. Although Jane believed that "the man in the street does contribute to victory or defeat",[52] official distrust of that individual provided a major reason for the instability of public opinion during the First World War. The loss of HMS *Audacious*, the Royal Navy's latest dreadnought, was successfully kept from the Germans for five weeks in the autumn of 1914, her loss not appearing in *Fighting Ships* until after the war. However, the public unease which such secrecy generated led to a frame of mind where rumours and panics found a ready seeding ground.[53] During the Russo-Japanese War, Jane had recognised the advantage to Japan of suppressing news of her naval losses,[54] but he had also pointed to the dangers of such a course. Riots followed the end of that war, as the population were ignorant of Japan's true position, and believed the peace terms to be too generous to the Russians.[55]

In June 1915 Jane attributed the failure of voluntary recruiting to the anodyne effect of: "the daily 'Great British Advance', 'Great Russian Victory', 'Decided French Success', 'Great Forward Movement' and all that kind of thing . . . The impression created is that we are winning easily, that there's no need to go".[56]

In the same month the Allied offensives on the Western Front were petering out with no territorial gains at a cost of over 126,000 casualties, 26,000 of them British [57].

Later in the war the main problem caused for *Fighting Ships*, by the censorship, was the cumulative delay in publication. The 1918 issue was not submitted to the British Government Press Bureau until September of that year, and was still in their hands when the war ended in November. Information became progressively outdated, as no reference was allowed to alterations or ships built since 1914. When the US Navy joined the Allies its photographs were also removed, "at the request of the Navy Department Washington". The same issue carried a notice under the heading of the Defence of the Realm Act, setting out how DORA prohibited the publication of silhouettes of British warships, but reserving the copyright of all such drawings previously used in *Fighting Ships*. Well might the editors of that issue have acknowledged: "the patience of our readers during the past three years . . . We think we may take legitimate pride in the fact that in spite of evergrowing difficulties *Fighting Ships* is the only British Naval Annual that carried on during the Great War".[58]

The Second World War contrasted strongly with the First, conforming more closely with Jane's belief that: "every war should be an absolute national affair, conducted by strong men who have forced their way to the top in face of everything and who hold their position by the confidence of the nation – a war of All for All. Press muzzling laws do not contemplate war on such a line, they contemplate wars conducted by committee sitting in camera".[59]

This was reflected in the radically different approach to handling news during the later conflict. This greatly enhanced public morale, although the news was often far worse. The new approach was evident in the treatment of *Fighting Ships* from 1939 to 1945. Censorship did cause delays, but illustrations of the Royal Navy continued to appear.[60] The censor even allowed some new information to creep through. This even included pictures of the "latest type of Aircraft Carrier" HMS *Illustrious* along with Hunt Class destroyers and clearer plans of the battleship *King George V*.

A greater contrast with the earlier war was the "enemy action affecting the premises both of the publishers and of the blockmakers" which had delayed publication of the 1940 issue.[61]

Jane's thoughtful comments on the harm which might follow excessive wartime reporting shows that his hostile attitude to censorship was not simply the reflex reaction of a hack concerned for his livelihood. War correspondents, he felt, should not accompany fleets in wartime, not for fear of their revealing movements, and "all the other stock arguments", but because: "incident is the breath of life to journalists whereas absence of incident is probably the more essential to successful naval war... recording of such weariness may be the means of transmitting a similar weariness to the nation".[62]

* * *

The British were unprepared not just for the possibility of war but also for the form it took. They were ignorant of the government's commitments to France which drew them into a major land campaign in Western Europe. Hardly anyone understood how industrial technology and population growth had ensured that such a war would be long and bloody. Similarly people were unaware of how submarines and mines had restored the savagery and indecisive characteristic of war at sea before the classic age of sail that culminated in Nelson's achievements. Instead of stirring deeds and glorious victories, there would be unremitting toil, and a murderous outbreak of the commerce raiding that Mahan had decried. *Heresies of Sea Power* had warned anyone who cared to read it, that a weaker naval power will always turn to the *guerre de course*, however ineffectual, for lack of a better alternative. However, as Churchill said, the British governing classes were, "a lot of ignorant people",[63] and while Germany was prepared for both peace and war, Britain was, "organized for nothing except party politics".[64]

The Government being temperamentally and politically unable to give a clear lead, it was left for the press to form public attitudes to the war. Much to his disappointment Jane was one of those upon whom this vital role devolved: "It is not for me to make battle signals and things of that sort. I am merely an 'ink slinger', too old to do anything but a little home job in my spare time. I can only kill Germans by deputy...".[65]

Although Jane was 49 when the war began, he was only two years older than his brother George Hugh, who served as a sergeant in the Rifle Brigade. Lieutenant Commander Henry Edgar Jane spent the war at Rosyth, having joined the Navy in 1896, while Cecil worked in the 'War Trade Intelligence Department', tracing neutral ships trading with the enemy. He was able to combine war work with his academic interests, writing pamphlets such as *The Action off Heligoland*, and contributing an essay on *Historical Analogies and the Naval War* to the 1915 issue of *Fighting Ships*.

Jane must have been bitterly disappointed not to play a more active role in the war, but he loyally supported the Admiralty, writing at length in defence of Churchill, Fisher and Sir John Jellicoe, the Commander-in-Chief of the Grand Fleet.[66] He soon needed to do so. People were not prepared for the slow pace of naval warfare, "the absolute dearth of news that matters", where even actions like the British battlecruisers' success at Dogger Bank were only minor incidents, "quite different to the war stories to which we were accustomed in the days of peace".[67] Despite Jane's urging that, "the object of war is not to provide headlines or interesting reading for the public",[68] the latter were unable to believe: "things are not really happening any slower than in any other war of either recent or ancient times . . . We read of the battles and remember them but the years of waiting we forget".[69]

Jane was not even sure that this time the waiting would be relieved by a new Trafalgar: "It is at least one of the possibilities that this war will end with the German fleet still in existence".[70] He had seen through the German plan: "to remain safe behind the impregnable fortification which stud the German coast in hopes that the British Battleships will come off the coast and allow themselves to be thinned down by submarines and destroyer attacks".[71] Unfortunately the public failed to draw the obvious inference that the Grand Fleet should keep well out of the way, and not go messing about off the Dutch coast. As early as September 1914 Jane had to answer the question, "Why doesn't the Navy do something?": "The ridiculous and irritating part of this question is that the Navy is doing something. To adopt a paradox, 'THE LESS IT DOES THE MORE IT DOES'".[72]

If the Navy had not maintained its constant watch over the North Sea, in such massive strength, then Britain could have gone the same way as Belgium. In the same month that Jane advanced the above proposition there appeared an English translation of *On War*, the masterpiece of the great German military philosopher, Clausewitz . Although there is no direct evidence that Jane had read this, he had hit upon the idea behind one of Clausewitz's less memorable headings: 'Possible Engagements are to be Regarded as Real Ones Because of their Consequences'. Such engagements can have significant results without ever being

185

fought,[73] a paradox that would have delighted Jane. The same concept lay behind Julian Corbett's teaching at the War Course, in Portsmouth, that: "a seemingly inactive navy, by holding the correct positions in force, was able to strangle her enemy from the sea. Spectacular moves were not necessary in this kind of war".[74]

One example of the process of strangulation was the British capture of Basra in December 1914, a key to the oil fields of the Middle East. The significance of the coup seems to have gone largely unrecognised, although it assured the oil supply on which an increasing number of Royal Naval vessels depended. Moreover, the initial success was almost effortless, thanks to "that British Navy which is popularly supposed to be doing nothing".

"It is the curse of modern conditions that the public is never permitted to see things in perspective . . . because it is incapable of envisaging any action in which Dreadnoughts do not appear in front of the footlights. It is, generally speaking, totally incapable of realising that British Dreadnoughts somewhere in the North Sea (apparently doing nothing) can possibly have any effect in the Persian Gulf thousands of miles away. But Basra and its capture all was accomplished in the North Sea and in the Mediterranean".[75]

At the very end of his journalistic career Jane returned, in a valedictory passage, to his theme that the navy had done its job too well. In the very nature of the war the navy would be regarded as a 'back number' he said, while the soldiers took the limelight, but: "The Navy will have seen to it that the soldiers land unmolested. The Navy will see to it that the soldiers get their supplies uninterrupted . . . It won't get much of the credit – but what of that? It will have done its job. The rest can slide. The job is 'For England'".[76]

If Jane did not expect the war at sea to provide dramatic spectacle, neither did he expect it to be over quickly. While Hilaire Belloc was stumping the country predicting that the end of the war was in sight by St Valentine's Day 1915,[77] Jane refused to believe stories about "demoralised German soldiers anxious to surrender: All these yarns about Germany being played out or fed up with the war are mostly sheer bunkum".[78] A month after St Valentine's Day, on the very day when the British called off their stalled offensive at Neuve Chapelle, Jane was writing in a very different vein from Belloc: "things seem to be pretty much where they were one, two or three months ago, and where they may keep on being almost indefinitely ... When the war began we were told that the Russians would be in Berlin in six weeks. Six months have passed since then, and the Russians are no nearer Berlin than ever they were ... A year or two ago everyone was explaining to everyone else that a general European war was impossible because no nation could stand more than a week or two of it without going bankrupt. But after 31 weeks of it everyone is going as strong as ever ... Even the poor old Turks manage to carry on somehow".[79]

Jane's views were not universally popular. He openly acknowledged as much in his articles in *Land and Water*. After his death, a critical, Liberal newspaper hinted that this may have been behind his sudden disappearance from that periodical's pages, in May 1915: "it was not very wonderful that the public eventually refused, with some asperity, to listen any longer to the expert who sought to prove to them that the Heligoland fight was a defeat for the British Navy and the Coronel disaster a victory".[80]

At Heligoland the Germans lost three light cruisers, but only after the intervention, at considerable risk, of the British battlecruisers. Jane had deprecated the hysterical acclamation of the action as a 'Great Naval Victory', which it was not when taken in the wider context of Anglo-German naval strength. In the case of Coronel, Jane's logic requires some explanation. In that action two elderly British armoured cruisers were sunk by crack gunnery of the Imperial German Navy. Lionel Yexley felt the disaster bore out Jane's words to the Navy League long before when he had criticised the legacy of Nelson. Coronel showed that fighting spirit alone could no longer be relied on to even the odds against overwhelming material superiority. The debate between the 'historical' school of naval thought and the 'material' school championed by Admiral Fisher had ended in favour of the latter.[81] Jane did not contest that: "The Germans gave us a licking ... The odds were all against us so we have nothing to be ashamed of".[82]

However, in *Land and Water*, he advanced a theory that Coronel showed how the Royal Navy's commerce protection policy was working. This had forced the German commerce raiders to stay together, and even risk an action, expending much of their irreplaceable ammunition in the process. Subsequently, the South Americans, who found their trade interrupted by the German success, became rather less accommodating towards von Spee's squadron, which could offer no alternative to British merchant ships, as long as the Royal Navy maintained its general superiority: "if the Germans are unable to get their sea trade in working order no matter how many British cruisers they may sink, it is still no victory for them since a victory must have results. The utmost achievement possible is to cause grave inconvenience to neutrals and to get themselves regarded as a general nuisance . . . And that in substance is defeat".[83]

In early 1915 the Allies attacked the Dardanelles, in the hope of knocking Turkey out of the war and joining up with Russia. Jane was again "somewhat severely criticised" for pointing out the obstacles which lay in the way of an operation widely expected to win the war without the inconvenience of fighting the Germans: "The public impression that forcing the Dardanelles is a mere parade is very erroneous. The actual task is one of stupendous magnitude, perhaps one of the greatest naval operations ever undertaken . . . Ships versus forts must ever be a hard task for the ships".[84] He also pointed to the risk from mines floated down the channel. In the event, the Allies' attempt to force the narrows failed with the loss of four major units to mines: HMS *Inflexible* damaged and three battleships sunk: HMS *Irresistible*, and the French ships *Ocean* and *Bouvet*. Jane returned to his theme in his final article in *Land and Water*: "As I have consistently insisted . . . the fort has immense advantages against the ship even without the aid of floating mines . . . which if at all efficiently protected from the shore can only be swept or counter-mined with the greatest difficulty".[85]

Long before the war Jane had argued that "no sane commander would attempt directly to engage forts on the chance of silencing them".[86] This was advice that should have been echoed by the government's professional advisers, principally Lord Fisher, who later testified of the Dardanelles venture that, "as a purely naval operation I think it was doomed to failure".[87] However, "the political members of the committee did too much of the talking and the experts too little".[88] Even when Fisher attempted to walk out of a cabinet meeting in protest, nobody thought to ask him to explain his objections to the scheme.[89] If that was how the government's senior naval adviser was treated, it is not surprising that more notice was not taken of a provincial writer.

Jane's untimely death prevented him from commenting on the only action of the war between the main battlefleets, at Jutland in May 1916. We may surmise, however, that he would not have been impressed by commentators who have viewed the battle as a German success, equating ships sunk with goals scored in a football match. He might even have described the escape of the German High Seas Fleet, as he had the flight of their battlecruisers after Dogger Bank: "a really fine speed sprint back to safety . . . good training for their engine room complements".[90] He would not have been surprised by the heavy losses among the British battlecruisers at Jutland, having recognised their less effective protection compared with their German counterparts.[91] What would have mattered to him, as a strategist rather than the personal friend of many of the casualties, would have been the result of the action. Despite later sorties in 1916 and 1918, the High Seas Fleet never seriously challenged the Grand Fleet again before the German surrender, and "a victory must have results".

The other aspect of the war on which he was unable to comment was the unrestricted submarine campaign launched by Germany in May 1916. Jane had generally deprecated the effectiveness of submarines for any other purpose, suggesting that their only chance of success would be, "to destroy ships without warning and generally act the pirate".[92] He was, however, aware of the threat that this presented to civilised limitations upon war, taking "everything back to the days of savagery".[93] We will never know whether he would have argued for the adoption of convoys, the eventual answer to the U-boat threat. Before the war he had argued against them,[94] but in 1907 the threat was squadrons of armoured cruisers not submarines. At that time these were still a largely unrealised possibility. Although a Russian submarine had been deployed at Port Arthur during the Russo-Japanese War, the first anyone had heard of the vessel was when the Japanese dredged it up from the harbour bottom after the war.[95] By 1915 matters had changed to such an extent that Jane could write: "If not fully up to the prophecy of Admiral Sir Percy Scott a year or so ago, all the present indications are that the capital ship will shortly be the submarine, all other vessels gradually becoming subsidiary and auxiliary to it".[96]

This, however, would be one prophecy that Jane would not live to see come true. The solution of "the problem of how submarines are to fight each other", would not be satisfactorily addressed until after another world war. In the summer of 1915 the darkness, historical and personal, was already beginning to close around Fred T Jane.

CHAPTER IX

THE END OF THE ROAD

ARLY in 1915 Fred T Jane was in Nottingham, where from his hotel he had: "the satisfaction of contemplating my own name in very large letters, announcing to all and sundry, that to the tune of many lantern slides, I am going to try to convince people who have never seen a warship in their lives, that it is the navy which enables them to carry on 'Business As Usual'".[1]

Starting at Eastbourne in February, Jane had lectured in 24 venues across the country, from Plymouth to Dundee by May. In Scarborough he inspected the damage done by the German bombardment in December 1914. In Dover he mocked the exaggerated effects of a German seaplane raid: "This aeroplane did come, but the blowing up only amounted to the partial destruction of somebody's cabbage patch, and the main 'moral effect' is due to local arguments as to whether the uprooted cabbages would have been edible or otherwise had they been immediately replanted".[2] Often it was hard to realise that the British were at war: "Down the street rushed news boys yelling 'Extra Special'. News of the War? News of the Fleet? Not a bit of it. Instead it was FOOTBALL FINALS".[3]

However, over in Belgium the guns could be heard: "British warships bombarding somewhere along the Belgian coast where the struggle for Calais is still in progress. It is very much war at Dover".[4] Perhaps for that reason, "Although the attendance was very good, there were still plenty of unoccupied seats" at Dover

Town Hall.[5] At Folkestone Jane received hearty applause from a "fairly large audience" presided over by the mayor.[6] In a countryside deserted except for women and old men, he witnessed the building of Kitchener's Army of volunteers, passing: "strange new cities stretching as far as the eye can reach – neat wooden huts with galvanised iron roofs and all the roads about them seas of mud".[7]

In Scotland a battalion exercise was disrupted when the back door of Jane's car flew open on a sharp bend, his reserve cigarettes flying out among the troops at the roadside. In the industrial heart of England, with its slagheaps and orange streams, the recruiting posters lacked any reference to the King, the people being, "mostly all Socialists". Nevertheless, Jane developed a faith in these industrial workers who were then under attack for the British Army's lack of munitions: "what a lot of drivel is being talked and written about shirking workers, munitions delayed by drink and all the rest of the gas . . . You suddenly tumble to it what fools all the old women in trousers are – theorising about things they know nothing about directly".[8]

His talks covered much the same ground as his newspaper columns, defending the Admiralty, and trying to engender a sense of proportion about the progress of the war. Some of Jane's comments are more indicative of what people thought was happening at the time than evidence of what actually did happen. The Germans did not, for example, attempt to invade England in 1914, despite Jane's claim that the Royal Navy had turned them back in a destroyer action.[9] He did, however, reject the wilder stories of pontoons several miles long and submarines packed like sardine-tins with motor-cyclists ready to spread mayhem across the English countryside.[10] In general Jane found his audiences inclined to trust the navy, thinking it: "will get along all the better without interference and advice from well-meaning people who know nothing about it".[11]

Although he showed slides of the naval leaders, there was more applause for Lieutenant Holbrook, who won the Victoria Cross taking his submarine through the Dardanelles. There was also a surprising degree of sympathy for Prince Louis of Battenberg, driven from his post as First Sea Lord by a disgraceful agitation against his German ancestry: "it was due to Prince Louis on the eve of war that the British Fleet was mobilised, and it was through him that the Fleet was kept together in case of war with Germany (after the naval manoeuvres of July 1914), and for that the British Empire owed him a big debt of gratitude, and as a nation they ought to be rather ashamed of the many things written about him in the sensational Press (hear, hear)".[12] Jane livened up the serious points with anecdotes, telling how, before the War, he had played quoits in a village pub with Captain von Müller, later of the German commerce raider, *Emden*. At the end Müller had been 25 to the good, which curiously was the number of ships he met before being sunk by HMAS *Sydney*.[13]

Early travel by car was no easy business. Jane missed filing one of his columns after a puncture, and nearly ran down a convalescent naval lieutenant, but his main problem would have been the weather. In *The Old Wives' Tale* one of Arnold Bennett's heroines dies from the effect of the journey from Stoke to Manchester, and a similar fate may have befallen Fred T Jane. In October 1915 he drove the hundred-odd miles from Portsmouth to Cheltenham in pouring rain becoming, "beastly wet and uncomfortable about the feet".[14] The next week's column was the last Jane ever wrote. Perhaps his health collapsed after his soaking. Certainly his colleague Francis McMurtrie remembered how: "During the last year or two of his life Jane's health was visibly failing",[15] although: "relying on the tough constitution which had stood him in good stead in the past, he consistently neglected danger signals".[16] At Christmas Lionel Yexley received a card from Jane, wishing him: "Sincere Christmas Greetings — Enemies at times, but no object in ill-will at Christmas".[17]

On 2 January 1916 Jane wrote to his solicitors, Messrs Biscoe-Smith and Blagg of 148 High Street, Portsmouth. He asked them to prepare a codicil to his will, promising that: "when you have put this into your incomprehensible legal jargon I will come down and sign it".[18] The main effect of the codicil was to provide a small income for his secretary, Evelyn Lawton, and appoint his brother Cecil sole executor. Jane seems to have considered more drastic changes as he wrote again on 8 January with instructions for an entirely new will, but nothing more was done about this. When the codicil was signed on 21 January Jane's address was given as 34a Palmerston Road, in Southsea's main shopping street. Before the war this had been an insurance office, over a chemist's shop, so it is not clear if Jane was living there or just using the premises as an office.

By Wednesday 8 March 1916 Jane was definitely residing

elsewhere, for on that date he was, "found dead in bed at his residence in Clarence Parade". The dead man: "had been attended during the past week or so by Dr Cole-Baker on account of an attack of influenza, and had also complained of heart trouble, but his sudden death came as a great shock".[19]

Fred T Jane was 50 years old. This is less than the ages attained by his siblings, George Hugh and Henry Edgar, but 50 was quite a respectable age for a period, when few men reached their sixties.[20] The informant on the death certificate was not Jane's wife or grown-up daughter, as might have been expected, but his brother Cecil, although he was not living locally, but in Hampstead. The certificate was signed by Dr Cole-Baker, who gave the causes of death first as 'Heart Disease Valvular' and secondly as 'Influenza Heart Failure'. Jane was buried with his first wife, Alice, in Highland Road cemetery, the Friday immediately following. The barest amendment was made to Alice's inscription:

> 'The Dead Who Are Remembered
> Still Live
> Also F. T. Jane
> Mar 1916'

Predictably the local press gave extensive coverage to the death of one of Portsmouth's more notable citizens. They remembered him as a friend of the navy, and a journalist "with a vigorous, popular, and breezy style of writing".[21] They recalled his activities as a Parliamentary candidate, Scout leader, kidnapper and volunteer with the Balmacedist Fleet. The Service press also treated him kindly. 'A Service Contemporary', described him as "always readable . . . although often eccentric", recalling Jane's early days in Gray's Inn Road, and his "very rare faculty among black and white men of making the sea move".[22] In *The Fleet* Lionel Yexley regretted the passing of his old sparring partner: "As a journalist *THE FLEET* constantly came into conflict with his views, but there was never any personal feeling in the matter and as recently as Christmas last Mr Jane sent along his good wishes".[23]

If Jane had parted with *Land and Water* in anger, there was no evidence of it in their send-off: "His annual *Fighting Ships* has long since been indispensable to all whose interest in Naval matters was more than superficial. Its compilation from year to year gave Mr Jane a knowledge of constructional and statistical detail altogether unique. But he was much more than a naval statistician.

He was an omnivorous reader, and as his published books show, had a wide and curious knowledge of ancient as well as modern sea practice".[24] The editor of *Aeroplane* had been working with Jane on the 1915 issue of *All the World's Aircraft*. He paid a tribute that is the more creditable for being apparently unsolicited: "The task of collaboration has been a pleasant one, for Mr Jane put into his work the same breezy sporting spirit which won him so many friends in the service. His death deprives me of a highly esteemed colleague with whom it was a continual joy to work".[25]

The Times noticed Jane's passing but briefly.[26] Perhaps there was more pressing news from Verdun, where the French had just recaptured the key position of Mort Homme. However, preceding the 16 lines spared for Fred T Jane were 90 devoted to 'Artist and Dilettante', Lord Ronald Gower. He had hated Eton, never sat finals at Cambridge, was a silent Member of Parliament for a rotten borough in the 1860s, and had written several books on art, although, "none of these can be called adequate". A strong advocate of cremation, he was notorious for his "violent antipathy to the tall or silk hat", but his main claim to fame was that his father had been 20th Earl of Sutherland. Even in death, the establishment and its third raters prevailed.

The mystery behind Jane's movements towards the end of his life are explained by the legal action subsequently required to disentangle his testamentary affairs. He contrived to leave two wills, besides the codicil previously mentioned. Both benefited his first daughter Dorothy and Muriel his widow, although it was: "difficult to ascertain exactly in what degree because the value of *Fighting Ships* and other publications was a fluctuating one".[27]

Jane's first will was made at the time of his remarriage, in December 1909, appointing two naval officers as his executors. One of these, Lieutenant Florian Usborne, was killed only a fortnight before Jane's own death, testing a hybrid airship/aeroplane intended to counter Zeppelins.[28] The second will was made in 1912, appointing Muriel and Dorothy as executors, along with Cecil Jane. Although this was properly signed and witnessed, Jane never returned it to the solicitors. Consequently they drafted the 1916 codicil as if it applied to the original will of 1909 which they still had. Cecil brought an action in support of the 1909 will with the codicil, in which he was supported by his niece Dorothy, now aged 20. The position of the defendant, that is Mrs Jane, is not clear, but she presumably claimed that the 1912 will was valid, without the codicil. The judge probably satisfied nobody, as he "pronounced for the will of October 22 1912 together with the codicil of January 21 1916, omitting from the latter the words referring to the 1909 will and the executors".[29]

He acknowledged that the testator may have intended the codicil to apply to the 1909 will, but the last duly executed will was in fact that of 1912. The codicil could not revive the previous will as it showed no specific intention to do so. In practical terms, Cecil Jane remained sole executor, and the bequest to Jane's secretary stood. She was to receive one pound a week from the profits of each of *Fighting Ships* and *All the World's Aircraft*, until she married, when the amounts would be halved. The remaining profits were to be shared by Muriel and Dorothy.

Under the terms of her marriage settlement, Muriel already received three eighths of these, which was unaffected by her husband's death. The publishers had a quarter of the profits, and Jane the remaining three eighths. Under the will, Muriel and

Lady's Mile Southsea: Jane died in the house indicated

196

Top: Blue plaque commemorating Jane's final residence. Bottom: The block
indicated has replaced the house shown opposite

197

Dorothy were to share this last portion, unless Muriel should marry again, in which case the whole of Jane's three eighths share devolved upon his daughter. However, this was subject to a rather odd restriction. In order to benefit from the bequest, Muriel and Dorothy had to: "undertake not to give or leave any money they inherit under my will to any clergyman priest minister or religious body".

Jane's attitude to the clergy was not generally hostile: he often treated them sympathetically in his novels, dedicating *His Lordship, the Passen, and We*: "To the Country Parsons of East Devon particularly my father". He had worked with local clergy in the Scout movement, and resented "being depicted as an enemy of religion", by an opponent of his views on sexual morality: "If there is one thing I believe in more than another it is religion . . . But there is religion and religion: that of the Founder of Christianity and a modern equivalent of the scribes and pharisees".[30] This he attacked as humbug, "more interested in seeing that there is a hell for simple immorality than in finding ways and means to buttress the backsliders".[31] On the other hand, he attacked the Church's often obstructive attitude towards prevention of the venereal disease then common in the Navy. This was a common enough concern in the service press.[32] It even surfaces, somewhat inappropriately, among the cold statistics of the *Statesman's Year Book* which Jane edited before the war.[33] Jane also objected to missionary activity. He believed this only caused trouble among the natives, costing the lives of the sailors sent to sort it out. He himself had lost a friend during the Benin campaign of 1897, the historical basis for the horrible punitive expedition to the bloodstained city of Bogon in *The Port Guard Ship*.

The minimal, almost abrupt, inscription on Jane's headstone can be explained by his own desire, "that I may be buried with as little expense as possible". However, perhaps nobody cared to provide a more extravagant memorial. Under cross-examination Jane's solicitor Mr Biscoe-Smith claimed that, "from the correspondence it appeared that the testator and his wife were on affectionate terms", but later admitted, "the testator was in fact separated from his wife", adding loyally that, "from the letters he evidently desired a reconciliation".[34] This not only explains the change in Jane's arrangements against his death, but also his leaving Bedhampton, his residence until the previous year.[35] His new apartment in Southsea, at the corner of Palmerston Road and Clarence Parade, had a view of Spithead across Southsea Common, where Jane's first wife Alice had loved to walk, and where the Royal Naval Memorial stands today. It was in a fashionable area, the MP Sir Bernard Falle living a few doors away. The rateable value was £120, twice that of Jane's old Southsea home in Elphinstone Road.[36] It seems unlikely therefore that Jane's move into Southsea was for economic reasons. The value of his estate was considerable for the day, £4,681/17/4d gross, or £3,930/10/9d after tax. His father, the Reverend John Jane, outlived Jane by seven years, leaving only £627 net. The combination of the change in address, with the codicil, definitely indicates a drastic alteration in Jane's domestic situation towards the end of 1915.

During the First World War Mrs Jane served in the Women's Voluntary Service, obtaining a passport photograph in 1914, presumably in order to work in France. Perhaps the Janes' affairs were already running into difficulties; prolonged separation arising from Jane's lecture tour or Muriel's voluntary work cannot have helped. Towards the end of the war, Muriel helped guard German prisoners of war working on a farm in Dorset where she met, and later married, Edward Tory.[37] He is remembered as a rough, bluff farmer, rather like William Cobbett, the author of *Rural Rides*, with his hunting pink hung up behind the door – a very different character from Muriel's wayward naval expert.[38] She always called her second husband 'Jack' to avoid recalling her brother, Ted Carré, whose submarine, E17, failed to return in August 1917. She never appears to have mentioned Jane by name, although a large studio portrait of him hung in her bedroom. Muriel's youngest son, Anthony, who as a child asked her about "the man on the wall", suggests that her memories may have been too painful to recall.[39] As will appear, she may have had good reason for such feelings.

* * *

The house at 26 Clarence Esplanade, where Jane died, was ironically destroyed by the aircraft which also put an end to the armoured ships to which he devoted so much of his life. However, in 1993 Portsmouth City Council fixed a blue commemorative plaque to the block of modern flats which was built there in the 1950s. Its words are as follows:

FRED T
JANE
1865–1916
Journalist & Author of
Jane's Fighting Ships
spent his last years in a
house which stood
on this site

Luckily, anyone interested in Fred T Jane can still find some other places worthy of pilgrimage. In Highland Road cemetery, Southsea, the headstone which Jane shares with Alice Beattie Jane has withstood the elements, although there has been no dynasty of Janes to fill the adjacent family plot. In Elphinstone Road, the house where he laboured to transform the early issues of *Fighting Ships* still displays the Boy Scouts' fleur-de-lys over the first floor bay window. Just around the corner stands St Jude's Church, where Jane married his second wife Muriel. Hill House, where they lived in Bedhampton, has fallen victim, however, to the speculative builders of the 1970s.

At Exeter, similar forces have swept away the world in which Fred T Jane grew up. The ancient church of St John's in Fore Street was already far gone in decay when it was bombed in May 1942, along with Bedford Chapel, while the old school buildings in the High Street were mostly demolished in Jane's day. Post-war reconstruction has concealed Exeter's original street plan, although the names of Bedford Road and Bluecoat Lane provide a clue to the historical connections of what is now the Princeshay shopping precinct. Time has been kinder to the new Exeter School, which Jane attended towards the end of his school career. Appropriately clutching a model ironclad he appears on a commemorative sculpture, set into the wall of Butterfield's original building, with other alumni of the school. Surprisingly, the Victorian brick elevations of Jane's tenement in Grays' Inn Road are still to be seen, on the left hand side, going north from the Yorkshire Grey, on the corner of Theobalds Road. The pub itself still presents a Victorian exterior, which Jane might recognise, with the figure of a red-coated cavalry trooper high above the traffic.

In the countryside, less change is apparent. At Upton Pyne, within the South East chapel, lies a figure in 16th century armour, much as Jane might have remembered when he described the Mohun effigies, with their noses sliced off by their Puritan enemies. Upottery lies safely away from the main road to Honiton. Here it is still possible to drink real ale in the Sidmouth Arms, while the vicarage still commands an unspoiled view across the water meadows, although it no longer houses the vicar. Between the pub and the vicarage stands the church, with its monuments to the lords of the manor. In the porch, John Jane is listed as Vicar for the years 1885 to 1923, while the 1914–18 Roll of Honour records the names of George Hugh and Henry Edgar. Over on the South East side of the graveyard lies their sister Helen, who never married and lived in the village until 1940, teaching in the Sunday School. Reverend John Jane's own memorial, which he shares with his wife, bears the additional inscription 'Also of Fred T Jane their eldest son born 6 Aug 1865 entered into rest 8 March 1916'.

As so often with human affairs, it is the abstract parts of Jane's legacy that have worn best. New hands and minds take up old ideas, and fit them to their own purposes. Jane's contract with Sampson Low ensured that *Fighting Ships* did not depend on his life alone, and his will made specific provision for its

The inscription added to Jane's parents' memorial at Upottery

201

continuation. Aware of his poor health, he had taken: "the precaution of arranging that in case of need the editorial responsibility should be confided to Dr Oscar Parkes, who had for some time been privileged to assist in the work of production".[40] Parkes had attracted Jane's attention by the quality of the illustrations he drew for the pre-war *Navy League Annual*, to pay for his medical studies.[41] He was also a collector of naval photographs. Subsequently Director of Naval Photographs at the Imperial War Museum, he acquired the early collections of Long and Symonds with the help of William Bieber. However, when Jane died Parkes was serving at Malta as a Naval Surgeon, before taking up an appointment in the Naval Intelligence Department in 1917.[42]

As Parkes was otherwise occupied, the responsibility for carrying on *Fighting Ships* initially fell upon his friend Maurice Prendergast, who had "the heartbreaking job of bringing out a naval annual during a war when everything was secret".[43] Parkes returned in time to help with the enormous post-war issue of 1919, introducing the first full page blocks, for HMS *Renown* and *Furious*. After 1922 Prendergast's failing sight forced him to retire, Francis E McMurtrie taking charge of the text and make-up of the book.[44] Coming from a naval family, but unable to serve for health reasons, McMurtrie had "for many years assisted in the revision of the book",[45] starting in 1906, when he had highlighted the previous year's misprints.[46] During the war he had compiled the lists of ships lost in action. When Parkes retired as editor in 1933, McMurtrie proved a worthy successor to Jane, combining his "card index mind" with an "almost physiological passion for accuracy".[47] McMurtrie did much to perpetuate the memory of *Fighting Ships'* founder through the biographical pieces he wrote for the 30th and 50th issues. Although not always accurate, these provide an invaluable starting point for the study of Jane. Sadly, McMurtrie's own collection of papers, which no doubt contained much information of the early days, was destroyed by his wife after his death from cancer in 1949.[48] Jane's original and priceless album, *Ironclads of the World*, still preserved in 1926, was presumably another of Mrs McMurtrie's victims.

The 50th anniversary issue, of 1947–48 still featured five ships from 1898, and reprinted a page from that issue showing a group of ironclads already obsolescent in 1898, including HMS *Northampton*. Perhaps the longest surviving ship from the early days was the *Presidente Sarmiento*, built by Cammell Laird in 1898 for Argentina, and still listed as a training ship in 1961. The long partnership between Parkes and McMurtrie provided a significant force for continuity. In their hands *Fighting Ships* consolidated its position as, "perhaps the most complete of naval books of reference", allowing: "the naval enthusiast to recognise at sight any man of war to whatever navy she belongs. It contains photographs of practically every man of war in the world, down to the gunboats of Manchukuo".[49]

Some years after Manchukuo had disappeared from its pages, *Fighting Ships* celebrated its 60th anniversary in 1958 by introducing the current double sized page layout. The issue's congratulatory introduction was signed by the First Sea Lord, Earl Mountbatten of Burma – by a happy coincidence the son of the same Prince Louis of Battenberg who had encouraged Jane, in the 1890s. Nothing could be more symbolic of how *Fighting Ships* has come to be accepted by generations of naval officers as an essential tool of their job. Although revolution may have been as "thick upon the naval world" in 1957 as it had been when Jane first coined the phrase in 1906, the essential concerns of *Fighting Ships* have not changed, even in the 1990s: "Page composition continues to be driven by the needs of supplying comprehensive operational data to the man in a hurry, for a quick answer. Much care is taken to prevent pages spilling over or cross-references being needed to answer straightforward questions".[50] The same editor also echoed Jane's concern for the intangible factors upon which naval success is founded, with his comment that it is "Always easier to write about technology than people, about weapon systems than operators, about organisation as opposed to morale".[51]

The combination of longevity with painstaking accuracy has made *Fighting Ships* a valuable historical source. Often cited by serious naval historians such as Arthur J Marder, or more recently John Sumida, it uniquely provides a consistent basis for comparative study of naval equipment over the years. The word 'Jane' even features in the Collins Dictionary as a noun signifying completeness and reliability.

All the World's Aircraft has enjoyed an even greater degree of editorial stability than *Fighting Ships*. Before the First World War Jane remarked how the periodical *Aeroplane* was, in its field, "the only publication I know of which is consistently level headed".[52]

Jane's first love: a destroyer preparing for sea in the 1890s

Its editor, Charles G Grey, had worked with Jane on the 1915 issue of the yearbook, taking over full responsibility after Jane's death. He continued as full time editor until 1949, establishing it on as sound a basis as its naval companion.

Jane's acceptance by a new generation of naval officers, not even born when *Fighting Ships* first appeared, underlines once more the paradoxical nature of a man who was so close to the navy but never really accepted by its leaders during his own lifetime. Paradox runs throughout Jane's life and character. In 1903 he brought a motorist before the Honiton magistrates for furious driving and bad language, but having obtained the conviction to make his point, paid the fine himself.[53] Able to see the wider strategic picture of the First World War at sea, Jane carried his delineation of the minute details of steam pipes and fighting tops almost to obsession: "If genius is the infinite capacity for taking pains then Mr Jane possesses it for his work could only have been brought to its present state of perfection by the most diligent research and unremitting care".[54]

Yet the *Times* could not implausibly allege that, "the grounds of his judgement are sometimes slender".[55] However, Jane's judgement was clear enough to see through the social hypocrisy of his time: the sexual double standard and class prejudice targeted in *The Incubated Girl* and *A Royal Bluejacket*. The same honesty, or perhaps naivety, lay behind his publication of anonymous letter-writers who hoped, "FT Jane is being well paid by C--- B--- for doing his dirty work" or who offered £5 reward for: "a dangerous lunatic known as Fred T Jane ... May your lying lips be put to silence".[56] Jane's response was to offer to hand himself over to the writer, if they would pay the money to a local charity. A less attractive side of this openness was the violent language with which Jane wrote of 'peace maniacs', 'slackers' and 'German baby-killers'. The same spirit moved him to reverse his motor car into some: "'knut' with plastered hair who was telling some other friends of his what a rotter he thought Kitchener was ... It didn't hurt him but I told him I was d----d sorry I hadn't killed him".[57]

The style of many of Jane's drawings reflects the impulsive rather than the particular side of his nature, reminding the onlooker of his assertion that in art, "subject was everything and it did not really matter how it was treated".[58] Despite his deeply serious approach to his work, and although he advocated "reading the heavier naval literature that goes more to the root of things", he could also float such ideas as sponsorship of naval manoeuvres by the ratepayers of the home ports, in order to encourage public interest in the outcome. His life was illuminated by dubious anecdotes and practical jokes. They can be seen as typical behaviour for the period, but in personal terms Jane's sense of humour can also be explained as a reaction against the serious side of his nature, and a relief from his total commitment to his work.

When he died Jane was generally remembered for his vivacity and as "a thorough sportsman"[59] who would be "mourned by more than those who could claim the privilege of his friendship, and they were many".[60] For all his jocularity and good-fellowship, however, he died alone and possibly not exactly as recorded in the newspapers. He must have been deeply frustrated by the unending squabbles with the censor and his inability to play any real part in the war. He had even lost his voice in his old standby the *Hampshire Telegraph*. His friends were dying and his clear appreciation of the war's bleak reality would have left little room for optimism that others, like Ted Carré, would come through safely. There is a family belief that Fred T Jane died by his own hand, shooting himself with a .32 calibre Colt revolver, while in low spirits as a result of his poor health and the collapse of his marriage. As Jane had been in the doctor's hands before his death no inquest would have been needed, and indeed he was buried with surprising promptness. The strongest argument against the story is the doctor's implicit breach of professional ethics in signing a false death certificate, an allegation not to be brought lightly against a man unable to defend himself. Dr Cole-Baker would have been seriously compromised had the truth come out. As a prominent Southsea physician, and Chairman of the Clinical Sub-Committee of the City Council's Education Committee he had a lot to lose, although his word would be the less likely to be doubted. Circumstances may have lent themselves to a 'cover-up'; perhaps a suicide attempt was bungled with heart failure as the outcome. That, however, is entirely conjectural as it is in the nature of a successful conspiracy that no contradictory evidence be left. It is, however, hard to understand why the straightforward Edward Tory who married Jane's widow should have made the claim, if she had not told him of it.[61]

Jane's death may help us resolve the central paradox of this strange man, with his curious mixture of painstaking accuracy and originality bordering on make-believe. Although his outward face was often broken by a smile, and his boisterous sense of fun would leave him to be "missed by a wide circle",[62] behind the public face was a more private individual who enjoyed his home comforts, and took his daughter with him on Field Days.

Perhaps the mask of the clown concealed the sad face of a man, who, with the pessimism of the true conservative, saw his country threatened at home by spies and party politicians, and abroad by the rising power of Germany and Japan, while its Empire proved not a source of strength, but weakness: "the 'Sons of Empire', 'Britain beyond the Sea', 'the men who can ride and shoot' and all those other phrases which sound so big and mean so little because the day for them is passing".[63] Even the dreadnoughts, for which he argued so vociferously, proved of limited value when the deterrent failed in August 1914: "The only guarantees of peace are 'bloated armaments' and these guarantees probably only postpone the fatal day. As we have since learned".[64]

Jane's wargaming clearly fits within this downbeat pattern. Playing games is one way of coming to terms with an unbearable reality, reducing the horrors of war to a morally neutral struggle between Red and Blue. The careful tabulations of *Fighting Ships* provide a useful distraction from the awful purpose of the ships themselves, in the same way that more recent strategic analysts have taken comfort from counting missiles and warheads. Fred T Jane was the original exponent of their trade, whatever his motivation. He remains a key figure in the provision of the technical information required to support the defence debate in a democratic society, in a form at once authoritative and easy to use: "A popular Government, without popular information or the means of acquiring it, is but a Prologue to a Farce or a Tragedy: or perhaps both. Knowledge will forever govern ignorance; And a people who mean to be their own Governors, must arm themselves with the power which knowledge gives".[65]

Often enough the 20th century has shown the first of these statements to be true. Fred T Jane helped make it possible for the people to arm themselves with knowledge. Only they can decide whether or not they wish to do so.

SOURCE REFERENCES

Sources are identified as follows:
1. For periodicals: title, year and page number.
2. For newspapers: title and date.
3. For books: author's surname, and initial if neccessary.
   Abbreviated titles are only given where more than one
   work by that author was consulted. However, books by
   Fred T Jane are only referred to by their abbreviated
   title.
   See the Bibliographies for full details of works
   consulted.
   See the Glossary for the acronyms used below.

CHAPTER 1:
1. HT 15/01/1910 & HT/FTJ 28/10/1912
2. Times 25.08.1915
3. Exonian April 1913
4. Fighting Ships 1911 Preface
5. HT/FTJ 14/8/1914
6. HT/FTJ 28/5/1915
7. Times 11/12/1902 & JRUSI 1903 p.171
8. Quoted by Bond: War & Society in Europe, 1870-1970 p.27
9. Bond p.13
10. Thompson D: Europe Since Napoleon p.322
11. Quoted by Read: The Age of Urban Democracy p.64
12. English Illus 1892-3 p.658
13. Heresies of Sea Power p.14-15
14. Read pp.88-90
15. The British Battle Fleet
16. British Battle Fleet vol. I p.271 & FS 1919
17. Marder: Anatomy of British Sea Power p.128
18. HT 26/6/1897
19. The Incubated Girl p129

20. Marder: Anatomy p.56
21. Clarke: Voices Prophesying War p.109
22. Offer: The First World War, An Agrarian Interpretation p.218
23. Times 2/6/1902 & 5/6/1902
24. Guppy: Homes of Family Names in Great Britain p.103
25. Hanks & Hodges: Dictionary of Surnames
26. Guppy p.109
27. HT 6/2/1904
28. Foster: Alumni Oxonienses p.801
29. Charnock: Biographia Navalis vol. VI p.180
30. Francis E McMurtrie: FS 1947-49 p.vii
31. McMurtrie: FS 1947-8 p.vii
32. Kelly's Commercial Directory for Devon & Cornwall 1873 p.705
33. Gentleman's Magazine 1863 vol.ii p380
34. Alumni Cantabrigenses p.198
35. Boase: Collectanea Cornubiensia p.999
36. Marshall: Royal Naval Biography vol. I (ii) pp.834-5
37. Gentleman's Magazine 1809 p.538
38. Boase p.462
39. Toulson: Companion Guide to Devon p.126-9
40. Kelly's Devon 1878 p.195
41. Exeter Flying Post 10/4/1878
42. Schools Inquiry Report 1868 vol.xiv p.303-5
43. Glendinning: Trollope p.16
44. FTJ 'Some School Reminiscences' Exonian Dec 1912
45. Exonian Dec 1912
46. Ibid
47. L Cecil Jane: FS 1916
48. McMurtrie: FS 1947-8 p.viii
49. HT 11/6/1915
50. HT/FTJ 27/11/1914
51. Exonian April 1913
52. 'In Memoriam': Exonian April 1916
53. 'In Memoriam': Exonian April 1916
54. Exonian Dec 1913
55. Ibid
56. Exonian Dec 1883
57. Schools Inquiry Report 1868 vol.xiv p.299
58. Exeter School p.147
59. Strand Magazine May 1904 p.161

60. HT/FTJ 5/6/1909
61. Read p.211
62. HT/FTJ 25/6/1910

CHAPTER 2:
1. L Cecil Jane: FS 1916 p.4
2. A&NG 18/3/1916
3. Incubated Girl p.133
4. Incubated Girl p.127
5. HT 19/1/1907
6. Ibid
7. English Illustrated 1892-3 p.705 et seq
8. Read p.248
9. Francis Edwards' Catalogue of Naval Books 1974
10. Marder: Anatomy p.133
11. PW 15/8/1889
12. HT/FTJ 11/7/1913
13. PW 7/8/1890
14. PW 4/9/1890
15. McMurtrie: FS 1947-48 p.viii
16. Marder: Anatomy p.45
17. Marder: Anatomy p.367
18. FS 1898-1900 Acknowledgements
19. English Illustrated 1893-4 p.534 et seq
20. McMurtrie: FS 1947-48 p.viii
21. FS 1914: Swiftsure & Triumph
22. FS 1911 Preface
23. FS 1898 p.82
24. PW 20/11/1890
25. ILN 23.3.1895
26. PW 24/1/1891
27. PW 7/3/1891 & 21/3/1891
28. FS 1916 p.4
29. Jacob & Pyke p.254
30. Torpedo in Peace and War p.59
31. Royal Bluejacket p.342)
32. HT/FTJ 12/12/1908
33. Read: p.402
34. The Incubated Girl p.60
35. Art Journal 1894 p.211
36. Read p.59
37. Photograph in The CAR 17/1/1906 p.296

38. See The Incubated Girl & The Lordship, The Passen and We
39. Read p.207
40. ILN 1906 p.466
41. IF Clarke: op cit
42. L&W 30/1/1915
43. Frewin: One Hundred Years of Science Fiction Illustration p.47
44. Clute & Nicholls p.638
45. Thomas
46. Bleiler pp.389-90
47. Robinson p.529
48. Robinson p.368
49. Torpedo in Peace and War p.14
50. Torpedo in Peace and War p.27
51. Torpedo in Peace and War p.81
52. Torpedo in Peace and War p.31
53. Torpedo in Peace and War p.63
54. McMurtrie: FS 1947-48 p.viii
55. Blake of the Rattlesnake p.21
56. Bayly p.76
57. Blake p.106
58. Blake p.8
59. IF Clarke p.78
60. To Venus in Five Seconds p.47
61. To Venus p.51
62. The Violet Flame p.245
63. Laurence Davies in Slusser & Rabkin p.64
64. To Venus p.25
65. To Venus p.98
66. Incubated Girl p.180
67. Incubated Girl p.54.
68. Incubated Girl p.58
69. Read p.41
70. To Venus p.98
71. Read pp.291 & 324-5
72. To Venus p.98
73. To Venus p.32
74. Bleiler p.392

CHAPTER 3:
1. McMurtrie: FS 1947-48 p.vii
2. Oscar Parkes: MM 1957 p.281-7

3. cf Hozier p.391-4 and Greene p.15
4. McMurtrie: FS 1926 p.6
5. ILN 9/6/1894
6. McMurtrie: FS 1947-48 p.vii
7. NA 1886
8. McMurtrie: FS 1926 p.6
9. JRUSI 1897 p.911
10. JRUSI 1900 p.1096
11. JRUSI 1899 p.828
12. FS 1909 p.6
13. JRUSI 1905 p.1224
14. English Illustrated 1893-4 p.544
15. McMurtrie: FS 1926 p.6
16. McMurtrie: FS 1947-48 p.ix
17. Port Guard Ship p.26
18. G&L 1945 p.48
19. The Engineer quoted in FS 1899
20. FS 1899 Introduction
21. HT 19/1/1907
22. McMurtrie: FS 1926 p.6
23. FS 1898 p.14
24. JRUSI 1903 p.858
25. Torpedo in Peace & War p.36
26. For Jane's awareness of this see IRN p.185 fn
27. McMurtrie: FS 1926 p.6
28. FS 1900 Preface
29. HT/FTJ 14/7/1911
30. Times 21/12/1897 & 22/12/1897
31. HT/FTJ 13/11/1914
32. McMurtrie: FS 1947-48 p.ix
33. HT 26/6/1897
34. JRUSI 1897 p.886
35. HT 26/6/1897
36. Riley: The Growth of Southsea as a Naval Satellite
37. PCRO Ratebook 1901 vol. A p.47
38. JRUSI 1899 p.828)
39. Times 10/2/1898
40. NWOJ Aug 1901
41. NWOJ Sep 1902
42. McMurtrie: FS 1947-48 p.ix
43. DT 3.7.1872 quoted by Read

44. HT/FTJ 18/4/1913
45. NA 1897 p.53
46. NA 1897: John Leyland: Recent Naval Literature
47. FS 1899 Preface
48. FS 1901 p.9
49. FS 1899 Acknowledgements
50. Macdonald: Camera pp.145-8
51. FS 1900 Preface
52. FS 1900 Preface
53. FS 1901 Preface
54. FS 1901 Preface
55. A&NG 1901 p.753
56. A&NG 1901 p.753
57. FS 1901 Preface
58. Biscoe-Smith
59. Undated Letter at PCRO 832A
60. Biscoe-Smith
61. PCRO 832A
62. Biscoe-Smith
63. Biscoe-Smith
64. PCRO 832A
65. FS 1901 Title page
66. PCRO 832A
67. PCRO 832A
68. McMurtrie: FS 1947 p.ix
69. HT 5/4/1902
70. Read p.23
71. Carew pp.47-53
72. Royal Bluejacket p.310
73. Port Guard Ship c. XVI
74. PCRO 832A
75. Stableford pp.127-31
76. PCRO 832A 8/3/1900
77. NWOJ 1903 p.106
78. See Marder: Anatomy p.148
79. Marder: From the Dreadnought to Scapa Flow vol. II p.9
80. See Wells: An Illustrated Social History of the Royal Navy p.57
81. Quoted by Marder: From the Dreadnought to Scapa Flow vol. I p.403
82. FS 1901 Preface
83. PCRO 832A

84. Read p.391

CHAPTER 4:
1. Engineer 9.12.1898
2. Strand May 1904
3. Ibid
4. Castle: JRUSI 1874 p.786-805
5. Colomb: JRUSI 1880 p.507 et seq
6. Ibid
7. quoted by Marder: Anatomy p.47
8. How To Play the Jane Naval Wargame p.9
9. Wilson A: War Gaming p.27
10. Chamberlain: JRUSI 1888-89 pp.525-537
11. Rules for the Jane Naval Wargame p.5
12. Hints on Playing the Jane Naval Wargame p.46
13. Rules p.6
14. Engineer 18.2.1898
15. Engineer 9.12.1898
16. Jane JRUSI 1899 p.148-160
17. Hints p.46
18. Times 7.2.1957
19. Schurman: Julian S Corbett, 1854-1922 p.32
20. Naval Review 1931 p.251
21. JRUSI 1899 p.158
22. Hints p.6
23. JRUSI 1899 p.159
24. Dreyer: The Sea Heritage p.36
25. Bennett: Charlie B. - A Biography of Lord Charles Beresford p.234
26. Offer p.230-232
27. Jane: JRUSI 1900 p.252-3
28. Scientific American 26/10/1901
29. King-Hall: Sea Saga p.312-3
30. Scientific American 26/10/1901
31. HT 2/1/1902
32. McMurtrie: FS 1947-48 p.x
33. HT 26.12.1908
34. Scientific American 26/10/1901
35. Marder: From Dreadnought to Scapa Flo vol. I p.401 quoting Admiral KGB Dewar
36. Naval Review 1931 p.241
37. Strand May 1904

38. Hints p.43
39. Hints p.45
40. FS 1905-6 p.444 & Hints p.27
41. Hints p.18
42. Strand May 1904
43. Times 21/4/1900
44. HT 6/2/1904: Mr Jane on Russia - Fact Compared with Fiction
45. HT 6/2/1904
46. Times 21/4/1900
47. IRN p.16
48. IJN p.255
49. IRN p.13
50. IRN p.103 The Battle of Viborg 1790
51. MM 1961 p.315
52. DNB & IRN pp 181-5 & Hobart: Sketches From My Life
53. Quoted in FS 1902
54. Times 21/4/1900
55. McMurtrie: FS 1947-8 p.ix
56. IJN p.279
57. IJN pp.284-5
58. IJN pp404-5
59. FS 1899 Preface
60. Engineer 7/10/1898 p.345
61. IJN p.49
62. IJN Preface
63. FS 1905-6 Preface
64. Connaughton: The War of the Rising Sun and Tumbling Bear p.175
65. IRN p.399
66. HT 6/2/1904
67. HT 18/11/1905
68. HT 19/11/1904
69. HT 19/11/1904
70. Offer pp.190-2
71. HT/FTJ 19/2/1915
72. Honan: Bywater: The Man Who Invented the Pacific War p.128
73. HT 19/11/1904
74. A&NG 1898 p.758

CHAPTER 5:
1. HT 15/12/1906
2. Times 21/4/1900

3. A&NG 1901 p.753
4. JRUSI 1903 p.858
5. FS 1911 Preface
6. HT/FTJ 21/3/1913: Winsome Winnie was Winston Churchill; Unalloyed Thief was Lloyd George, Chancellor of the Exchequer; and Mrs Pankhurst led the Suffragette's fight for Votes for Women
7. HT/FTJ 3/4/1909
8. HT/FTJ 20/3/1909
9. HT/FTJ 3/4/1909
10. See Schurman op. cit. for Corbett's career
11. Marder: Dreadnought to Scapa Flo Vol II p.218-222
12. HT/FTJ 20/11/1914
13. JRUSI 1903 p.171 et seq
14. Quoted by Sumida; In Defence of Naval Supremacy p.38
15. Schurman p.71
16. Times 11/12/1902
17. Times 15/12/1902 & 16/12/1902
18. Heresies p.177
19. HT 16/6/1906
20. FR 1902 p.456
21. Heresies p.7
22. Heresies p.11
23. Heresies p.7
24. TLS 20/8/1906
25. A&NG 1906 p.560
26. L&W 21/11/1914
27. Heresies p.164
28. Heresies p.139
29. L&W 5/12/1914 & 10/4/1915
30. Heresies p.139
31. HT/FTJ 12/6/1909
32. Times 5/7/1902
33. FR 1902 p.454
34. Compare the last pre-Dreadnoughts, the 1904 Nelson class, with the King Edwards: FS 1914
35. Your Navy as a Fighting Machine p.17
36. FS 1903 fp & Part III
37. Your Navy as a Fighting Machine p.17
38. Parkes: British Battleships p.466
39. Sumida p.45-6

40. FS 1919: Historical Note under Dreadnought
41. McMurtrie FS 1947-48 p.x
42. Jane: JRUSI 1899 p.155
43. IRN p.92
44. Engineer 4/11/1898 p.442
45. Schurman p.34
46. IRN p.572
47. HT/FTJ 6/10/1906
48. ILN 6/10/1896 p.466
49. HT 6/10/1906
50. A&NG 24/3/1916
51. HT Pictorial Souvenir 1799-1949
52. HT/FTJ 5/1/1907
53. HT/FTJ 14/3/1903
54. HT/FTJ 9/3/1907
55. HT/FTJ 16/2/1907
56. HT/FTJ 1/5/1909
57. HT/FTJ 29/01/1910
58. McMurtrie: FS 1947-48 p.xi
59. HT 24/10/1903
60. HT/LY 27/11/1914
61. HT 24/10/1903
62. FR 1902 p.454
63. Carew p.23
64. Marder: Anatomy p.356
65. HT 12/12/1903
66. Marder: Anatomy p.56
67. FR 1902 p.445
68. HT/FTJ 27/7/1907
69. HT 27/7/1907
70. Autocar 30/11/1912
71. PCRO PR/vi/1-5
72. MMC Sales leaflets 1903-7 at Beaulieu Motor Museum
73. HT 05/12/1903
74. MMC advertising material 1907, Beaulieu Motor Museum
75. Autocar 30/6/1906
76. CAR 16/10/1904
77. McMurtrie: FS 1947-8
78. Motor Car Journal 25/02/1905
79. HT 15/10/1904
80. HT 12/05/1906

81. CAR 21/11/1906
82. Motor Car Journal 11/02/1905
83. Motor Car Journal 15/04/1905
84. CAR 14/05/1911
85. HT 7/11/1903
86. McMurtrie: FS 1947-8
87. Ibid
88. PCRO: Vospers 100 Years
89. CAR 25/5/1910
90. HT 13/3/1907. A cockney is said to be a Londoner born within the sound of Bow Bells (church) in the east end of London. Cockney dialect and rhyming slang baffles many a tourist.
91. FS 1910 Advertisement
92. McMurtrie: FS 1947-48
93. Autocar 1912 pp.1131-33
94. Michael Frostick: The Mighty Mercedes p.165
95. Autocar Ibid
96. HT 19/05/1991: Mr Jane and the Sheep
97. Autocar Ibid
98. Autocar Ibid

CHAPTER 6:

1. Wells p.43
2. HT/FTJ 19/2/1910
3. Carew: The Lower Deck of the Royal Navy 1900-39 p.53-58
4. HT 12/12/1903
5. Carew p.40-46
6. Carew p.27-31
7. Carew p.21
8. HT/FTJ 2/3/1907
9. Wells pp.54 & 84
10. HT/FTJ 24/2/1911
11. HT/FTJ 2/6/1911
12. HT/FTJ 15/6/1907
13. HT/FTJ 22/8/1913
14. HT/FTJ 12/9/1913
15. Fleet 1928 p.71
16. Carew p.82
17. HT 11/7/1903 Interview FTJ
18. HT 11/7/1903
19. Times 10/1/1906

20. HT 11/7/1903 Interview FTJ
21. Read p.164
22. HT 18/5/1903
23. HT 6/1/1906
24. HT 13/1/1906
25. HT 20/1/1906
26. HT 13/1/1906
27. HT 20/1/1906
28. HT 20/1/1906
29. HT 20/1/1906
30. Ibid
31. Ibid
32. HT 16/2/1910
33. HT/FTJ 16/6/1911
34. Carew p.73-4
35. Royal Navy List Jan 1909 p.717
36. A&NG 1909 p.247
37 Royal Bluejacket p.353
38. HT 16/1/1904
39. HT/FTJ 1/7/1910
40. HT/FTJ 5/6/1909
41. A&NG 1909 p.247
42. The Death Certificate gives the following cause of death: 'Dilatation & curetting of uterus. Shock 6 hours. Cardiac Syncope'
43. HT 19/12/1908
44. Ibid
45. Ibid
46. HT/FTJ 19/12/1908
47. Ibid
48. Engineer 8/8/1902
49. Exonian Dec 1912 p.95
50. HT/FTJ 14/7/1911
51. Ibid
52. HW Wilson quoted in HT 15/12/1906
53. HT/FTJ 01/01/1910
54. HT/FTJ 27/07/1907
55. HT/FTJ 21/12/1907
56. Clark DG: Labour's Lost Leader p.67
57. EN 28/1/1909
58. PT 6/2/1909

59. EN 28/1/1909
60. Quoted by Clark DG p.61
61. PT 6/2/1909 and EN 29/1/1910
62. EN Interview with Grayson 29/1/1909
63. EN Interview with Wilson 29/1/1909
64. Daily Mail Interview with Jane 30/1/1910
65. Clark DG p.161
66. HT/FTJ 6/1/1911
67. HM Hyndman "Further Reminiscences", quoted by Clark DG p.61
68. Clark DG ch.8-10
69. McMurtrie FS 1947-48 p.xi
70. Clark DG p.164
71. PT 6/2/1909
72. HT/FTJ 19/6/1909

CHAPTER 7:
1. McMurtrie: FS 1947-8 p.xi
2. FS 1902 p.275
3. FS 1902 p.358
4. Times 20/7/1907
5. HT/FTJ 19/6/1909
6. ATWA 1910-11 Preface
7. ATWA 1909 Preface
8. ATWA 1909 p.53
9. ATWA 1909 Preface
10. Times 11/1/1911
11. McMurtrie: FS 1947-8 p.x
12. Read p.430-1
13. ATWA 1914 Preface
14. HT/FTJ 14/7/1911
15. ATWA 1912 Preface
16. ATWA 1914 Preface
17. TLS 10/9/1914
18. HT 14/3/1911
19. HT/FTJ 12/3/1910
20. HT/FTJ 28/8/1909
21. HT/FTJ 7/8/1909
22. HT 2/10/1909
23. ATWA 1910-11 p.278
24. Gange: Memories of Yesteryear p.4
25. HT/FTJ 28/8/1909

26. HT/FTJ 25/4/1913
27. HT/FTJ 28/8/1909
28. HT/FTJ 5/8/1910
29. McMurtrie: FS 1947-8 p.xi & WWW vol.vi
30. Grove: Fleet to Fleet Encounters pp.61 & 64
31. HT/FTJ 9/5/1913
32. HT 10/7/1909
33. HT 1/8/1913
34. HT 25/7/1913
35. HT/FTJ 25/4/1913
36. A&NG 29/10/1904
37. HT/FTJ 12/12/1908
38. HT/FTJ 10/7/1909
39. HT 10/7/1909
40. Ibid
41. HT/FTJ 10/7/1909
42. HT/FTJ 7/8/1909
43. PT 18/12/1909 Boy Scout's Notes
44. HT 14/10/1910
45. HT 14/10/1910
46. PT 17/3/1916 Boy Scout's Notes
47. Gange p.4
48. Bedhampton & Havant Boy Scouts Magazine
49. HT/FTJ 27/11/1914
50. Photographed in October 1914: PCRO 1034A/7/76-7
51. Exonian Dec 1914
52. HT 7/4/1911
53. EA Tory
54. PT 6/11/1909
55. EN 20/12/1909
56. PT 25/12/1909
57. A&NG 1912 p.582
58. EA Tory
59. EA Tory
60. Autocar 1912 pp.1131-33
61. PCRO PR/VI/5 p.68 & EA Tory
62. Grubb: The History of Bedhampton & Cook: Tales of Ancient
    Wessex pp.65 & 98
63. EA Tory
64. HT 13/3/1907
65. JT Carre & EA Tory

66. Quoted in Bennett title page
67. Quoted by Bennett p.226
68. Bennett p.240-1
69. HT/FTJ 17/8/1907
70. HT/FTJ 31/7/1909
71. HT/FTJ 21/8/1909
72. Wells p.39
73. HT/Nauticus 20/3/1909
74. PT 20/3/1909
75. HT 20/11/1909
76. HT 20/11/1909
77. Ibid
78. HT 15/01/1910
79. HT 15/1/1910
80. Ibid
81. ILN 1910 p.138
82. Autocar 1912 p.1131-2
83. HT/FTJ 9/12/1910
84. Carew p.74
85. HT/FTJ 16/2/1910
86. Ibid
87. McMurtrie:FS 1947-48 p.x
88. HT 6/11/1914
89. BBF vol. I p.v
90. BBF vol. I p.viii
91. BBF vol I p.x
92. HT 6/11/1914
93. BBF vol. I p.2
94. BBF vol. I p.203
95. BBF vol. II p.110
96. BBF vol. II p.102
97. BBF vol. II p.10
98. FS 1906-7 Preface
99. FS 1908
100. FS 1908 Preface
101. FS 1906-7 Preface
102. HT 1/7/1910
103. FS 1911 Preface
104. FS 1906-7 Preface
105. FS 1908 Preface
106. FS 1914 Preface

107. FS 1909 Preface
108. FS 1908 Preface
109. FS 1913 Preface
110. FS 1911-1912
111. FS 1909 Preface
112. FS 1914
113. Biscoe-Smith
114. Ibid
115. Ibid
116. Ibid
117. Ibid
118. FS 1907 Preface
119. TLS 1914 p.402
120. Ibid
121. Ibid
122. HT/FTJ 5/6/1909
123. HT/FTJ 22/8/1913

CHAPTER 8:
1. HT 7/8/1914
2. HT 31/7/1914
3. HT/FTJ 14/8/1914
4. NR 1931 p.240
5. HT/FTJ 14/7/1911 & HT 21/7/1911
6. HT 15/01/1910
7. JRUSI 1910 p.673 & A&NG 1912 p.991
8. A&NG 1913 p.775
9. HT 6/1/1906
10. Andrew: Secret Service p.60
11. HT/FTJ 13/1/1911
12. IRN p.449
13. FR 1902 p.456
14. HT/FTJ 9/9/1910
15. Andrew p.61
16. HT/FTJ 22/5/1909
17. Edmonds III/5/2 chapt.20 p.2
18. Edmonds III/5/2 chapt.20 p.16
19. French: Spy Fever - Historical Journal 1978 p.361
20. HT 18/6/1915 & 25/6/1915
21. HT 4/6/1915
22. Andrew p.70
23. HT 14/8/1914

24. HT 25/9/1914
25. HT/FTJ 27/11/1914 & 16/7/1915
26. HT/FTJ 6/11/1914
27. HT 7/8/1914
28. French pp.368-9
29. HT/FTJ 6/11/1914
30. HT/FTJ 23/10/1914
31. HT/FTJ 9/10/1914
32. L&W 6/2/1915
33. HT/FTJ 27/11/1914
34. HT 28/5/1915
35. Your Navy as a Fighting Machine (Introduction)
36. AN Wilson: Hilaire Belloc p.223
37. L&W 26/12/1914
38. AN Wilson p.225
39. Times 7/9/1915
40. FS 1915 Preface
41. Ibid
42. The World's Warships 1915 Preface
43. PT 10/3/1916
44. HT/FTJ 23/7/1915
45. Ibid
46. FS 1915 Preface
47. HT/FTJ 23/7/1915
48. HT/FTJ 27/11/1914
49. Heresies p.234
50. FR 1902 p.456
51. Heresies p.244 & p.241
52. Ibid
53. Terraine: Impacts of War 1914 and 1918 p.80
54. HT 19/11/1904
55. Heresies p.238
56. HT/FTJ 25/6/1915
57. Wilson T: The Myriad Faces of War p.144
58. FS 1918 Preface
59. Heresies p.244
60. McMurtrie: FS 1947-48 p.xii
61. McMurtrie: FS 1940 Preface
62. Heresies p.244
63. Quoted by Marder Dreadnought to Scapa Flo vol. II p.222
64. Quoted by Read p.456

65. HT/FTJ 8/1/1915
66. L&W 30/1/1915
67. HT/FTJ 29/1/1915
68. L&W 6/2/1915
69. HT/FTJ 29/1/1915
70. HT 25/9/1914
71. L&W 22/8/1914
72. HT/FTJ 11/9/1914
73. See Michael Howard: Clausewitz p.42 quoting On war p.181
74. Schurman p.152
75. L&W 12/12/1914
76. HT/FTJ 8/10/1915
77. HT 27/1/1915
78. HT/FTJ 8/1/1915
79. HT/FTJ 12/3/1915
80. Daily News & Leader: quoted in EN 10/3/1916
81. HT/LY 27/11/1914
82. HT/FTJ 13/11/1914
83. L&W 19/12/1914
84. L&W 6/3/1915
85. L&W 6/3/1915
86. Heresies p.133
87. Quoted by Marder Dreadnought to Scapa Flo vol II p.218
88. Lord Crewe quoted by Ibid p.222
89. Ibid p.221
90. HT/FTJ 29/1/1915
91. L&W 19/12/1914
92. HT/FTJ 12/2/1915
93. HT/FTJ 26/2/1915
94. Heresies p.177
95. Fighting Machine p.48
96. L&W 10/4/1915

CHAPTER 9:
1. HT/FTJ 19/3/1915
2. HT/FTJ 30/4/1915
3. Ibid
4. Ibid
5. DE 30/4/1915
6. FH 1/5/1915
7. HT/FTJ 19/3/1915
8. HT/FTJ 30/4/1915

9. FH 1/5/1915
10. HT/FTJ 30/10/1914
11. HT/FTJ 16/4/1915
12. DE 30/4/1915
13. FH 1/5/1915
14. HT/FTJ 1/10/1915
15. McMurtrie: FS 1926 p.7
16. McMurtrie: FS 1947-48 p.xi
17. HT/LY 23/12/1915
18. Times 30/3/1917
19. PT 10/3/1916
20. Thompson P: The Edwardians p.69
21. EN 9/3/1916
22. A&NG 18/3/1916
23. Fleet 1916 p.119
24. L&W 16/3/1916
25. PT 24/3/1916
26. Times 10/3/1916
27. Times 30/3/1917
28. Abbot: The British Airship at War p.35-6
29. Times 30/3/1917
30. HT/FTJ 27/2/1909
31. Ibid
32. HT/FTJ 30/1/1909 & HT 13/2/1909
33. SYB 1911 p.844
34. Times 30/3/1917
35. EN 9/3/1916
36. PCRO Ratebooks 1911/1921
37. EA Tory
38. JT Carre
39. EA Tory
40. McMurtrie: FS 1926 p.7
41. Times 4/7/1958
42. Mariner's Mirror 1957 p.281-7
43. Parkes: FS 1934 Vale
44. McMurtrie: FS 1926 p.7
45. McMurtrie: FS 1926 p.7
46. FS 1906
47. Times 24/2/1949 & FS 1949-50
48. Honan p.272
49. TLS 9.1.1937

50. FS 1993-94 Introduction
51. Ibid
52. HT/FTJ 25/4/1913
53. HT 19/9/1903
54. HT 18/3/1903
55. Times 21/4/1900
56. HT/FTJ 16/4/1910 & 29/1/1910
57. HT/FTJ 28/5/1915
58. HT 19/1/1907
59. PT 17/3/1916
60. L&W 16/3/1916
61. EA Tory
62. A&NG 18/3/1916
63. Heresies p.181
64. HT/FTJ 19/2/1915
65. James Madison to WT Barry 4/8/1822

APPENDIX

EMPLOYEES & SUPPLIERS LISTING JANE'S INFORMATION GROUP, 1997

UK Employees

AARON, Chris
AHMAD, Viqar
ALI, Zeenat
ALLEN, Denise
ANDERSON, Brian
ANGELINI, Fabiana
ASHTON, John
ATKINS, Martyn
BACH, Karine
BALL, Marion
BARNES, Brigitte
BARKER, Philip
BARRICK, Diana
BEAL, Clifford
BEAVER, Paul
BEECHENER, Jenny
BERRY, Jean
BETTS, Jennie
BETTS, Tara
BLAKE, Lorna
BOAKYE, Irene
BORRAS, Kevin
BOX, Kevan
BOXALL, Janine
BRENCHLEY, Jack
BRIGDEN, Gary
BROWN, Jean
BROCKWELL, Suzanne
BRUNAVS, Claire
BRYANT, Frank
BRYANT, Michael
BRYANT, Nick
BUNTEN, Kathy
BURNS, Diana

BURNS, Dominic
BUTINA-CORBY, Vera
BYRNE, Helen
CANNON, Stephen
CARRINGTON, Penny
CHAPMAN, Colin
CHAPMAN, Rosemary
CHILES, Marian
CHISHOLM, Annabel
CHRISTMAS, Emma
CLAYTON, Alison
CLARKE, Jackie
CODRINGTON, Alice
CONDRON, Alan
COPE, Carolyn
CRANDON, Lisa
DALLAS, Roland
DALY, Mark
DAVID, Michele
DAVIES, Erika
DAWKINS, Gina
DAWSON, Elizabeth
DAY, Michelle
DE OLIVEIRA, Sergio
DILIETO, Brenda
DODDS-ELY, Louise
DURKIN, Michael
DURHAM, Simon
DYER, John
EDGERTON, Wendy
ERSKINE, Sarah
FAULKNER, Keith
FELSTEAD, Peter
FENWICK, Joanne
FILHO, Fernando
FIRMAGER, Marc

FISHER, David
GALE, Melanie
GALLAGHER, Carol
GEMMILL, Karen
GETHING, Mike
GIBBONS, Sarah
GILBERT, Marc
GLENDINNING, Elizabeth
GODFREY, Susan
GORDON, Charlotte
GRAY, Lisa
GREEN, James
GRINT, Charles
HANKS, Martin
HARDING, Harriet
HARTNELL, Kerry
HARRIS, Carole
HATWELL, Michelle
HEAVER, Ann
HEFFER, Karen
HIPKISS, Sally
HOLLIGAN, Annette
HORROCKS, Lorna
HOWARD, Peter
HOWE, Sean
HOYLE, Craig
HUGGETT, Malcolm
HUMPHREYS, Amelia
HUTCHINSON, Bob
INGLES-LE NOBEL, Johan
IRONS, Rebecca
JACKSON, Sharon
JAMES, Anthony
JANSSEN LOK, Joris
JEACOCK, Rob
JEFFERIES, Jenny
JESSUP, Chris
JOHNSON, Tracy
JONES, Kathryn
JOWETT, Ruth
KARNIOL, Robert
KAY, Ian
KAY, Simon
KEMP, Damian
KEMP, Ian
KENT, Judith
KERR, Analisa
KEW, Laura
KEW, Patricia
KINGHAM, Anthony
KNIGHT, Alexander
KORNELL, Susie
LAMBERT, Sue
LANGLEY, Jacquie
LAVERICK, Bernard
LAWRENCE, Christine

LAWRENCE, Jane
LEATHWOOD, Alistair
LEE, Reg
LEMESURIER, Charles
LENHAM, Fay
LESLIE, Anne
LEWIS, Karen
LIM, Serena
LOGAN, John
LOPEZ, Celso
MARTIN, Steven
MARSHALL, Claire
MASLIN, Colin
MASON, Gary
MAYHEW, Sandra
McCARTHY, Deborah
McDOUGALL, Shiona
McFARLANE, Gary
McQUEEN, Stephen
MICHELL, Simon
MIOTTO, Fabio
MILLER, Edward
MILTON, Margaret
MOORHOUSE, Simon
MOON, Jo
MOORE, Linda
MORRIS, Christopher
MOYES, David
MURPHY, Lynette
NG, Julia
OFFER, Carol
OFFEY, Lesley
O'NEILL, Ruth
OSBORN, Graeme
PATEL, Dilpa
PAYNE, Julia
PENGELLEY, Rupert
PETERS, Timothy
POND, Emma
POTTER, Keith
PORTER, Claire
PORTER, Margaret
PRATT, Danny
PUCKERING, Harry
PYE, Jeffrey
RANSOM, Gary
REED, Carol
REEDER, Julie
RICKETTS, Alan
RICKETTS, Paul
ROBERTS, Pauline
ROLINGTON, Alfred
ROVERY, Melanie
RUSSELL, Jenny
RYAN, Noel
SAMUEL, Lynne

SANTOS, Antonio
SCOTT, Richard
SEYMOUR, Janet
SHAW, Julianne
SHIPTON, David
SHONS, Florina
SCHWARZ MORTENSEN, Christine
SIMMANCE, Ruth
SIMMONS, Katherine
SLADE, Anita
SNEATH, Catherine
SPARK, Stephen
STANIFORD, Sulann
STANLEY, Barbara
STATON, Mike
STIMSON, Jane
TANDY, Ian
TAYLOR, Ruth
THOMSON, Peter
TODMAN, Howard
TUCKER, Susan
TURNER, Sue
VAN DER HOEK, Matthew
VARNDELL, Christine
ULPH, Stephen
VIOL, Cornelia
VUKIC, Alexandra
WALDEN, Alfred
WALTON, Hazel
WARD, Dave
WATKINS, Christine
WEBB, Mary
WELCH, Tony
WELLS, Nicola
WEST, Richard
WILLIAMS, Julie
WILLIS, Katherine
WITHERS, Murray

Cleaners

FLYNN, Sheila
GARNER, Gina
GEORGE, Carrie
GILL, Colin
GILL, Derek
GILL, Val
JOHNSON, Doris
PEACHEY, Val
PIKE, Rita
WEBB, June.

US Employees

AYRES, Sandra
BAXTER, Peter
BELANI, Sonia

BELANI, Rahul
BOATMAN, John
BRIA, Joseph
CHAPMAN, Matt
CHETOPUZHAKARAN, George, Paul
CHIAO, Deborah
CHOPRA, Anju
CLAUSEN, James
CONRAD, Dawn
DAKE, Laura
EVERS, Stacey
FOSTER, Catrina
GOSS, Shamus
GRIFFITH, Glenn
HAYES, Scott
HENDERSON, Crystal
HEWISH, Mark
HICKMAN, Sharon
HINES, Karen
ISLAM, Khandaker
JACKSON, Linda
KNOTT, Shawn
KRAVITZ, Brett
LEITAO, Louie
LOUGHMAN, Robert
LUCAS, Tracy
MAHON, Tim
MATESKI, Mark
McHALE, Joe
McNEELY, Lori
MEISSNER, Colleen
MICARE, F, Gina
MICHLOVIZ, David
MODEN, David
MORRIS, Cynthia
MORRIS, Patrick
NEAL, Deborah
NUTE, Maureen
PETTY, Robert
PHAM, Thu
PORRATA, Veronica
RAMAGE, William
SARAN, Mohit
SEBRING, Clay
SHAVATT, Maria
SMITH, Lois
SMITH, Linda
STARR, Barbara
STEINBERG, Matt
STUBBS, Darryl
TENCZA, Elizabeth
TINGEN, Sharon
VASKO, Andrew
VELTHAUS, Sally
VENZKE, Ben
WATT, Mark.

WESTBROOK, Rachel

Editors,
Correspondents &
Contributors

ABBOTT, James
ALLEN, Roy
BARKER, John
BICKERS, Charles
BOYLE, Daniel
BURNS, David
BUSHELL, Chris
BUSHELL, Susan
BUTTERWORTH-HAYES, Philip
CARR, David
CARVELL, Roger
CITRINOT, Luc
CULLEN, Tony
ENDRES, Günter
ENGLISH, Adrian
FISHER, Scotty
FITZSIMONS, Bernard
FOSS, Chris
FOWLER, Robert
FOXWELL, David
GALEOTTI, Mark
GANDER, Terry
GILL, Tony
GOULD, Dr Rick
GOULDING, James
GOURLEY, Scott R
GRAMSON, Peter
GREENMAN, David
GUNSTON, Bill
HEITMAN, Helmoed-Romer
HENDERSON, Keith
HEYMAN, Major Charles
HOBSON, Sharon
HOGG, Ian
HOOTON, Ted
JACKSON, Paul
JERRAM, Mike
KING, Major Colin
KITCHERSIDE, Peter
KUNZ, Richard
LENNOX, Duncan
LESTAPIS, Jacques de
MENEFEE, Sam P
MILLER, David
MUNSON, Ken
O'LEARY, A P (Les)
PASCOE, Rod
PATTISON, Tony
PEACOCK, Lindsay
PHILLIPS, Stephen

PORTNOI, Paul
RACKHAM, Peter
REED, John
RICHARDSON, Doug
RIDER, David
SHARPE, Captain Richard - OBE RN
SCHWARTZ, Adele
SMITH, Dr Chris
SCRASE, Terry
STEELE, Harry
STRACHAN, Ian
STONE, Brian
STREETLY, Martin
SOWTER, Robert
TAYLOR, John W R - OBE
TOMPKINS, Paul
WALTERS, Brian
WATTS, Tony
WILLIAMSON, John
WILSON, Andrew
WISE, John
WOOLLEY, David
YATES, Chris.

List of agents (Worldwide)

GULLIFER, Brendan
Havre & Gullifer (Pty) Ltd; BILYK, L
Brazmedia International S/C Ltda;
FÉVRIER, Patrice
Jane's Information Group France;
WEHRSTEDT, Dr Uwe
MCW; MILLER, Jeremy
Major Media Ltd; BEN-YAACOV,
Oreet
Oreet International Media;
Ediconsult Internazionale Srl;
THOMPSON, Gillian
The Falsten Partnership; SAI, Hoo
Siew
Major Media Singapore Pte Ltd;
CHINN, Young-Seoh
JES Media International; IGLESIAS,
Jesus Moran
Varenga Exclusivas Internacionales;
HANSON, Kimberley
MELCHER, Cathy
SCHULZE, Kristin
Global Media Services.

Thomson Corporation

BROCKMANN, Nigel
BROWN, Michael
BRYFONSKI, Deidria
BURGESS, Pat
CAMPBELL, Fiona

CLARK, Desmond
CULLEN, Bob
EHLERS, Dawn
FISHER, David
FRIEDLAND, Edward
GLYNN, Barry
GOLDSMITH, Michael
GREEN, Jenny
GRIFFITHS, Jeremy
HALL, Bob
HARRINGTON, Dick
HARRIS, Michael
HARRISON, Nigel
HEGGENER, Peter
HESTER, Brian
HINCHMORE, Barry
JACKSON, Mick and Casey
JENKINS, John
KALLEBERG, Dottie
KIRBY, Mike
KNIGHT, Mark
LAMERTON, Deborah
LASSNER, Keith
LUCAS, David
MARRAFFA, Basil
MELTZER HUGHSON, Amy
RILEY, Simon
RUTT, Jim
PAUL, Gordon
PAUL, Tom
THOMSON, David
THOMSON OF FLEET, Lord and Lady
THOMSON, Lynn
TIERNEY, Pat
TORY, John
VEATOR, Chris
WESTGATE, David

Ex-Thomson

BOSWELL, Ralph
CROOM, David
GILL, John
DUNCAN SMITH MP, Iain
KIERNAN, Bob
LILLIS, Charlie
RAINEY, George

SHOVLIN, Gary
THOMAS, Sarah.
WEBB, Rupert

UK Suppliers

Amadeus Press Ltd
Biddles Ltd
Butler & Tanner Ltd
CCI Europe Ltd
COMPTON, Barrie
Deltaset
Disctronics
E T Heron Ltd
Hobbs the Printers Ltd
Huntcard Ltd
MFK Group Ltd
MultiMedia Services
Price Waterhouse
Strakers
The Scanning Gallery
Riverside
Visual Graphic Supplies Ltd

US Suppliers

HANSON, Kim
SCHULZE, Kristen
MELCHER, Cathy
CIOTA, Mike
Global Media Services; BUTLER,
    Della
ZIP Mailing; BERSOFF, Ed
BTG; FOUSHEE, Dolora
Merkle Computer Systems; CLARKE,
    Desmond
Kentucky Distribution Center;
    BANKER, Ellen
Art Litho; LINKOUS, Brian
GC Creations.

GLOSSARY

AA:	Automobile Association
AB:	Able Bodied Seaman
A&NG:	Army and Navy Gazette
aeronef:	An imaginary word for a fictional airship
BBF:	British Battle Fleet
BSAA:	Boy Scouts Assistance Association
CAR:	CAR Illustrated
DE:	Dover Express
DNB:	Dictionary of National Biography
DT:	Daily Telegraph
EN:	Evening News
FH:	Folkestone Herald
fn:	footnote
FS:	Fighting Ships, including All The World's etc
FTJ:	Fred T Jane
G&L:	Globe and Laurel
homo:	Man as a physical organism lacking in spirit, heroism etc
HP:	Horse Power
HT:	Hampshire Telegraph
HT/FTJ:	Hampshire Telegraph: Jane's Weekly Causerie
HT/LY:	Hampshire Telegraph: Lionel Yexley's Weekly Column
IJN:	Imperial Japanese Navy
ILN:	Illustrated London News
IRN:	Imperial Russian Navy

JP:	Justice of the Peace
JRUSI:	Journal of the Royal United Service Institute
knut:	Young man dressed in the height of fashion for 1915
L&W:	Land and Water
maj:	major or elder
MM:	Mariner's Mirror
MMC:	Motor Manufacturing Company
mph:	Miles per Hour
NA:	Naval Annual
NID:	Naval Intelligence Department
OS:	Ordnance Survey
PT:	Portsmouth Times
PW:	Pictorial World
RM:	Royal Marines
RMLI:	Royal Marine Light Infantry
RN:	Royal Navy
RUSI:	Royal United Service Institute
tertstertius:	or third
vir:	Man as a spiritual being, possessing courage, and virtue
WO:	Warrant Officer
WVS:	Women's Voluntary Service

Weights and Measures:

Inch (abbrev in.) = 2.4 cm ('centipedes' to Jane's mechanic)

Foot (Abbrev ft.) = 12 inches

Money:

(1) Penny: An old unit of currency abbreviated to d.

(2) Shilling: An old unit of currency equivalent to five new pence. Contained twelve old pence - abbreviated to 's' or 'sh'.

(3) Pound: Contained twenty shillings. Approximately the weekly earnings of an Edwardian labourer.

(4) Guinea: Antique unit of currency equivalent to £1-1s-0d ie £1.05p in post decimalisation money. Used for expensive items like race horses, and wargames, being handsomer than straight pounds.

Dates:

Dates of references are given in the British format: Day/Month/Year, but including the century, for example 8/3/1916 or 8th March 1916.

WORKS PUBLISHED BY FRED T JANE
1892-1917

All About the German Navy: Illustrations of German Fighting Ships: 1915 Sampson Low & Co, London (New & Revised edition).

All About the German Navy: Illustrations of German Fighting Ships: 1917 Sampson Low & Co, London.

All About the United States Navy: 1917 Sampson Low & Co, London (compiled by W Tyrrell).

All the World's Aircraft: 1912 Sampson Low Marston & Co, London (renamed annual).

All the World's Airships: 1909 Sampson Low Marston & Co, London (first issue of annual — reprinted 1969).

All the World's Airships: 1910 Sampson Low Marston & Co, London (second issue of annual).

All the World's Fighting Ships 1898: 1898 Sampson Low Marston & Co, London (first issue of annual — reprinted 1969).

All the World's Fighting Ships 1899: 1899 Sampson Low Marston & Co, London (second issue of annual).

All the World's Fighting Ships 1900: 1900 Naval Syndicate (third issue of annual).

The Angel of the Revolution: by G C Griffiths, 1893 Tower Publishing Co, London (illustrations only).

Blake of the Rattlesnake: 1895 Tower Publishing Co, London (illustrated).

The British Battle Fleet: Its Inception and Growth...: 1912 S W Partridge & Co, London (first edition in one volume).

The British Battle Fleet: Its Inception and Growth...: 1915 Library Press, London (second edition in two volumes).

The Captain of the Mary Rose: by William Laird Clowes, 1892 Tower Publishing Co, London (illustrations only).

Ever Mohun: 1901 John Macqueen, London (frontispiece).

Heresies of Sea Power: 1906 Longmans & Co, London.

Hints on Playing the Jane Naval Wargame: 1902 Sampson Low Marston & Co, London.

How the Jubilee Fleet Escaped...: by P L Stevenson, 1899 Simpkin, Marshall & Co, London (illustrations only).

How to Play the Naval Wargame... Official Rules: 1912 Sampson Low & Co, London (reprinted 1990 by Bill Leeson).

The Imperial Navy: in *British Dominions Year Book*: 1916.

The Imperial Japanese Navy: 1904 W Thacker & Co, London (illustrated – reprinted 1984).

The Imperial Russian Navy: 1899 W Thacker & Co, London (illustrated).

The Imperial Russian Navy: 1904 W Thacker & Co, London (second edition – reprinted 1983).

The Incubated Girl: 1896 Tower Publishing Co, London.

The Iron Pirate: by Max Pemberton, 1893 Cassell, London (frontispiece only).

The Jane Coastal Operations Wargame: 1903 Sampson Low Marston & Co, London.

Jane's Historic Aircraft: 1916.

Jane's Pocket Aeronautical Dictionary: 1918 Sampson Low & Co, London (compiled by C G Grey).

The Lordship, The Passen, and We: 1897 A D Innes & Co, London.

Naval Supremacy: Who? ...: by A M Laubeuf, 1908 Siegle Hill & Co, London (introduction).

Olga Romanov or the Syren of the Skies: G C Griffiths, 1894 Tower Publishing Co, London (illustrations only).

The Ought-to-Go: 1907.

Per Mare No.1: Fred T Jane's Illustrated Naval Annual: 1895 Tower Publishing Co, London (illustrated).

The Port Guard Ship: 1899 Hurst & Blackett, London.

Recognition Book of German Torpedo Craft: 1912 Sampson Low & Co, London.

A Royal Bluejacket: 1908 Sampson Low & Co, London.

Rules for the Jane Naval Wargame: 1898 Sampson Low Marston & Co, London.

Silhouettes of British Fighting Ships: 1914 Sampson Low & Co, London.

Silhouettes of German Fighting Ships: 1914 Sampson Low & Co, London.

The Torpedo Book: ... sketches of Torpedo Craft: 1897 Neville Beeman, London (illustrations only).

The Torpedo in Peace and War: 1898 W Thacker, London (illustrated).

The Torpedo in Peace and War: 1904 W Thacker, London (second edition).

To Venus In Five Seconds (a Tale): 1897 Innes & Co, London (illustrated).

The Violet Flame: 1899 Ward Lock & Co, London (illustrated).

War Lessons To Date: 1915 Daily Post, Liverpool (introduction).

Warships at a Glance: Silhouettes of the World's Fighting Ships: 1914 Sampson Low & Co, London.

The World's Warships: 1915 Sampson Low & Co, London (first issue of annual).

Your Navy as a Fighting Machine: 1914 F & C Palmer, London.

MISCELLANEOUS BIBLIOGRAPHY

Abbot, P: The British Airship at War, 1985 Terence Dalton Ltd.

Andrew, C: Secret Service, 1985 Heinemann.

Anonymous: Return of Owners of Land 1873, 1873 official statistical compilation.

Bayly, Adm Sir L: Pull Together: The Memoirs of Admiral Sir Lewis Bayly, 1939 Harrap & Co.

Bennett, Capt G: Charlie B: A Biography of Lord Charles Beresford, 1967 Peter Dawnay Ltd, London.

Bleiler, E F: Science-Fiction: The Early Years, 1990 Kent State University Press, Ohio, USA.

Boase, C G: Collectanea Cornubiensia: Collection of Topographical & Biog Notes relating to Cornwall, 1890 Netherton and Worth, Truro, Cornwall.

Bond, B: War and Society in Europe 1870–1970, 1984 Fontana Paperbacks.

Brassey, Lord: The Naval Annual 1886–1919, Griffin, Portsmouth.

Burke, J B: *Genealogical & Heraldic Dictionary of the Peerage and Baronetage*, 1852 Colburn & Co, London.

Carew, A: *The Lower Deck of the Royal Navy 1900–39: Invergordon in Perspective*, 1981 Manchester University Press, Manchester.

Charnock, J: *Biographia Navalis... From the Year 1660 to the Present Time*, 1798, London.

Cianfrani, T: *A Short History of Obstetrics and Gynaecology*, 1960 Blackwell Scientific Press.

Clark, Dr D G: *Victor Grayson: Labour's Lost Leader*, 1985 Quartet.

Clarke, I F: *Voices Prophesying War: Future Wars 1763–3749*, 1992 Oxford University Press.

Colomb, P H: *The Duel: A Naval Wargame*, 1878 Griffin, Portsmouth.

Cook, Col J H: *Tales of Ancient Wessex*, c.1930

Dangerfield, G: *The Strange Death of Liberal England*, 1966 MacGibbon & Kee.

Dixon, C: *Ships of the Victorian Navy*, 1987 Ashford Press Publishing, Southampton.

Dreyer, Adm Sir F: *The Sea Heritage*, 1955, London.

Featherstone, D F: *Naval Wargaming*, 1965 Stanley Paul.

Foster, J: *Alumni Oxonienses: Members of the University of Oxford 1500–1886*, 1891 J Parkes & Sons, Oxford.

Frewin, A: *One Hundred Years of Science Fiction Illustration*, 1988 Bloomsbury Books, London.

Frostick, M: *The Mighty Mercedes*, 1961 Dalton Watson.

Gange, M: *Memories of Yesteryear*, 1982 St Thomas' Church, Bedhampton.

Glendinning, V: *Trollope*, 1993 Pimlico, Essex.

Graves, A: *Royal Academy of Arts: Complete Dictionary of Contributors 1769–1904*, 1906 Henry Graves & Sons, London.

Greene, F V: *The Campaign in Bulgaria*, 1903 Hugh Rees Ltd, London.

Griffiths, G C: *The Angel of the Revolution: A Tale of the Coming Terror*, 1893 Tower Publishing Co, London.
Olga Romanov or the Syren of the Skies: A Sequel to The Angel of the Revolution, 1894 Tower Publishing Co, London.

Grove, E: *Fleet to Fleet Encounters*, 1991 Arms & Armour Press.

Grubb, Rev P H W: *The History of Bedhampton*, undated leaflet.

Guppy, H B: *Homes of Family Names in Great Britain*, 1890 Harrison & Sons, London.

Hanks, P and Hodges, F: *Dictionary of Surnames*, 1988 Oxford University Press.

Hobart, A C: *Sketches from the Life of the late Admiral Hobart Pasha*, 1887 Longmans Green & Co, London.

Hobbs, Rev A J H, BA: *Notes on the History of UpOttery Church, Devon*, 1941 Dimond & Co, Honiton, Devon.

Honan, W H: *Bywater: The Man who invented the Pacific War*, 1990 Macdonald & Co.

Houfe, S: *Dictionary of British Book Illustrators & Caricaturists 1800–1914*, 1978 Antique Collectors Club.

Hough, R: *First Sea Lord: An Authorised Biography of Admiral Lord Fisher*, 1977 Severn House Publishing Ltd.

Howard, M: *Clausewitz*, 1983 Oxford University Press.

Hozier, Capt H M: *The Russo–Turkish War*, 1877 William Mackenzie, London.

Jacob and Pyke: *Hampshire at the Opening of the Twentieth Century*, 1904 M T Pyke, Brighton.

P Kennedy: *The Rise & Fall of British Naval Mastery*, 1991 Fontana Press.

King-Hall, L: *Sea Saga: Diaries of Four Generations of the King-Hall family*, 1935 Victor Gollancz, London.

Clowes, Sir W Laird: *Four Modern Naval Campaigns: Chilean War 1891*, 1970 Cornmarket Press.
Naval Pocket Book, 1895-1914 Thacker.
The Captain of the Mary Rose: A Tale of Tomorrow, 1892 Tower Publishing Co.
The Royal Navy: Its History From Earliest Times Vol 1-7, 1897 Samson Low Marston.

Love, F C: *Hampshire Telegraph Pictorial Souvenir 1799-1949*, 1949 Portsmouth.

Low, Lt C R: *Her Majesty's Navy Including its Deeds and Battles*, 1892 JS Virtue & Co Ltd.

Macdonald, G: *Camera — Victorian Eyewitness*, 1979 ET Batsford Ltd, London.

Marder, A J: *Anatomy of British Sea Power: British naval Policy 1889-1905*, 1972 Frank Cass.
From the Dreadnought to Scapa Flow Vol 1 1904-1914, *The Road to War*, 1972 Oxford University Press.
From the Dreadnought to Scapa Flow Vol 2 1914-1916, *The War Years to Jutland*, 1972 Oxford University Press.

Marshall, J: *Royal Naval Biography*, 1831, London.

Mackay, K (ed): *Exeter School 1880-1983*, 1984 Exeter School, Exeter.

Mitchell, W F & Elgar, F: *The Royal Navy 1872-1880: In a Series of Illustrations from Original Drawings*, 1881 Griffin.

Nicholls, P: *Encyclopedia of Science Fiction*, 1979 Granada Publishing.

Offer, A: *The First World War: An Agrarian Interpretation*, 1991 Oxford University Press.

Padfield, P: *Aim Straight: A Biography of Sir Percy Scott*, 1966 Hodder & Stoughton, London.

Parkes, O: *British Battleships: Warrior 1860 to Vanguard 1950*, 1957 Seeley.

Peacock, S: *Hampshire Studies: Parliamentary Elections in Portsmouth*, 1981 Portsmouth City Record Office, Portsmouth.

Pevsner,N and Lloyd, D: *Hampshire & the Isle of Wight*, 1967 Penguin.

Read, D: *The Age of Urban Democracy: England 1868–1914*, 1994 Longman.

Read, D (ed): *Edwardian England*, 1982 Croom Helm & HA.

Riley, Dr R C: *The Growth of Southsea as a Naval Satellite and Victorian Resort*, 1972 Portsmouth City Council, Portsmouth.

Robinson, Cmdr C N: *The British Fleet*, 1896 George Bell & Sons.

Schurman, D M: *Julian S Corbett 1854–1922: Historian of British Maritime Policy*, 1981 Royal Historical Society.

Slusser, G & Rabkin, E S (eds): *Flights of Fancy — Armed Conflict in Science Fiction and Fantasy*, 1993 University of Georgia Press.

Smith, D C: *H G Wells — Desperately Mortal*, 1986 Yale University Press.

Stableford, B: *Scientific Romance in Britain 1870–1950*, 1985 Fourth Estate, London.

Stevenson, P L: *How the Jubilee Fleet Escaped Destruction and The Battle of Ushant*, 1899 Simpkin Marshall & Co, London.

Sumida, J T: *In Defence of Naval Supremacy: Finance Technology & British Naval Policy 1887–1914*, 1993 Unwin Hyman, Boston, Massachusetts.

Terraine, J: *Impacts of War: 1914 & 1918*, 1993 Leo Cooper.

Thomas, S: *Pall Mall Magazine: Index to Fiction 1893–1914*, 1983 University of Queensland.

Thompson, D: *Europe Since Napoleon*, 1983 Pelican Books.

Thompson, P: *The Edwardians: The Remaking of British Society*, 1992 Routledge.

Toulson, S: *Companion Guide to Devon*, 1991 Harper Collins.

Venn, John: *Alumni Cantabrigenses: A Biographical of all Known Students etc... to 1900*, 1922 Cambridge University Press.

Walford, E: *County Families of the United Kingdom*, 1879 Hardwicke & Boyne, London.

Wells, Capt J: *An Illustrated Social History of the Royal Navy 1870–1982*, 1994 Alan Sutton/Royal Naval Museum.

Weyer, B: *Taschenbuch der Kriegsflotten XV Jahrgang 1914*, reprinted 1968 J F Lehmann's Verlag, Munich.

Wilson, A: *War Gaming (originally The Bomb and the Computer)*, 1970 Pelican Books.

Wilson, A N: *Hilaire Belloc*, 1984 Hamish Hamilton.

Wilson, T: *The Myriad Faces of War: Great Britain and the Great War*, 1988 Polity Press.

PERIODICALS CONTAINING WORK BY FRED T JANE

Autocar: Famous Cars in Retirement IX: A 1907 8 litre Benz Racer (1912 November 30th)

Black & White: Illustrations of Naval Subjects (1890–1895)

Book Buyer: Henry Reuterdahl (1902 June)

CAR Illustrated: Diary of a Motor Man (series) (1904–1905)
Garage Yarns (series) (1910)
Miscellaneous humourous articles (1910–1911)

Contemporary Review: The British Ship of War (1898 February)
A Problem in the Far East (1898 March)
Seaworthiness of Destroyers (1901 November)

Edinburgh Review: Submarines and Aircraft (1915 January)

Engineer: Miscellaneous comment on naval matters including
'Dockyard Notes' (1896–1904)
Naval Manoeuvres & Their Value (1896 July 8th)
The Naval Wargame (1898 February 18th)
Jane Naval Wargame at the United Service Institute (1898 June 24th)
Jane Naval Wargame (1898 December 16th)
The Classification of Warships (1900 March 9th)
The Recent Belleisle Experiment (1902 August 8th)

English Illustrated Magazine: Hartmann the Anarchist: The Great City's Doom (1892–1893)
Queenstown to Sheerness in Torpedo Boat No. 65 (1892–1893)
Romance of Modern London (I): London Railway Stations (1892–1893)
Romance of Modern London (II): In the Small Hours (1892–1893)
Romance of Modern London (III): Round the Underground (1892–1893)

Life on Board a Torpedo Catcher (1893–1894)
The New Navies (with Laird Clowes) (1893–1894)

Fortnightly Review: The Maine Disaster & After (1898 April)
Apotheosis of the Torpedo (1901 August)
The Navy: Is All Well? (1902 March)

Forum: Naval Warfare Present and Future (1897 October)
Naval Lessons of the War (1898 November)

Hampshire Telegraph: 'Weekly Causeries': Column in Naval Chronicle (1906–1911)
'Weekly Causeries': Column in Naval Chronicle (1913–1915)

Illustrated London News: Illustrations of Naval Subjects (1892–1896)
Dreadnought Broadside (1906 October 6th)

Land & Water: The War By Air (occasional column) (1914–1915)
The War On Water (weekly column) (1914–1915)

Pall Mall Magazine: Guesses at Futurity (1894–1895)

Pictorial World: Illustrations of Naval Subjects (1889–1891)

RUSI Journal: The Jane Naval War Game (1899 February)
Tactics in the Jane Naval War Game (1900 March)
Are 12" Guns in Battleships Best Value for the Weight? (February 1903)

Sandows's Magazine: Hazlitt of the Chih Yuen (1899)

Scientific American: Naval Wargame between US & Germany (1902 1903)
Comparison of German Battleship WETTIN with the MAINE (1903 June 13th)
Russian Naval Guns (1904 May 28th)

Scientific American Supplement: Classification of Warships (1900 April7th)
Naval Wargame (1901 October 26th)
Recent BelleIsle Experiment (1902 August 30th)

Statesman's Year Book: Naval Correspondent (1904–1914)

Stories: The Naval Secret Service (1898)

World's Work: What the Torpedo Can Do (1904 June)

KEY EVENTS IN THE STORY OF FRED T JANE 1865-1923

1840 John Jane born at Brownquinn, St Winnow - 5th November

1842 Caroline Sophia Todd born at Church Street, Liskeard - 22nd April

1864 John Jane marries Caroline Sophia Todd at Clifton, Bristol - 8th September

1865 John Frederick Thomas Jane (FTJ) born at Richmond - 6th August

1866 Rev John Jane becomes curate at St Austell

1867 George Hugh Jane born in St Austell - 15th June

1869 Helen Caroline A Jane born at St Austell - 18th February

1871 Rev John Jane becomes curate at West Teignmouth

1873 Henry Edgar Jane born Catherine Terrace, West Teignmouth - 19th October

1874 Rev John Jane appointed to Bedford Chapel, Exeter

1876 Rev John Jane becomes rector St John-with-St George, Exeter

1877 FTJ starts at Exeter School - 12th September

251

1878 Rev John Jane becomes rector of Upton Pyne, Exeter

1879 Lionel Cecil Jane born at the Rectory, Upton Pyne - 28th July

1881 Rev John Jane becomes curate for Alphington Devon

1882 Edith Muriel Carre born at Weymouth - 22nd Mar
Bombardment of Alexandria by British Fleet - 11th July

1883 FTJ leaves Exeter School - December

1885 FTJ goes to London aged 20
Gwendoline Morwenna Kinsman Jane born in Exeter Close - 29th January

1886 Rev John Jane becomes vicar of UpOttery - 4th January

1890 FTJ's 'New Channel Squadron' appears in Pictorial World - 10th July
FTJ attends RN Manoeuvres in HMS Northampton - August

1891 Chilean War: Blanco Encalada torpedoed - 9th April

1892 FTJ illustrates 'The Captain of the Mary Rose'
FTJ's 'Battle on the Minefield' appears in ILN - 20th August
FTJ marries Alice Beattie at Trinity Church, Holborn - 17th September

1893 FTJ illustrates 'The Angel of the Revolution'

1894 FTJ exhibits 'Frankenstein of the East' at Royal Academy
The Janes move to 12a Edith Terrace Fulham
Sino-Jap War: Chinese defeated at Battle of the Yalu - 17th September
FTJ illustrates 'Hartmann the Anarchist'
FTJ's articles appear in English Illustrated Magazine
FTJ's 'Guesses at Futurity' begins in Pall Mall Magazine - October

1895 FTJ's first novel: 'Blake of the Rattlesnake' - September
'Per Mare #1: Fred T Jane's Illustrated Naval Annual' - July
The Janes move to 18 Chesilton Road Fulham - December

1896 'The Incubated Girl'
FTJ exhibits 'Roman Galleys of Today' at Royal Academy
Stella Dorothy Alice Jane born at 18 Chesilton Road, Fulham - 14th November

1897 'To Venus In Five Seconds'
Diamond Jubilee Review at Spithead - 26th July
'The Lordship, The Passen, and We' - 4th October
FTJ staying at 6 Elphinstone Road Southsea - December
Prince Henry of Prussia and German squadron visit
Portsmouth - 21st December
'The Torpedo Book'

1898 'The Torpedo in Peace and War'
The Janes move to 17 Elphinstone Road, Southsea
'All the World's Fighting Ships': 1st Issue - January
'The Jane Naval Wargame' - June
FTJ demonstrates the Jane Naval Wargame to the RUSI -
17th June
Spanish-American War: Battle of Santiago - 3rd July

1899 'Hazlitt of the Chih Yuen' appears in Sandow's Magazine
'The Violet Flame'
FTJ illustrates 'How the Jubilee Fleet escaped...'
FTJ visits Russian Naval dockyards - January
'All the World's Fighting Ships': 2nd Issue - Feb
'The Imperial Russian Navy' 1st edition - December
FTJ demonstrates the Jane Naval Wargame to the RUSI -
6th December

1900 'The Port Guardship'
'All the World's Fighting Ships': 3rd Issue - July

1901 'Ever Mohun'

1902 FTJ lectures at RUSI on 12" Gun Battleships - 6th June
'Hints on Playing the Jane Naval Wargame' - December
FTJ outrages RUSI over Protection of Commerce in
Wartime - 10th December

1903 'The Jane Coastal Operations Wargame etc'
Cuniberti's 'Ideal Battleship' described in 'Fighting Ships'

1904 'The Imperial Japanese Navy'
'The Imperial Russian Navy' 2nd edition
Japanese attack Port Arthur, starting Russo-Jap War - 8th
Feb
Death of Rear Admiral H J May - 25th May
Sir John Fisher becomes First Sea Lord - 21st October

1905   Russo-Japanese War: Battle of Tsushima - 27th May

1906   General Election: FTJ beaten at Portsmouth - 17th January
        'Heresies of Sea Power' - June

1907   'The Ought-to-Go'
        FTJ becomes naval correspondent of 'Standard'
        newspaper
        FTJ's first column appears in Hampshire Telegraph - 5th
        January

1908   'A Royal Bluejacket' - November
        Death of Alice Beattie Jane - 10th December

1909   Abduction of Victor Grayson - 28th January
        1st Boy Scout Motor Field Day - 3rd July
        FTJ crashes aeroplane during test flight on Dartmoor -
        September
        'All the World's Airships' 1st Issue - November
        FTJ marries Edith Muriel Carre - 18th December

1910   Battle of Unicorn Gate during General Election campaign -
        13th January

1911   FTJ's mother, Caroline Jane, dies at Upottery - 1st Mar
        FTJ's daughter Barbara Jane born at Hill House,
        Bedhampton - 11th July

1912   'Recognition Book of German Torpedo Craft'
        'All the World's Aircraft' 1st Issue - April
        'How to Play the "Naval Wargame"... Official Rules' - May
        'The British Battle Fleet' 1st edition - October

1914   Great Britain declares war on Germany - 4th August
        'Silhouettes of British Fighting Ships' - September
        'Silhouettes of German Fighting Ships' - September
        'Your Navy as a Fighting Machine' - September
        U9 sinks HMS Aboukir, Hogue and Cressy - 22nd
        September
        Prince Louis Battenberg resigns as 1st Sea Lord - 29th
        October
        British disaster at Coronel: HMS Good Hope & Monmouth
        sunk - 1st November

Australian Cruiser SYDNEY sinks EMDEN at Cocos Islands
- 9th November
Battle of the Falkland Islands - 8th December
'Warships at a Glance'

1915 'All About the German Navy'
'The British Battle Fleet' 2nd edition
'The World's Warships' (annual)
FTJ writes 'Submarines and Aircraft' for Edinburgh
Review - January
Battle of Dogger Bank - 24th January
Sinking of Lusitania - 7th May
FTJ's last column appears in Hampshire Telegraph - 8th
October

1916 FTJ changes Will, appointing Cecil sole executor - 21st
January
FTJ dies at 26 Clarence Parade Southsea aged 50 - 8th Mar
FTJ buried in Highland Road cemetery - 10th Mar
Battle of Jutland - 31st May

1917 'All About the US Navy' compiled from Fighting Ships
Legal action leaves Cecil Jane sole executor of FTJ's will -
29th March

1918 'Jane's Pocket Aeronautical Dictionary' compiled by CG
Grey

1923 FTJ's father, the Rev John Jane, dies at Exeter - 20th March

EDITORS OF FIGHTING SHIPS

1898–1915	Fred T Jane
1916–1917	Maurice Prendergast
1918–1922	Oscar Parkes with Maurice Prendergast
1923–1929	Oscar Parkes with Francis E McMurtrie
1930–1934	Oscar Parkes
1935–1948	Francis E McMurtrie
1949–1973	Raymond Blackman
1974–1988	Captain John Moore RN
1988–to date	Captain Richard Sharpe RN

EDITORS OF ALL THE WORLD'S AIRCRAFT:

1909–1915	Fred T Jane
1916–1936	Charles G Grey
1937	Charles G Grey with Leonard Bridgeman
1938–1958	Leonard Bridgeman
1959–1990	John WR Taylor
1991–1994	Mark Lambert
1995–to date	Paul Jackson

FIGHTING SHIPS CONTRIBUTORS 1898-1916

"Two of the New School"
- 1902 Critique of major navies' 1902 manoeuvres.

A British N. O.
- 1906 Seestern 1906: German war story.

Adm Sir J O Hopkins
- 1902 Intermediates.

Anonymous
- 1901 Signalling Progress.
- 1902 German Charges, Shells, Fuzes etc.
- 1902 Gunnery: New Mounts etc.
- 1902 Vickers, Canet, Bofors & Krupp M.1901 Guns.
- 1903 Aerostatics Progress.
- 1903 Naval Manoeuvres.
- 1903 Submarine Progress.
- 1903-05 Strategy & Tactics.
- 1905 Summary and Photos of the War.
- 1907 Salving of HMS *Montagu*.

Anonymous/Gyro
- 1901-05 Torpedo Progress.

Anonymous/Mark X
- 1901-05 Gunnery Progress.

Charles de Grave Sells
- 1903-08 Types of Water Tube Boiler.
- 1903-14 Progress of Warship Engineering.
- 1908 Types of Turbine.
- 1908 Warships Fitted with Turbines.

FIGHTING SHIPS CONTRIBUTORS 1898-1916

Col V Cuniberti & Matsuo
- 1901 Views Upon the Battleship Question.

Col V Cuniberti RIN
- 1902 New Battleship Designs.
- 1903 Ideal Warship for the British Navy.
- 1905 A Blockade Battleship.
- 1906 Another Ideal Future Battleship.
- 1908 20,000 Ton Warship of Future.
- 1912 Battleship of the Future.

F T Jane
- 1899 Notes on the Spanish American War.
- 1900 The BelleIsle Experiment.
- 1902 Notes on Submarine and Aerial Warfare.
- 1902 Reconstruction.
- 1902 Torpedo: General Progress & Experiments.
- 1902 Torpedo: New Elswick Submerged Tube.
- 1905 Reconstruction.
- 1905 Revised Rules for Jane Wargame.
- 1905-6 New Construction.
- 1907 British Trade Manoeuvres.

Gyro
- 1904 Torpedoes and Submarines.

Ingenieur C G Bjorkemann
- 1902 Maj Unge's Aerial Torpedo.

IRN
- 1905 The War: Russian Viewpoint.

J J Bennett
- 1902 Fuel Expenditure in the British Navy.

Kap Lt Bruno Weyer
- 1902 New Krupp Armour (Cast Nickel Steel).

L Cecil Jane
- 1915 Historical Analogies and the Naval War.
- 1916 Special Memoir of Late FT Jane.

FIGHTING SHIPS CONTRIBUTORS 1898-1916

Lt A Rice RN

● 1910 Reserve of Electrical Power.

Mark X

● 1907 Armour and Armament.

Mars

● 1907 Influence of Coastal Defence.

Nippon

● 1905 The War: Japanese Viewpoint.

Official

● 1902 US 12" AP HE Trials.

Percival A Hislam

● 1910 National Expenditure and Naval Strength.

Prof W Hovgaard

● 1908 Proposed New Conning Tower.
● 1909 Protection of B'ships from Submarine Attack.
● 1910 Further Development of Seagoing Battleship.

Rear Adm Borresen

● 1901 Tactical Value of Submarine Boats.
● 1904 Battle of the Azores.

Symposium

● 1901 Have Submarine Boats a Future?
● 1901 The Six Best Types of Battleship.

Various

● 1902 Coaling Records.
● 1902 Different Types of Water Tube Boilers.
● 1906 Russo-Japanese War.

W A Bieber

● 1905-6 Subsidised Merchant Ships.
● 1907-14 World Merchant Ships.